READING DREAM

READING DREAMS

THE INTERPRETATION
OF DREAMS FROM
CHAUCER TO SHAKESPEARE

EDITED BY
PETER BROWN

WITH AN INTRODUCTION BY
A. C. SPEARING

OXFORD
UNIVERSITY PRESS

OXFORD
UNIVERSITY PRESS

Great Clarendon Street, Oxford OX2 6DP

Oxford University Press is a department of the University of Oxford.
It furthers the University's objective of excellence in research, scholarship,
and education by publishing worldwide in

Oxford New York

Athens Auckland Bangkok Bogotá Buenos Aires Calcutta
Cape Town Chennai Dar es Salaam Delhi Florence Hong Kong Istanbul
Karachi Kuala Lumpur Madrid Melbourne Mexico City Mumbai
Nairobi Paris São Paulo Singapore Taipei Tokyo Toronto Warsaw

and associated companies in Berlin Ibadan

Oxford is a registered trade mark of Oxford University Press
in the UK and in certain other countries

Published in the United States
by Oxford University Press Inc., New York

British Library Cataloguing in Publication Data

Data available

Library of Congress Cataloging in Publication Data

Brown, Peter, 1948–
Reading dreams : the interpretation of dreams from Chaucer to
Shakespeare / Peter Brown.
Includes bibliographical references (p.   ).
1. English literature—Early modern, 1500–1700—History and
criticism. 2. Dreams in literature. 3. English literature—Middle
English, 1100–1500—History and criticism. 4. Psychoanalysis and
literature—England—History. 5. English literature—Psychological aspects. I. Title.
PR428.D74B76 1999 820.9'353—dc21 98–51995

ISBN 0–19–818363–1

1 3 5 7 9 10 8 6 4 2

Typeset by Jayvee, Trivandrum, India
Printed in Great Britain
on acid-free paper by
Bookcraft Ltd.,
Midsomer Norton, Somerset

Editor's Preface

On a train-ride from a dispiriting conference at Gregynog, my colleague Andrew Butcher provided the inspiration and intellectual excitement that were to result in *Reading Dreams*. Its conception and realization owe much to him. The essays themselves began life in the 'Culture and Society' seminar which forms part of the postgraduate programme in Medieval and Tudor Studies at the University of Kent. David Aers, Peter Brown, Andrew Butcher, and Kate McLuskie each gave a paper in a series of meetings on the subject of dreams. Our discussions were sufficiently lively and controversial to suggest that we had the makings of a book, and so other scholars were invited to submit essays in complementary areas. We were fortunate to attract the interest of Peter Holland, Steven Kruger, Kathryn Lynch, and A. C. Spearing, all of whom are well known for their distinguished studies of medieval and Renaissance dreams.

We wanted the book to be interdisciplinary; to cross back and forth between the medieval and Renaissance periods in order to identify intellectual and artistic continuities, as well as differences; to adopt a variety of analytical methods; to include both literary and non-literary material; to embrace a diversity of theories; above all to make the cultural study of dreams interesting and challenging. Whether or not we have succeeded in these aims will be evident in the pages that follow.

I acknowledge with gratitude a personal research grant from the British Academy which enabled me to employ Felicity Dunworth as a part-time assistant during the editorial phase of *Reading Dreams*. Her cheerful hard work and eye for detail, as well as her knowledge of the periods covered, represent a significant contribution to what follows. I have also benefited from some teaching relief generously provided by the School of English at Kent.

Canterbury
April 1997

Contents

Notes on the Contributors

DAVID AERS is James B. Duke Professor of English and Director of the Center for Medieval and Renaissance Studies at Duke University.

PETER BROWN is Senior Lecturer in English and Director of the Canterbury Centre for Medieval and Tudor Studies at the University of Kent at Canterbury.

PETER HOLLAND is Professor of Shakespeare Studies at the University of Birmingham, and Director of the Shakespeare Institute, Stratford-upon-Avon.

STEVEN KRUGER is Professor of English at the University of Alberta.

KATHRYN LYNCH is Professor of English at Wellesley College, Massachusetts.

KATHLEEN MCLUSKIE is Professor of English at the University of Southampton.

A. C. SPEARING is William R. Kenan Professor of English at the University of Virginia, and a Fellow of Queens' College, Cambridge.

Abbreviations

ABC	Chaucer, *An ABC*
ABR	*American Benedictine Review*
AHDLMA	*Archives d'histoire doctrinale et littéraire du moyen âge*
AK	*Archiv für Kulturgeschichte*
AM	*Annuale Mediævale*
BD	Chaucer, *Book of the Duchess*
BHR	*Bibliothèque d'Humanisme et Renaissance*
Bo	Chaucer, *Boece*
CEACrit	*College English Association Critic*
ChauN	*Chaucer Newsletter*
ChauR	*Chaucer Review*
CT	Chaucer, *Canterbury Tales*
DUJ	*Durham University Journal*
EETS	Early English Text Society
ELH	*Journal of English Literary History*
ELN	*English Language Notes*
ES	*English Studies*
EStn	*Englische Studien*
GP	Chaucer, General Prologue to the *Canterbury Tales*
HF	Chaucer, *House of Fame*
HR	*History of Religions*
JEGP	*Journal of English and Germanic Philology*
JRMMRA	*Journal of the Rocky Mountain Medieval and Renaissance Association*
JWCI	*Journal of the Warburg and Courtauld Institutes*
LGW	Chaucer, *Legend of Good Women*
LitHist	*Literature and History*
MÆ	*Medium Ævum*
MED	H. Kurath, S. M. Kuhn, J. Reidy, and R. E. Lewis (eds.), *Middle English Dictionary* (Ann Arbor, Mich., 1952–)
MiltonS	*Milton Studies*
MLN	*Modern Language Notes*
MLQ	*Modern Language Quarterly*
MP	*Modern Philology*
MS	*Mediaeval Studies*
MSE	*Massachusetts Studies in English*
NLH	*New Literary History*

NM	*Neuphilologische Mitteilungen*
NPT	Chaucer, Nun's Priest's Tale
NQ	*Notes and Queries*
NS	new series
OS	original series
PardT	Chaucer, Pardoner's Tale
PL	*Patrologia Latina*, ed. J.-P. Migne, 221 vols. (Paris, 1844–64)
PLL	*Papers on Language and Literature*
PMLA	*Publications of the Modern Language Association of America*
PQ	*Philological Quarterly*
RES	*Review of English Studies*
ResLit	*Respublica Litteraria*
RIP	*Rice Institute Pamphlet*
RPL	*Res Publica Litterarum*
RUO	*Revue de l'Université d'Ottawa*
SATF	Société des Anciens Textes Français
SMiss	*Studia Missionalia*
SN	*Studia Neophilologica*
SP	*Studies in Philology*
SQ	*Shakespeare Quarterly*
SR	*Studies in the Renaissance*
SS	*Shakespeare Survey*
SStud	*Shakespeare Studies*
STC	A. W. Pollard and G. R. Redgrave, *A Short-Title Catalogue of Books Printed in England, Scotland, and Ireland, and of English Books Printed Abroad 1475–1640*, 2nd edn., rev. W. A. Jackson, F. S. Ferguson, and K. F. Pantzer, 3 vols. (London, 1976–91)
SumT	Chaucer, Summoner's Tale
TC	Chaucer, *Troilus and Criseyde*
TSE	*Tulane Studies in English*
UTQ	*University of Toronto Quarterly*
WBP	Chaucer, Wife of Bath's Prologue
WBT	Chaucer, Wife of Bath's Tale

Introduction

A. C. SPEARING

Dreaming is a form of sleeping experience that simulates waking experience: it occupies the whole field of consciousness and is extended (however illogically) in the dimensions of space and time; but, so far as I can recapture it in memory, it has a number of characteristics that differentiate it from being awake. Though sometimes extremely vivid, dreaming is in general elusive, and less easily remembered than waking experience. Further, it is not under the control of my conscious will: I cannot decide whether to dream or what to dream, and when dreaming I seem to be less in command (perhaps I should say, even less in command) of what happens than in waking life. Again, while dreaming I cannot choose to do anything else—for example, to write down what I am dreaming. But of all the distinctive features of dreaming, two seem to have an especially close connection with the phenomenon addressed by many of the essays in this collection, the use of dreams as frames for or events in fictional narratives. First, dreaming feels charged with significance: unlike events in waking life, nothing in a dream seems to be trivial or unimportant. (This is true of the *experience* of dreaming, regardless of any theories as to the causation of dreams. In reality they may be, as some would argue, insignificant waste products of the mental processes that enable us to function efficiently when awake, but they still *feel* significant as we experience them.) Second, dreaming does not make sense in the same way as waking life. The latter feature may be a consequence of the former. In waking life many occurrences can be dismissed as insignificant and the remainder can then be shaped into 'normal' sense, but if in dreaming no occurrence feels insignificant, then waking methods of making sense will not work, and some other method will seem necessary. (Hence the many systems proposed for the interpretation of dreams, from Artemidorus to Freud and his successors.)

These two characteristics help to explain why most people have felt that at least some dreams demand interpretation rather than dismissal, and why dreams have been so popular as frames for and incidents in literary texts—which also claim to be more charged with significance than everyday life. Jean-Paul Sartre, in a famous passage in his first novel, distinguished between living and telling: 'When you are living, nothing happens. The settings change, people come in and go out, that's all. . . . But when you tell about life, everything changes . . . events take place one way and we recount them the opposite way.' In a novel, for example:

'It was dark, the street was empty.' The sentence is tossed off casually, it seems superfluous; but we refuse to be taken in and we put it aside: it is a piece of information whose value we shall understand later on. And we have the impression that the hero lived all the details of that night like annunciations, promises, or even that he lived only those that were promises, blind and deaf to everything that did not herald adventure.[1]

As is noted by contributors to this collection, dreams survive only as subsequently narrated, but my impression is that dreaming too, however fleeting and strange, has some of the qualities of an experience told along with those of an experience lived. This is another way of describing the effect noted by Sartre elsewhere, that in dreams 'events occur as if not being able not to happen'.[2]

The appeal of this book's theme is the compelling ubiquity of dream experience, and the special attraction of the essays it contains is the variety of their approaches to 'reading dreams'. They range over a long period from the fourteenth to the seventeenth century, with ventures back into classical antiquity and the earlier Middle Ages and forward as far as David Lynch's *Blue Velvet*. The collection thus implies a welcome questioning of the indispensable yet dubious periodization that divides 'medieval' from 'Renaissance' or 'early modern'. The ideological motivation that originally produced the idea of a dark and unchanging *medium aevum* between antiquity and modernity is often forgotten in the apparent naturalness of consensus and, as David Aers observes, this periodization has in recent years formed the basis for 'profoundly unhistorical' assertions about the 'newly interiorated subject'[3] of early modernity. The representations of dreams and visions in medieval texts, as discussed in this volume, demonstrate clearly enough that medieval writers fully grasped the concept of the 'interiorated subject'. A major problem here has been the confusion of interiority with individuality.

---

[1] J.-P. Sartre, *Nausea*, trans. R. Baldick (Harmondsworth, 1965), 61–3.

[2] J.-P. Sartre, *The Psychology of Imagination*, trans. B. Frechtman (New York, 1966), 220.

[3] I take this phrase from F. Barker, *The Tremulous Private Body: Essays on Subjection* (London, 1984), 52.

The dream's content may not be individualized, for it may claim to offer a vision of absolute truth rather than a glimpse of what is peculiar to one dreamer's mind and body or (like dreams such as those in *The Kingis Quair* or the English poetic sequence of Charles of Orleans) a turning-point in his understanding of his waking situation. But whatever its content, the space of the dream is unquestionably that of an interiority that can only be called subjective. Steven Kruger's brilliant analysis of ways in which the ' "somatizing" of dream theory' produces 'a merging or crossing of medical and moral discourses' in later medieval texts such as Chaucer's *Book of the Duchess* and Henryson's *Testament of Cresseid* is only one demonstration of the value of studying both dream theories and literary dreams with scholarly attention if we are to gain a truer understanding of the history of the subject.

The variety of approaches in *Reading Dreams* is not only a matter of period and periodization but of the critical and scholarly methods adopted by the contributors. These include Kathryn Lynch's scrupulous deployment of traditional source-studies (again across the supposed gap between medieval and Renaissance), David Aers's vigorously polemical discussion of the ethics of interpretation, and the richly informative surveys of post-medieval dream interpretation by Peter Holland and of the multiple functions of dreams in early modern drama by Kathleen McLuskie. One aim that emerges from the whole collection is to historicize—to place dreams and their interpretation more exactly in specific cultural contexts, which means in turn to define those contexts more exactly through the inclusion of new material and new understanding—and inevitably this raises questions about the possibilities and limits of historicization. In discussing the work of the several contributors (though I cannot avoid some fairly bland summary), I focus on the challenges they offer, which often means focusing on areas of doubt and disagreement. But I have learned more from this collection than from most books I have read in recent years, and what I have learned has made me long to be able to rewrite my own book, *Medieval Dream-Poetry*, now over twenty years old, so as to remedy some of its distortions and blindnesses.

Peter Brown, in his 'On the Borders of Middle English Dream Visions', engages at an early stage with the difficulties of historicization, towards which his attitude seems to me honourably ambivalent. Enquiring why there should be such a concentration of dream poetry among the major English poems of about 1350–1400, he refers to the changes in philosophical outlook offered as explanations by previous

scholars (Lynch and Kruger among them), and argues that these historical contexts are unsatisfactory in being 'represented in causative,
monolithic, and general terms. To be convincing, the historical context
needs to be more specific, more complex, more circumstantial.' He is
surely right, and it might be added that the field of medieval philosophical discourse is still so alien to all but a few experts (who are often in disagreement among themselves) that we take great risks in attempting to
translate it into readily intelligible terms, usable for an understanding of
the rise and fall of literary genres. Moreover, the notion of cause in
human history is so dubious that we should surely hesitate in employing
it to explain what we actually understand much better, literary texts.
The causes of the First World War, a sequence of events overwhelm-
ingly documented and still just within living memory, are ferociously
disputed; what chance then is there that we shall be able to define historical causes for the proliferation of English dream poems in the far
more distant era of the late fourteenth century?

Brown turns instead to something internal to these texts, the 'key literary mechanism' of falling asleep and entering a dream, which he sees
as 'a powerful device for signalling a state of altered consciousness'.
This apparently simple statement embodies an important insight.
Brown notes the varied circumstances in which poets begin their
dreams—times, places, and, above all, the range of personal situations
that tend to conduce to 'a state of inwardness and anxiety', and thus to
a heightened degree of receptivity. The following shift from wakefulness to sleep is not necessarily from one world to another, for, as Brown
puts it, 'the dream world is not to be thought of as wholly different from
waking experience, but in some measure a different account of it'. In my
view, this is probably truer of the late medieval dream poems with
which he is concerned than of earlier medieval visions, which can open
the dreamer's mind to a realm of absolute truth totally different from his
waking world. But by the late fourteenth century even *Pearl*, a poem in
which the dreamer is detached from his body and carried to the very
brink of St John's heavenly city, also contains details that can be interpreted as reflecting his waking experience. The Pearl maiden's apparent
detachment from human feelings belongs to her heavenly situation as a
bride of the Lamb and one of those who 'þurȝoutly hauen cnawyng'
(859),[4] but at the same time it can be interpreted through the dreamer's

---

[4] *The Poems of the Pearl Manuscript: Pearl, Cleanness, Patience, Sir Gawain and the
Green Knight*, ed. M. Andrew and R. Waldron, York Medieval Texts, 2nd ser. (London,
1978).

eyes as having something of the innocent but painful callousness natural to the small child she was when she died.

Next comes what seems to me the most illuminating move in Brown's argument: if 'the onset of dreaming indicates a state of altered consciousness', may it not be as much a symptom as a cause of that alteration? If so, 'the existence of a dream boundary is not in itself crucial to the meaning of the poem'. Numerous examples illustrate the truth of this observation. In some French *dits amoureux* a dream boundary is lacking where in other generically similar poems a boundary is present. Similarly in poems existing in variant versions, even those such as *Piers Plowman* and the Prologue to *The Legend of Good Women* that are the work of major poets, dream boundaries may be shifted or omitted without the changes seeming to be specially significant. Thus the dream itself may be no more than 'one option among many for signifying a state of altered consciousness'.

I find this fully convincing. In *Medieval Dream-Poetry*, I arbitrarily confined myself to poems where a dream boundary is explicitly present, but even at the time I sensed uneasily that this meant excluding others not essentially different in kind. The implication is that the dream poem, characterized by an explicit dream framework, is not a distinct genre, but rather occupies an important area in a more vaguely divided generic spectrum. We badly need such insights into the largely unformulated generic systems that helped to shape medieval writing; without them we are liable to seek laboriously for subtle significance in differences that might have been perceived by medieval readers as relatively trivial.

In the closing stages of his essay Brown returns to the problem of historicization. Given that dreams are 'well suited to the representation and analysis of alienation, of a sense of lost authority, or of a searching for connections that have become hidden, tenuous, or problematic', does the late medieval efflorescence of dream poetry occur as 'a response to those economic, social, political, and religious conditions which were likely to produce a sense of fragmentation, of lost identity, of questionable authority'? He notes the suggestive analogy between this aptness of the dream to explore what Kruger has elsewhere called 'areas of betweenness'[5] and the concept of liminality theorized by Victor and Edith Turner as focused in pilgrimage (itself a frequent theme in medieval dream poems). Yet at the same time Brown is aware of the

---

[5] S. F. Kruger, *Dreaming in the Middle Ages*, Cambridge Studies in Medieval Literature 14 (Cambridge, 1992), 129.

danger of the 'abstracting, generalizing, and universalizing tendencies' inherent in the use of such theorization to relate literary texts to their cultural moment. The danger is real, but we are left with a powerful stimulus to apply ideas of the liminal to specific poems in what we can discover of their specific contexts.

In 'Medical and Moral Authority in the Late Medieval Dream', Steven Kruger's unusual focus on the connection between dreams and bodily sickness splendidly illuminates his two literary examples. Most readings of Cresseid's vision of the planetary gods in Henryson's *Testament of Cresseid* have indeed been marked by 'the simple allegorizing and spiritualizing tendencies' that he attributes to earlier scholarship. Yet this poem gazes unflinchingly at the 'spottis blak, | And lumpis haw' of leprosy, a physical 'seiknes incurabill' imposed by the gods as punishment for Cresseid's blasphemy—the 'sclander and defame iniurious' involved in blaming Cupid and Venus for the consequence of her own 'leuing vnclene and lecherous' (339–40, 307, 284–5).[6] As the deities of classical paganism, the gods want things both ways: they control specific aspects of human behaviour, yet refuse to accept responsibility for that behaviour's outcome. But they are also the planets of medieval natural and medical science, and so the dream in which Cresseid sees them can be interpreted as a symptom of 'melancholic humour occasioned by incipient leprosy'. Melancholy stimulated dreams, especially those of dark-coloured things such as the 'gyte full gay of gray' and the 'gyte . . . gray and full of spottis blak' (164, 260) worn respectively by Saturn and the moon, the planets appointed to assess Cresseid's punishment. Kruger is right to argue that what is important in this terrifying and powerfully complex vision is not any contradiction between the medical and the moral but rather the 'mutual reinforcement' of these two discourses, of the body and of the spirit.

It might be useful, though, to invoke a larger context. Recent study of late medieval religious practice has shown it to be characterized by approaches to the transcendent *through* the bodily. This is true in areas as various as the cult of the eucharist and the growing importance of devotions (associated especially though by no means exclusively with women) that focus on Christ's bodily sufferings and take bodily forms such as weeping and refusal of food.[7] Kruger writes later that 'The

---

    [6] R. Henryson, *The Testament of Cresseid*, in *The Poems of Robert Henryson*, ed. D. Fox (Oxford, 1981). All subsequent quotations from Henryson are from this edition.
    [7] e.g. M. Rubin, *Corpus Christi: The Eucharist in Late Medieval Culture* (Cambridge,

complex medieval Christian ideology of body—one that embraces a "proper" (masculine) gendering and heterosexual positioning of the male body—also recognizes that a truly masculine attitude towards body pushes beyond embodiment, towards spiritual transcendence.' If 'incarnation' were substituted for 'embodiment', it would become clearer that in the later Middle Ages there is no single 'Christian ideology of body', however complex. Certainly we can find writings, such as *The Cloud of Unknowing*, that have as their goal a spiritual transcendence beyond even God's incarnation; but a more powerful stream of devotion places a positive value on embodiment and sees the body as the primary means of access to divinity. Given the traditional association of the body with femaleness, we might perhaps expect to find a move towards female dreamers in the poetry of the later Middle Ages. No such move is in evidence, though it is true that in Kruger's other main example, *The Book of the Duchess*, Alcyone's refusal to eat, and her swooning and weeping, followed by her dream of Ceyx's 'dreynte body' (92, 103, 107, 195), might be seen as pagan correlatives to these religious developments.[8] As Kruger observes, 'Alcyone's illness . . . eventuates in a dream linked to both body and divinity'. In general, however, what we find is not female dreamers achieving transcendence through the body, but male dreamers whose bodies are feminized, whether by religious devotion or by passionate love or equally passionate empathy.

Kruger's argument, that in the *Book of the Duchess* obsessive returns to 'the question of melancholy' produce a dream that is at once '(morally or spiritually) instructive' and '(somatically) corrective', is ingenious and enlightening. This is especially true of its bearing on the poem's treatment of gender, which Kruger sees as complex and fluctuating. In the speaker of the prologue, 'a certain gender undefinedness or ambiguity' may be recognized as a symptom of the feminization—the loss of rational self-control—produced by melancholy. The disappearance of the diagnosis of heterosexual love-sickness found in the prologue's source, Froissart's *Paradys d'Amours*, leaves the speaker with only an undefined malady that is 'agaynes kynde' (16) and thus 'potentially "queer"'. (It might be worth considering whether the 'gender undefinedness' of Chaucer's prologue has any connection with the absence from English of certain gendering features of French grammar. Froissart's *je* is grammatically

1991); C. W. Bynum, *Fragmentation and Redemption: Essays on Gender and the Human Body in Medieval Religion* (New York, 1991).

   [8] *The Riverside Chaucer*, 3rd edn., ed. L. D. Benson, (Boston, Mass., 1987). Except where stated, quotations from Chaucer's works are from this edition.

specified as masculine before his love-object is identified as feminine and female. The loss of grammatical gender may have larger implications.)

The Alcyone episode, Kruger argues, heterosexualizes the situation through the narrator's sympathetic identification with her, but at the same time reinforces 'questions we might have about the narrator's "masculinity"'. The dream works 'more rigorously to secure the narrator's heterosexual and "masculine" identity', first in the hunt, then in the encounter with the knight. That encounter is potentially homoerotic, but its homoeroticism 'is deflected . . . into a male homosociality that operates to secure a bond between men through the (fantasmatic) heterosexual exchange of women'. Here again my feeling is that a larger context, without invalidating these provocative observations, might put them in a somewhat different perspective. Kruger reads the Chaucerian 'I' as the label of a being who in principle possesses the ontological consistency attributed to waking persons in real life, one whose gender and sexual orientation then appear in different lights as the poem proceeds, moving ultimately towards 'correction' and stability. Suppose, though, that we were to see the textual 'I' as no more than a grammatical focus for meanings unstably diffused over the whole text? And suppose that, even in late medieval dream poems where the 'I' is to some degree individualized and may even share some of the poet's biography (a development not yet reached in the *Book of the Duchess*), that 'I' still retained some of the instability of reference that belongs to writing as opposed to speech and to dreaming as opposed to waking? Surely we should expect the oneiric 'I' to be less stable than the ego of waking life—for to dream may be to descend below the gender hierarchies of the cultural realm and to re-enter an underlying psychic androgyny.

For Chaucer, several forces besides the revalorization of the bodily in late medieval Christianity help to destabilize the literary effect of gender. One is the loosening of existing gender identification involved both in Middle English textuality and in dreaming. Another is the pressure towards a more specific feminization exerted by late medieval courtliness, with its aestheticization of daily life and its cult of passionate feeling (as in Richard II's uncontrolled grief at the death of Anne of Bohemia). A third and fourth can be seen in the early dream poems in the first-person responses to the suffering of female characters such as Alcyone in the *Book of the Duchess* and Dido in the *House of Fame*. As a male reteller of classical stories, Chaucer is feminized by his inability to change what was authoritatively set down in the Latin books written and read by men, those stories

That clerkes had in olde tyme,
And other poetes, put in rime
To rede and for to be in minde . . .

(BD 53–5)

And he is further feminized by his inability to resist identification with suffering women and to control the sorrow aroused in him by their sorrow:

Such sorowe this lady to her tok
That trewly I, that made this book,
Had such pittee and such rowthe,
To rede hir sorwe that, by my trowthe,
I ferde the worse al the morwe
Aftir to thenken on hir sorwe.

(95–100)

Heroic masculinity, exemplified in the Theseus of the Knight's Tale, also feels *pittee* and *rowthe* for women, but there sympathy stimulates action directed to the redress of female suffering;[9] the poet is no hero and can only weep helplessly with female victims. I am suggesting that it may be helpful to look beyond the medical perspective introduced by Kruger, illuminating though it is; if my response to his essay leads in directions he might be unwilling to take, I hope that will be accepted as a tribute to its rewardingly provocative power.

David Aers, in his concise and exhilaratingly combative study, 'Interpreting Dreams: Reflections on Freud, Milton, and Chaucer', has the splendid idea of comparing the methods of dream interpretation adopted by Freud in the case history of Dora with those found in literary representations of dreams by Chaucer and by Milton. His predominant concern is with the functions of power and gender in the interpreter's relation to the dream and its dreamer; and, in the real-life case of Freud and Dora, his indignant sympathy with the teenaged girl who is doubly victimized by middle-aged men is generous and heartening.[10] Dora suffers first Herr K.'s sexual assault, then Freud's own 'imperialistic discourse', imposing alien meanings on her experience. Freud treats Dora as a mere text, subject to an exegesis that will always serve to confirm his

---

[9] Cf. B. Nolan, *Chaucer and the Tradition of the Roman Antique*, Cambridge Studies in Medieval Literature 15 (Cambridge, 1992), 266–8.

[10] Compare the more nuanced treatment in L. Appignanesi and J. Forrester, *Freud's Women* (London, 1992), ch. 5.

preconceived assumptions—his stupefyingly arrogant ' "No" signifies the desired "Yes" ' is only the most egregious instance cited—and such treatment is rightly seen by Aers as a kind of rape. Dora's dreams are among the objects of interpretation. Aers describes the mode of exegesis as 'allegorical', and he invites comparison of Freud's facile sexual allegorization of objects such as Dora's reticule with the employment of a similar allegorical mode 'to sustain different metaphysics' in patristic scriptural commentary—the theme of his own first book, *Piers Plowman and Christian Allegory*.

What makes Freud's approach 'imperialistic' is its avoidance of dialogue, its refusal to engage with Dora's own responses to and interpretations of her dreams and other experiences. Aers points to a similar 'imperialism' in *Paradise Lost*, in Adam's interpretation of Eve's dream in Book V. For Eve, the dream is associated with a 'complex and contradictory set of feelings', but Adam takes no interest in these, and his monologic interpretation thus 'reinforces received divisions of power and authority around the construction of gender'. Finally, Aers moves further back in time to discuss dream interpretation in three poems by Chaucer; and here, while still wanting to cheer him on, I feel more uncertainty as to what can be learned from such cases. The Wife of Bath explains in her Prologue how she told Jankyn, her fifth husband, that she dreamed he attempted to kill her, 'And al my bed was ful of verray blood'. She interpreted this favourably, on the ground that 'blood bitokeneth gold' (581–3). But she tells *us* that the dream was really a fiction, learned from her mother, and Aers comments that 'The sequence almost invites any potential interpreter . . . to occupy the position of a knower who has the ability to track a road to the dreamer's hidden inner world, a road the dreamer herself cannot follow without an exegete's help. The invitation turns out to be both lure and trap . . .'. To be too confident of one's ability to interpret the dream would certainly be a mistake; but, given that we cannot engage in dialogue with the Wife, I see no reason why we should not guess at what such an invented dream might reveal beyond what she tells us about herself, so long as we do not pretend that our guesses are more than guesses. If we imagine the Wife as the fictive equivalent of a real person (as I think Aers does, and as the references to her in the Merchant's Tale, the epilogue to the Clerk's Tale, and the ballade to Bukton seem to indicate that Chaucer did), why should we not also speculate about her motives, whether conscious or unconscious, for inventing this dream and its meaning? The concept of unconscious motivation may be dangerous in lending itself so readily to authoritarian glossing, and medieval people certainly did not see it in the same way as we do, but it can scarcely be abolished.

The case of Chauntecleer's dream in the Nun's Priest's Tale is more straightforward, and here Aers's argument that 'dream texts and their interpretations are appropriately approached through attention to the social relations within which they are produced' seems entirely convincing. The third Chaucerian case, Troilus' dream of Criseyde and the boar in *Troilus and Criseyde* Book V, glossed in turn by Troilus himself, by Pandarus, and by Cassandra, well illustrates Chaucer's awareness that dreams resist single interpretations, and that interpretation itself, far from being objective, is almost invariably shaped by the interpreter's interests. Whether we can learn from it of the 'consequences of an interpretation that breaks away from the dialogic mode' I doubt. Does Chaucer ever represent interpretation as dialogic? Even Chauntecleer and Pertelote seem to interpret past each other rather than engaging in dialogue, for their views of Chauntecleer's dream derive from opposing preconceived theories about dreams in general. And while we ought to resist the treatment of people as texts, what are we to do with texts, which cannot answer back? Dialogism can perhaps be understood as an attitude rather than a method; and Aers's own attitude, pulling no punches but implicitly inviting equally hard counter-punches, is one I welcome and admire.

The argument of Kathryn Lynch's carefully documented 'Baring Bottom: Shakespeare and the Chaucerian Dream Vision' is that Shakespeare was an 'astute reader' of the tradition of medieval dream poems, and that *A Midsummer Night's Dream* correspondingly reflects the ambiguity of dream in antique and medieval theory—'sometimes the insignificant product of anxiety and preoccupation, but sometimes the messenger of profound truth'. Shakespeare, in an age that regarded Chaucer as an 'intellectual, learned, and philosophical writer', would, she suggests, have responded to 'the medieval poet's generic sophistication and philosophical complexity'. The question of how Shakespeare read Chaucer, what *kind* of poet he saw his great predecessor as being, is indeed fascinating, and has scarcely been raised even in the best comparative studies.[11] Shakespeare, after all, never writes, as Spenser does, specifically about *poetic* tradition, never indicates that he sees Chaucer

---

[11]   e.g. A. Thompson, *Shakespeare's Chaucer: A Study in Literary Origins* (Liverpool, 1978); E. T. Donaldson, *The Swan at the Well: Shakespeare Reading Chaucer* (New Haven, 1985).

as father; and one reason may well be that his theatrical medium severs him from this learned tradition and from the figure of the poet as the 'I' of his writing. And whereas Chaucer reveals by quotation and reference his sense of a tradition of learned inspiration going back through the Trecento to antiquity, and Spenser similarly evokes that tradition as one that now includes Chaucer too, such features are quite lacking from Shakespeare's writing. In all his work, Shakespeare never mentions Chaucer or any other English poet except Gower, the quaintly archaic Chorus of *Pericles*; the allusion to Marlowe as the 'dead shepherd' of *As You Like It* stands conspicuously alone as an indication of Shakespeare's sense of belonging to an English poetic tradition.[12] Perhaps he knew himself to be greater poet than those English predecessors he had read, as Spenser could not have known himself to be a greater poet than Chaucer? Or perhaps, as is suggested by the constant evocation of theatrical themes in his poetic language, he was so much a man of the theatre that that was the tradition which meant most to him—and to his audience? The chance of approaching an answer to these questions makes Lynch's project especially welcome.

Her account of the *Legend of Good Women* is perceptive and often original; I especially liked her remark that the God of Love's 'literal ability to see signals his inability to perceive deeply or figuratively', so that, by a telling paradox, 'Cupid's sight . . . figures his blindness'; and sight and blindness are unquestionably major themes of the *Dream*. But when Lynch urges against another recent scholar that the *Legend* is a main source for Shakespeare's Pyramus and Thisbe, arguing that the fact that Shakespeare had access to other Renaissance versions of this story 'fails to prove that Chaucer's *Legend* was not an additional source', she raises troubling questions about the value of source-studies, as conceived in terms of scientifically demonstrable influence and indebtedness. How can we prove that a poet did *not* use a particular source, given that it was available to him? And, more important, how would it change our

[12] The allusion, in III. v, is to *Hero and Leander*, not to any of Marlowe's plays. Surrey is a character in *Henry VIII*, but not in his role as poet; he also appears in *Sir Thomas More*, and is referred to there as 'our honoured English poet' (III. i)—improbably, since he was only 18 when More was executed—but this is in a passage not attributed to Shakespeare. Shakespeare places poets on the fringe of classical history in *Julius Caesar* and *Timon of Athens*. It would be pleasant if he had taken the opportunity to pay tribute to his own poetic predecessors by including them in his English histories—Chaucer in *Richard II* or *1 Henry IV* (where he might have begged the continuation of his pension), Lydgate in *Henry V* or *1* or *2 Henry VI* (perhaps requesting payment from Duke Humphrey), Skelton or Wyatt in *Henry VIII* (Wyatt could have composed the lute-song in III. i)—but he did not.

understanding of the *Dream* if we could know that Shakespeare was or was not indebted to Chaucer for his presentation of Pyramus and Thisbe? I believe Lynch to be right that he was, but I am not sure how much it matters. A consequence of her admirably comprehensive and scrupulous approach is that such minor issues can distract the reader's attention from more important insights, such as her discussion of ways in which the 'series of competing perspectives on the action' in the *Dream* is analogous to the 'juxtaposition of competing perspectives' made possible by the dream framework in medieval poems, and her suggestion that for both Chaucer and Shakespeare the dream vision 'becomes a form that embodies the infinite regressiveness of language and its self-undermining deconstructions'.

The *Legend* is not of course the only Chaucerian source for the *Dream*, though it is the one for which Lynch marshals evidence most illuminatingly. A different area in which 'juxtaposition of competing perspectives' may be found is the characterization of Theseus, and if Shakespeare was a careful reader of Chaucer he would have found competing versions, taken from different sources, of this classical hero-villain in the *Legend*, the Knight's Tale (from which he took the frame narrative of the wedding of Theseus and Hippolyta, and at least the name of Egeus), and the *House of Fame*. Shakespeare's Theseus, as recent scholars including Peter Holland have noted, may be 'ardent and tolerant' but he also bears traces of the 'sexual betrayal and death' that darken other phases of his complex legend. Lynch shows how these conflicting characteristics all appear in Chaucer's retellings, where they are sometimes linked in subtle ways: thus the *Legend* includes not only the story of Ariadne, in which Theseus is an unscrupulous betrayer, but also, in its Prologue, a reference to the Knight's Tale, where he is a 'noble duc' (873). She goes further, finding in the Knight's Tale itself hints of a Duke Theseus who is less than noble. In this she is supported by other twentieth-century critics, but I must say that I think this view mistaken. Chaucer is careful to exclude references to Theseus as betrayer from the Knight's Tale, and the exclusion is silent, unlike, say, the exclusion of information about the Amazons, to which he calls attention in his opening lines. Only 'resisting readers' of the tale will find in it the darker side of Theseus that emerges elsewhere in Chaucer's work and, likely enough under Chaucerian influence, in *A Midsummer Night's Dream*.

The richest reward of Lynch's study comes at its conclusion, where she puts Chaucer and Shakespeare alongside each other, sees them as 'sceptics of a similar cast of mind', but also distinguishes tellingly between them. Chaucer is, in Sheila Delany's phrase, a 'skeptical fideist', one who 'must turn, finally, to faith and theology for a solution to those problems he cannot untangle himself. Shakespeare, in contrast, moves past the limits of reason; he makes his scepticism finally an opening for the possibility of belief, and belief that finds its ground within, rather than outside, itself.' I find this distinction remarkably fruitful. For the medieval poet imagination confuses and deceives; for the Renaissance playwright imagination—explicitly a central theme of *A Midsummer Night's Dream* as it is not of Chaucer's dream poems— has the capacity to be truly transformative and creative. Chaucer deals in complexity, Shakespeare in mystery. The *Legend of Good Women* is one of the places where Chaucer comes closest to addressing the power that makes him a poet, but neither there nor elsewhere in his work is there any equivalent to the moonlight that in the *Dream* pervades rational Athens as well as the lawless wood outside. Coleridge was to envisage moonlight as 'the imaginative Poesy of Nature' which 'spreads its soft shadowy charm over all, conceals distances, and magnifies heights, and modifies relations; and fills up vacuities with its own whiteness, counterfeiting substance; and where the dense shadows lie, makes solidity imitate Hollowness; and gives to all objects a tender visionary hue and softening'.[13] We might not wish to follow Frank Kermode in seeing the *Dream* as unequivocally visionary,[14] but I do not believe we distort it in finding in it a foreshadowing of a Romantic idea of imagination.

Peter Holland has recently edited *A Midsummer Night's Dream*,[15] and in ' "The Interpretation of Dreams" in the Renaissance' he valuably extends the discussion of Renaissance dreams and dream interpretation in his introduction to that edition. Like Aers, he begins from Freud and moves backwards. Freud saw Descartes's famous dreams of 1619, which resolved his indecision about his career, as 'Träume von oben', which the dreamer himself is best able to interpret; but for Freud this meant that they came from a higher level of the dreamer's own psyche, whereas to Descartes, even while he was still sleeping, they seemed to be Macrobian *somnia*, prophetic dreams, and of divine not natural origin.

[13] S. T. Coleridge, *Aids to Reflection*, ed. J. Beer, in *The Collected Works*, vol. ix (Princeton, 1993), 393.
[14] F. Kermode, 'The Mature Comedies', in J. R. Brown and B. Harris (eds.), *Early Shakespeare*, Stratford-upon-Avon Studies 3 (London, 1961), 211–27.
[15] W. Shakespeare, *A Midsummer Night's Dream*, ed. P. Holland, The Oxford Shakespeare (Oxford, 1994).

As Holland observes, 'there seems something pleasingly paradoxical in the way that these dreams, enabling causes for the development of an ontological epistemology based on rationality, on the process of thought itself, are defined by the dreamer through their non-human agency'. Descartes was unusual in his certainty as to the prophetic status of his dreams. Renaissance interpreters, adding little to the dream theories they inherited, saw most dreams as being of natural origin, shaped by and permitting the diagnosis of the dreamer's 'complexion' or balance of humours. Holland's main concern is with the 'range of formulations' within this context for the problem of 'the possible prophetic purpose and non-human agency of dreams'.

His material is fascinating. Reginald Scot denied that modern dreams could be revelatory, and showed contempt for interpreters. Archbishop Laud doubted the value of his dreams even when they were apparently prophetic, yet recorded them in his diary all the same—perhaps an illustration of the fact that what characterizes dream experience is above all that it *feels* charged with significance. Montaigne claimed to dream little himself, but often wrote of the significance of others' dreams; for him, waking was a kind of dreaming, and sleeping dreams were 'nothing more than a transfer and reformulation of the day-residue'; thus 'The act of analysing the waking self is sufficient to account for the material of dreams.'

As Holland shows, dreams appear in an even wider variety of contexts in Renaissance than in medieval writings. They continued to be used as literary constructs to frame material not readily acceptable when presented directly: Kepler enclosed his scientific writing about the moon in a dream framework. Vives went back behind Macrobius to the *Somnium Scipionis* itself, and showed interest in 'the "lucid dream", the dream in which the dreamer is aware of dreaming and, while asleep, analyses the dream experience'; his commentary is itself a 'mocking meta-dream'. Discussion of the many possible views of the causes and significance of dreams, a recurrent element in medieval dream poems (as in the *House of Fame* and *Piers Plowman* B. VII), was greatly extended in Renaissance writings. In a multivocal discussion of dreams in Jean Bodin's *Colloquium of the Seven*, Salomon, representing Judaism, 'consistently argues for the significance of dreams', against the predominant scepticism; and Leon Modena, a seventeenth-century Venetian rabbi, saw 'dream interpretation and dream divination' as 'regular parts of his activities'. This last case especially illustrates the need to place 'dreams and their interpretation within a specific culture'. This is a valuable emphasis, shared with other contributors to the collection, and Holland offers enticing glimpses of the large stock of Renaissance records of dreams, their interpretation, and attitudes towards them. Ideally, we might hope one day for a comprehensive archive of Renaissance dreams; it might even include European colonies in the New World.

Spanish culture is illustrated by the recording of over 400 dreams by a young woman, Lucrecia de León, in the late 1580s: these included many seen as seditious and heretical, and got her into trouble with the Inquisition. Spanish priests, like the Venetian rabbi, saw dream interpretation as part of their work, and thus in Spain this was an area of conflict, as apparently in England it was not, between 'the community and the systems of authority'.

The most interesting dream theory that Holland unearths is that of Jerome Cardan. His study of dreams included discussion of his own dream diary, an 'almost unprecedented' phenomenon; and he saw all dreams, even those that might be prophetic, as 'composed of memory-images'. Nothing so original or logically argued is to be found among English writers. The most substantial discussion is Thomas Hill's sixteenth-century treatise, entitled in *unheimlich* anticipation of Freud *The most pleasaunte Arte of the Interpretacion of Dreames*. Hill relies heavily on Aristotle and Averroes, yet sometimes apparently fails to understand them. He values the art of interpretation highly, but his attempt to synthesize the wide range of available dream theories is 'unsystematic, leaping from topic to topic arbitrarily; Hill fails to find a way of setting out dream theory any more completely as a rational, organized science than his predecessors had done'. Finally Holland turns to the learned and energetic if undiscriminating discussion of dreams in Thomas Nashe's *Terrors of the Night* as a vivid evocation of the pleasure found in dream interpretation in the period with which he is concerned. His pioneering survey of this field itself conveys pleasure along with knowledge; I long to know more, and hope Holland will take his investigations further.

Kathleen McLuskie begins her essay, 'The Candy-Colored Clown: Reading Early Modern Dreams', with a scintillating account of images of dreaming in David Lynch's *Blue Velvet* and of the complex effects they produce for contemporary cinema audiences. Her statement of the model this establishes for scholarly reading of early modern dreams, especially those in drama, her chief interest, is worth quoting at length:

In its complex intertextuality and its play with vulgar Freudianism, *Blue Velvet* seems very much of its time. Yet the range of cultural reference which every spectator must bring to this film offers a model of the complexities required to provide an adequate account of dreams in earlier cultures. Lynch is able to play with images of dreaming since he is making films in a long tradition which associates films with dreaming, and which uses dreams and dream sequences as part of the language of the cinematic 'dream factory'. Reading dreams in early modern culture requires a similar attention to the connections between dreams and theatre, to the available models for the interpretation of dreams, and to the ways in which this cultural raw material contributes to the development of a dramatic and theatrical language of representation.

This is excellently put, but it seems to me to propose an unattainable ideal. The 'cultural raw material' with which Lynch works is in fact material already cooked many times over: like the pies of Chaucer's Cook, it was already 'twies hoot and twies coold' when it came to him. Moreover, this material is intimately known to Lynch's audience as part of the cultural literacy of their age; but we cannot hope to have anything like such intimacy with the material used by creative artists in early modern times. The best we can hope for, as the fruit of dedicated scholarship, is a partial knowledge of literary and pictorial traditions, and of some social history; much of the 'dramatic and theatrical language of representation' must remain unintelligible to us, to such an extent that we shall frequently not know whether we understand it or not. To pretend otherwise is to lend the cloak of academic authority to intellectual fashion and personal fantasy. Ideally, yes, we should aim to historicize, and we should do our utmost to fulfil this aim; but we should also remain aware that the further back we go the more insufficient our utmost will be.

In practice, McLuskie's wide-ranging study of dreams in early modern drama is rarely open to such objections. In plays such as *The Comedy of Errors* and *The Taming of the Shrew* dreams are envisaged 'as alternative realities which parallel the reality of waking existence', while in others 'The association of dreams with both pleasure and loss . . . allows them to serve as powerful images for the experience of love.' Again, 'The sense that theatre was a dream could be turned into an expression of the transitoriness of all human experience', as in *The Tempest*. But the attitudes towards dreams expressed by play-characters may seem 'frustratingly limited', and here McLuskie takes up Montrose's attempt[16] to find a deeper meaning in Bottom's vision in

---

[16] L. A. Montrose, ' "Shaping Fantasies": Figurations of Gender and Power in Elizabethan Culture', *Representations*, 2 (1983), 61–94.

A Midsummer Night's Dream than the play itself makes explicit. Montrose, employing the characteristic anecdotal method of new historicism, begins by comparing Bottom's dream with one recorded by the astrologer Simon Forman, who was also a keen playgoer, in his diary for 1597. In this fascinating dream, recalled in detail that authenticates and tantalizes, Forman meets Queen Elizabeth (as aged as she was by then in reality), strikes up a friendship, makes a dirty joke to her, and awakes as she is about to kiss him. Montrose offers an interpretation in terms of Oedipal fantasy, and comments that 'Bottom's dream, like Forman's, is an experience of fleeting intimacy with a powerful female who is at once lover, mother, and queen'.[17] McLuskie observes that behind this psychoanalytic interpretation, which 'makes no concession to genre or literary tradition', lies Jameson's concept of a 'cultural unconscious' unknown to Forman or Shakespeare themselves, but 'revealed by the theoretical tools of a later age'. The method employed produces 'a coherence which seems more satisfying, because more complete, than the simple connections made by the characters in the play between dreams and waking aspirations'. A discussion of this point between McLuskie and Aers would be welcome. The desire to find a totalizing interpretation may itself be totalitarian (or 'imperialistic'); and it is a desire aroused by dreams as much as by works of literature. Perhaps Jameson and Montrose are excessively monologic, too ready to disregard the directly experienced manifest levels of literary or oneiric texts. Yet can we be forbidden to propose *possible* interpretations that are not dialogic, or compelled to read plays and dreams only in the terms they themselves make available? In the case of literary analysis, if not in that of psychoanalytic therapy, totalizing interpretations may themselves provoke the very dialogue (among interpreters) that they seem to forbid.

'Coherent explanations' were also the aim of early modern dream interpreters, though their assumptions differed from ours, and where they employed 'allegorical and symbolic correspondences' to reveal prophecy, we may want to employ methods that will elicit hidden truths about the dreamer's psychology. An intriguing example McLuskie introduces is that of Ben Jonson's dream of his son's death, seen by Jonson as prophetic but by a modern scholar as expressing Jonson's guilt about his wish to abandon his family. I am sufficiently a product of the post-Freudian age to find in the psychoanalytic interpretation an

---

[17] L. A. Montrose, '"Shaping Fantasies", 65.

irresistible insight, though I would not wish it simply to replace Jonson's own reading. And indeed, McLuskie later suggests that by the seventeenth century dreams were in practice sometimes read as products of an interior unconscious. She returns to the dreams of Laud discussed by Holland, but puts them in a different context, which enables us to set one kind of contemporary interpretation against another. Prynne, Laud's bitter enemy, published selections from the archbishop's diary with his own commentary, especially on the recorded dreams, and though 'there was no hard and fast distinction between the superstitious Prynne and the rational archbishop', the two men did see specific dreams in quite different terms. For Prynne, the dreams were prophetic revelations of Laud's political ambition and concealed Catholicism; Laud protested against this 'imperialistic' appropriation, and in McLuskie's view saw his own dreams in terms of a 'modern sense of . . . identity' for which incoherence could point to meanings beyond the reach of consciousness.

Dreams in early modern plays follow various contemporary models and resist generalization. McLuskie shows that *Sir Thomas More* includes in an inner play an account of a dream taking 'the old-fashioned form of a medieval dream vision', alongside the anxiety dreams recounted by Lady More and Margaret Roper, which are more realistic but still use topical allusion and literary symbolism. The play also echoes contemporary disputes about dream interpretation. It might be added that this is another respect in which the supposedly insuperable barrier between medieval and Renaissance depends on dogma rather than observation. In Chaucer's *Troilus and Criseyde*, two centuries earlier, we can already find different kinds of dream coexisting within a single complex work. In Book V, before Troilus' dream of Criseyde and the boar, a clear and coherent narrative that seems to demand some kind of symbolic decoding, come his fragmentary nightmares of frightening landscapes and capture by his enemies,

> And therwithal his body sholde sterte,
> And with the stert al sodeynliche awake,
> And swich a tremour fele aboute his herte
> That of the fere his body sholde quake;
> And therwithal he sholde a noyse make,
> And seme as though he sholde falle depe
> From heighe o-lofte . . .
>
> (V. 253–9)

Here no interpretation is necessary, for the nightmares are among the symptoms of anxiety that directly affect his body.[18]

By contrast, the 'narrative coherence and poetic eloquence' with which Clarence describes his dream in *Richard III* mean that it lacks 'the compressed inconsequentiality of real dreams'. McLuskie sees that this dream has more than one function: it reveals simultaneously an internal conflict in Clarence's mind and the ironic shaping of the play's events. Here too, I would add, we can find in an early modern work traces of earlier conceptions of dreams. Clarence evokes a Dantean vision of punishment after death and of a transcendent justice beyond the play's political realm. In doing so he continues the classical and medieval conception of dream not just as prophecy of the future but as vision of transcendent truth, of another world that lies beyond the reach of the senses in their daily waking operation but can be grasped by the psyche in a state of special perceptiveness. McLuskie's last instance of a dramatic dream is that of Vittoria in Webster's *White Devil*: its meaning is ambiguous and 'is not made clear by a set of simple allegorical or prophetic correspondences'. If this essay's conclusion seems disappointingly indefinite, it is true in that to the extreme variety of the material discussed, which resists any simple categorization or summation; perhaps it also reflects the impossibility of living up to the ideal of historical reading proposed in the opening discussion of *Blue Velvet*.

Looking back over these essays, I notice again how strongly they confirm that in past centuries, as in that now ending, people have been unable to rid themselves of the feeling that dreams matter. Suspicion that they do not matter, and that their apparent meaningfulness is merely deceptive, has been stronger in some periods and some cultures than in others; modes of explanation and interpretation have undergone striking changes; but the feeling that dreams do convey messages, and that *somnia ne cures* is prudent advice that cannot be followed, has always survived. The depressing optimism of modern neurophysiology, which notes that the human brain operates on no more power than a refrigerator light bulb, and sees a dream as no more than 'a momentary interception by the conscious mind of material being sorted, scanned,

---

[18] They seem likely to be Macrobian *phantasmata*, the 'visual images at sleep onset' described by a modern scientist as 'more likely than dreams to be either fleeting or unstructured, and far less likely to be integrated into a sustained and episodic narrative frame; and they may be associated with, or terminated by, the abrupt sensation of falling'. J. A. Hobson, *The Dreaming Brain* (New York, 1988), 8.

sifted, or whatever' during sleep,[19] seems unlikely to change this situation. What can be the evolutionary value of the sense, created by dreaming itself, that dream experiences are charged with significance, if this is merely an illusion? If it is an illusion, it has at least been richly productive for storytellers and writers as far back as their activities can be traced, and it will doubtless continue to be richly productive for scholars who study these activities.

[19] C. Evans, *Landscapes of the Night: How and Why We Dream* (London, 1983), 141.

1. On the Borders of Middle English Dream Visions

PETER BROWN

There is an extraordinary concentration of English dream visions in the second half of the fourteenth century. Of the thirty or so major English poems composed between 1350 and 1400, no fewer than a third are dream visions while others, such as Gower's *Confessio Amantis* and the *Canterbury Tales*, have strong links with the genre.[1] Poets of the alliterative revival, including their chief representatives, Langland and the *Pearl*-poet, no less than Chaucer, regarded the dream vision as an essential medium for what they had to say. Why should this have been so? What did the genre offer to poets that they found particularly useful and attractive? It cannot have been novelty. For a century and more, the *Roman de la rose* had been available as an influential model, demonstrating the genre's wide variety of applications. Within and behind it lay the enduring effects of Macrobius and the Bible.[2]

Some immediate stimulus to reconsider the dream vision as a viable and useful genre may have derived from its mid-century revival in French courtly poetry, but this explanation would be restricted largely

I have read versions of this paper at the Canterbury Centre for Medieval and Tudor Studies, University of Kent; the Centre for Medieval Studies, University of Reading; Emmanuel College, Cambridge; and the University of Auckland, New Zealand. It has benefited greatly from the ensuing discussions. Andrew Butcher has made many suggestions for improvement and I have also received valuable help from Alison Wiggins. The faults which remain are my own.

[1] D. Pearsall, *Old English and Middle English Poetry*, Routledge History of English Poetry 1 (London, 1977), 296–7; J. V. Cunningham, 'The Literary Form of the Prologue to the *Canterbury Tales*', MP 49 (1952), 172–81.

[2] On the literary tradition see A. C. Loftin, 'Visions', in J. R. Strayer (ed.), *Dictionary of the Middle Ages*, vol. xii (New York, 1989), 475–8; K. L. Lynch, *The High Medieval Dream Vision: Poetry, Philosophy and Literary Form* (Stanford, 1988), 1 and 46; C. Erickson, *The Medieval Vision: Essays in History and Perception* (New York, 1976). On the influence of Macrobius see C. H. L. Bodenham, 'The Nature of the Dream in Late Mediaeval French Literature', MÆ 54 (1985), 74–86; A. M. Peden, 'Macrobius and Mediaeval Dream Literature', MÆ 54 (1985), 59–73; J. S. Russell, *The English Dream Vision: Anatomy of a Form* (Columbus, Oh., 1988), 60.

to Chaucer. In any case, Machaut and his followers were not so much reinventing the dream vision as continuing a French tradition rooted in the *Rose*.[3] In England it was otherwise. From about 1350 until the end of the century, the long-existing and familiar literary currents expressed through the dream vision became revitalized, charged with new possibilities, and the stimulus to original compositions. This phenomenon cannot be attributed to the chance cross-pollination of literary ideas. Instead, we need to ask (*a*) What was so distinctive, attractive, and different about the dream vision? (*b*) What was special in the circumstances of the writers that made them regard this genre as particularly relevant, to the point of giving it preferential treatment? and (*c*) Which theoretical approach might enable further exploration of the dream vision within its historical context?

Recent studies of the genre have begun to map out some explanatory hypotheses. Kruger relates the dream vision in its late medieval phase to the then current theories of dreaming. He finds in the productions of Langland, Chaucer, and others a distinct kind of 'middle vision' corresponding to a theoretical category of dream. As Macrobius' *somnium* is half-way between dreams caused by divine inspiration and those caused by physical or mental disorder, so its literary counterpart is situated in a similarly ambiguous position. Positing a 'growing distance between humanity and divinity' in the later medieval period, Kruger sees the late medieval English dream vision as a means of negotiating the increasingly tenuous connections between mundane reality and the transcendent world. Its ability to respond to an acute sense of 'betweenness' helps to account for its popularity.[4]

Russell attributes the late medieval flowering of the genre to a 'confluence of literary and philosophical currents'.[5] Lynch is more confident about the way in which the genre responds to historical change. She quotes Jauss and Fowler to the effect that 'genres are not instruments for prescribing meaning after the fact or classifying it afterward, but for interpreting and producing meaning in the moment, for a specific work and for a specific historical time'. She adds: 'it is now more crucial than ever to try to rehistoricize genres, to recover not just their internal laws but the mechanics by which historical developments exert pressures

---

[3] See M. M. Pelen, 'Machaut's Court of Love Narratives and Chaucer's *Book of the Duchess*', *ChauR* 11 (1976–7), 128–55.

[4] S. F. Kruger, *Dreaming in the Middle Ages*, Cambridge Studies in Medieval Literature 14 (Cambridge, 1992), 129–30.

[5] Russell, *English Dream Vision*, 195.

on those laws'. And yet hers remains, like Russell's, a history (and mechanics) of ideas: the 'extraliterary historical conditions' turn out to be 'synchronically . . . the context of contemporary philosophical discourse' and 'diachronically . . . how philosophical change influenced the reception of the late classical visionary dialogue into the medieval tradition and how that dialogue in its turn sought to speak to its own time'.[6]

It is that last phrase, 'its own time', which begs the question. What was special, distinctive, characteristic, about the time when the authors of these dream visions wrote that might have made them (and philosophers too) want to speak to it in particular ways? For there is surely something unsatisfactory (though not wrong) about the historical contexts proposed by Kruger, Russell, and Lynch, in that each is represented in causative, monolithic, and general terms. To be convincing, the historical context needs to be more specific, more complex, more circumstantial, embracing economic factors as well as philosophical discourse, and social and political history as much as religious matters.

By building on the work of Kruger, Russell, and Lynch, how might it be possible to produce a more satisfactory historical account of the dream vision as it appears in English literature of the second half of the fourteenth century? In the first place, by describing and analysing what is, after all, crucial and distinctive about the genre, namely the illusion that, prior to writing his poem, the author has made a transition into, and out of, a dream. Such a procedure might help to root Kruger's theory of betweenness more securely in literary evidence. In this respect, Lynch is surely right to suggest that, in order to understand the historical context more fully, we first need to pay closer attention to the phenomenon which it produced. Much of what follows is therefore descriptive in nature, the data deriving from a range of English writers, but with reference to the French context, particularly as it affected Chaucer.[7] Largely excluded from the discussion are visions—religious or otherwise—which do not involve a dream, although, as we shall see, it is sometimes useful and necessary to take these undreamed visions into account.[8] Much of the material will be familiar, but it builds into a

    [6] Lynch, *High Medieval Dream Vision*, 5–6, 8, and 9–10.
    [7] I have taken as my guide B. A. Windeatt (ed. and trans.), *Chaucer's Dream Poetry: Sources and Analogues*, Chaucer Studies 8 (Cambridge, 1982). Cf. J. M. Davidoff, *Beginning Well: Framing Fictions in Late Middle English Poetry* (London, 1988), ch. 3.
    [8] Peden, 'Macrobius', 63; cf. Russell, *English Dream Vision*, 45, and Lynch, *High Medieval Dream Vision*, 15.

detailed picture of the key literary mechanism, and shows how it functioned as a powerful device for signalling a state of altered consciousness. Thus the first part of this chapter attempts to answer question (*a*) above. The second, shorter, part, in answer to questions (*b*) and (*c*), is more speculative in nature. It argues for the suitability of theories of liminality in attempting to root the Middle English dream vision more securely in its historical context.

It is not difficult to see why, a priori, later medieval poets found the dream such a useful means of framing their narratives. As a rhetorical device it has numerous advantages. It intrigues and engages the interest of an audience by appealing to a common experience and by inviting its members to become analysts or interpreters. It allows for the introduction of disparate and apparently incongruous material. It encourages and facilitates the use of memorable images. It permits the author to disavow responsibility for what follows. It invokes an authoritative and impressive tradition of visionary literature. It provides a way of dealing with a wide variety of subjects: divine prophecy; erotic adventure; political or philosophical speculation; apocalyptic vision. It offers a point of entry into a representational mode (sometimes allegorical) which is less restrictive than, say, the conventions of realist narrative.[9]

But the aesthetic or functional capabilities of the dream vision are not my immediate interest. Instead my topic is the significance of the boundary between waking and sleeping. I wish to ask what this genre can disclose about the meaning of the dream experience as understood by the authors concerned, and therefore by their audiences. To this end my focus narrows to the moment when the narrator falls asleep to enter a dream. What is the significance of this moment within the 'richly developed register of expression' which dream-vision poets commanded?[10] Any attempt at an answer must pay attention both to the preconditions of dreaming, and to the afterlife of the dream, as well as to the dream threshold itself.

The external circumstances of the dream are sometimes given with a remarkable degree of specificity.[11] In *Pearl*, the poet is emphatic about

[9] Cf. S. Delany, *Chaucer's House of Fame: The Poetics of Skeptical Fideism* (Chicago, 1972), 37–8.

[10] R. R. Edwards, *The Dream of Chaucer: Representation and Reflection in the Early Narratives* (Durham, NC, 1989), p. xv.

[11] B. Nolan, *The Gothic Visionary Perspective* (Princeton, 1977), 146–8.

the place and time: 'þat spot' in 'þat erber grene | In Auguste' (37–9).[12] Chaucer gives 'The tenthe day now of Decembre' as the date of his dream at the beginning of the *House of Fame* (63). There are precedents for this specificity of time and place in the book of Ezekiel: 'Now it came to pass in the thirtieth year, in the fourth month, on the fifth day of the month, when I was in the midst of the captives by the river Chobar, the heavens were opened, and I saw the visions of God' (1: 1: 'Et factum est in trigesimo anno, in quarto, in quinta mensis, cum essem in medio captivorum iuxta fluvium Chobar, aperti sunt caeli, et vidi visiones Dei'), as well as in Apocalypse, where St John has his revelation 'on the Lord's day' (1: 10: 'in dominica die').[13] Such details authenticate the dream or vision which follows, but they also invest it with an air of significance.[14] The time and place may have profound personal associations, or they may represent a fateful or divinely ordained conjunction.

Not unusually the setting is a natural one, and the time spring or summer.[15] The C-text of *Piers Plowman* begins 'In a somur sesoun whan softe was þe sonne', while the prelude to a subsequent dream finds the dreamer lingering by a wood to hear birdsong, 'Blisse of þe briddes'. He lies down under a lime-tree and 'Murthe of here mouthes' lulls him to sleep (C. X. 61–7).[16] For Chaucer in the *Legend of Good Women* it is spring, especially the month of May, when 'fowles synge, | And . . . floures gynnen for to sprynge' (37–8), which lures him from his books and makes him a prey to dream experiences. It is May, 'when mirthes bene fele' and 'softe bene the wedres' when the poet of the *Parlement of the Thre Ages* begins his dream adventure (1–2).[17] Similarly, the narrator of *Wynnere and Wastoure* is wandering in bright sunshine along the bank of a stream near an impressive wood, by a pleasant meadow, as his

[12] *Poems of the Pearl Manuscript*, ed. Andrew and Waldron.

[13] This and subsequent quotations from the Bible are taken from the Vulgate, using *Biblia sacra iuxta vulgatam Clementinam*, ed. A. Colunga and L. Turnado, 4th edn., Biblioteca de Autores Cristianos 14. 1 (Madrid, 1965); with translations from *The Holy Bible: Douay Version Translated from the Latin Vulgate (Douay A.D. 1609: Rheims, A.D. 1582)* (London, 1956).

[14] Cf. E. Baumgartner, 'The Play of Temporalities; or, The Reported Dream of Guillaume de Lorris', in K. Brownlee and S. Huot (eds.), *Rethinking the Romance of the Rose: Text, Image, Reception*, Middle Ages ser. (Philadelphia, 1992), 21–38: 23–4.

[15] R. Tuve, *Seasons and Months: Studies in a Tradition of Middle English Poetry* (Paris, 1933; repr. Cambridge, 1974), 99–122.

[16] W. Langland, *Piers Plowman: An Edition of the C-Text*, ed. D. Pearsall, York Medieval Texts, 2nd ser. (London, 1978). Subsequent citations from the C-text are from this edition.

[17] *The Parlement of the Thre Ages*, ed. M. Y. Offord, EETS os 246 (Oxford, 1959).

experience begins (1–46).[18] In the later fourteenth century, the English spring countryside seems to have been full of dreaming poets. One wonders why they never met.

The landscapes through which they move, and which so beguile them, have a marked tendency to be idealized, to resemble paradise.[19] After the *Wynnere and Wastoure* poet has wandered, sunlit, by his stream, forest, and meadow, he finds many flowers unfolding beneath his feet. As he lies down beside a hawthorn bush, the thrushes vie with each other in song, woodpeckers hop among the hazel bushes, wild geese peck at the bark, jays jangle, and other birds twitter. The noise of birds and the rushing stream keep the narrator awake until dusk (36–44). The landscape of the *Parlement of the Thre Ages* is brimming with natural life. There are, again, a wood, a stream, and flowers—'The primrose, the pervynke, and piliole þe riche' (9), dew-drenched daisies, and burgeoning blossom swathed in pleasant dawn mists—and birds (cuckoos, wood-pigeon, thrushes), but other beasts too: as day breaks, harts and hinds make their way to the hills, foxes and polecats go to earth, hares crouch by hedges, then go quickly to their forms (1–20). Another dawn scene, in the F-version of the *Legend of Good Women*, finds Geoffrey Chaucer, or his narrative persona, enthralled by the beauty of the daisy, kneeling and waiting for one to unclose 'Upon the smale, softe, swote gras' (F118), the flower being an epitome of ideal natural beauty, 'For yt surmounteth pleynly alle odoures, | And of riche beaute alle floures' (F123–4). The birds meanwhile, glad that winter is past and that they have escaped the hunter, sing in defiance of the fowler, and croon love-songs to each other. Especially in the case of Chaucer, the influence of the *Rose*—part of which he may have translated as the *Romaunt of the Rose*—is everywhere apparent, with its opening in May, a 'tyme of love and jolite', burgeoning nature, and birdsong (49–95).

What are we to make of such preludes to dreaming? However specific, however detailed, they are not novelistic descriptions designed to give each composition a sense of uniqueness. Were that so, we would not find similar details across several poems by different authors. We are, of course, in the presence of a set of conventions which a poet might invoke in order to prepare an audience for a dream.[20] But that should not

---

[18] *Wynnere and Wastoure*, ed. S. Trigg, EETS os 297 (Oxford, 1990).
[19] Nolan, *Gothic Visionary Perspective*, 136–9.
[20] A. C. Spearing, *Medieval Dream-Poetry* (Cambridge, 1976), 17–18.

be taken to imply that the poet is himself a somnambulist, reaching absent-mindedly for hand-me-down details once the beginning of a dream vision is in prospect.[21] The stream, the forest, the sound of birds, a paradisal landscape are all signifiers to be deliberately deployed, in various kinds of combination and in varying degrees of elaboration, to create particular kinds of meaning.[22]

There is a notable alternative setting—one which, again, is not restricted to an individual writer. It is that of the bedchamber. Jean Froissart's *Paradys d'Amours* begins there (1–32), as does Chaucer's *Book of the Duchess*, influenced by the *Paradys*.[23] Chaucer's insomniac narrator, sitting up in bed, calls for a book 'To rede and drive the night away' (49). In it he finds Ovid's tale of Ceyx and Alcyone. Impressed by the discovery, within that narrative, of a God of Sleep, he resolves to give Morpheus some gorgeous, if imaginary, gifts: a feather-bed stuffed with white doves' down, striped with gold, and clad in fine black foreign satin; and many pillows, covered in soft French linen from Rennes and 'al that falles | To a chambre' (238–58). Such an opening—and this is part of its point—belies expectation and contrasts with the familiar landscape opening, creating a world which is confined rather than free, and artificial rather than natural.

A dreamer is by definition alone, solitary, separated from social activity.[24] Langland's dreamer is 'walkynge myn one' (C. X. 61), while Nicole de Margival reports in his *Dit de la panthère d'Amours* (c.1300) that he was 'loing de mon païs' (53: 'far from my own country').[25] Solitude may be an expression of being lost. Langland's dreamer wanders aimlessly 'wondres to here' (C, Prol. 4), an activity which later finds him by 'a wilde wildernesse' (C. X. 62). The *Wynnere and Wastoure* dreamer is 'in the weste wandrynge myn one' (32) before his encounter with the paradisal landscape. In the *House of Fame* 'Geoffrey' falls

---

[21] Lynch, *High Medieval Dream Vision*, 3–4. Cf. Davidoff, *Beginning Well*, 73.

[22] P. Piehler, *The Visionary Landscape: A Study in Medieval Allegory* (London, 1971), 13. Most of these signifiers are conveniently illustrated by the opening lines of Sir John Clanvowe's *The Boke of Cupid*, ed. V. J. Scattergood, in *The Works of Sir John Clanvowe* (Cambridge, 1965), lines 1–90. Cf. J. Gower, *Vox Clamantis*, ed. G. C. Macaulay, in *The Complete Works of John Gower*, iv: *The Latin Works* (Oxford, 1902), 20; *The Major Latin Works of John Gower:* The Voice of One Crying *and* The Tripartite Chronicles, trans. E. W. Stockton (Seattle, 1962), 49.

[23] J. Froissart, *Le Paradis d'Amour; L'Orloge amoureus*, ed. P. Dembowski, Textes Littéraires Français (Geneva, 1986); Windeatt, *Chaucer's Dream Poetry*, 41–2.

[24] Russell, *English Dream Vision*, 116.

[25] N. de Margival, *Le Dit de la panthère d'Amours*, ed. H. A. Todd, SATF (Paris, 1883); Windeatt, *Chaucer's Dream Poetry*, 127.

asleep like someone exhausted after a pilgrimage (111–18). Here, as elsewhere with the image of the lost and errant dreamer, there may be an allusion to the idea current in ancient literature and traditional tribal culture that, during sleep, the soul steps out of its bodily boundaries and wanders in other, no less real, worlds.[26]

Insomnia is another circumstance which dreamers must endure before the dream begins. In the *Book of the Duchess*, Chaucer's luxurious bedding is invented as a propitiatory gift to the God of Sleep, for the narrator begins by complaining:

> I have gret wonder, be this lyght,
> How that I lyve, for day ne nyght
> I may nat slepe wel nygh noght.
>
> (1–3)

—sentiments which Froissart would have recognized. Not unexpectedly, it is often in the limbo-land between sleeping (or trying to sleep) and waking that dreams begin, as in Guillaume de Machaut's *Dit de la fonteinne amoureuse*[27] and Clanvowe's *Boke of Cupide* (86–90).

More sombrely, but inevitably, given the implications of sleep, the dreamer can seemingly be on the brink of death.[28] The *Pearl*-poet slips into a heavy sleep, a 'slepyng-slaȝte' (59), where 'slaȝte' can mean 'slaughter' or 'death by violence' as well as 'stroke' and 'blow'. Langland's narrator, before one dream, has grown, 'wery of the world' (C. XX. 4), while the dreamer of the *Book of the Duchess* declares with fear: 'drede I have for to dye' (24). This state of inertia should be contrasted with the heightened sensual awareness of the narrator before his dream in poems like *Wynnere and Wastoure*, the *Parlement of the Thre Ages*, and Chaucer's *Legend of Good Women*.

Solitude, insomnia, wandering, a sense of death, are each expressive of the dreamer's mental and emotional condition. He tends to be

---

[26] See J. S. Lincoln, *The Dream in Primitive Cultures* (London, 1935), 27; W. Wolff, *The Dream—Mirror of Conscience: A History of Dream Interpretation from 2000 B.C. and a New Theory of Dream Synthesis* (New York, 1952), 8, and see p. 24; see also Spearing, *Medieval Dream-Poetry*, 8; Lynch, *High Medieval Dream Vision*, 49–50; B. Tedlock, 'Zuni and Quiché Dream Sharing and Interpreting', in id. (ed.), *Dreaming: Anthropological and Psychological Interpretations*, School of American Research Advanced Seminar ser. (Cambridge, 1987), 105–31: 113–16.

[27] G. de Machaut, *The Fountain of Love (La Fonteinne amoureuse) and Two Other Love Vision Poems*, ed. and trans. R. B. Palmer, Garland Library of Medieval Literature 54, ser. A (New York, 1993), lines 61–71 and 1563–8.

[28] Russell, *English Dream Vision*, 55.

preoccupied, in a state of inwardness and anxiety, an anxiety which derives from loss of confidence as well as uncertainty about the nature, sources, truth, and application of dreams. St John was 'in the spirit on the Lord's day' (Apocalypse 1: 10: 'in spiritu in dominica die') before experiencing his vision.[29] One recalls Dante's state of dislocation at the beginning of *Inferno*, alone in the dark wood, 'pieno di sonno' (I. 11: 'full of sleep').[30] The dreamer of the *Book of the Duchess* is numb, 'mased' (lost in a maze) with preoccupation:

> Al is ylyche good to me—
> Joye or sorowe, whereso hyt be—
> For I have felynge in nothing,
> But as yt were a mased thyng,
> Alway in poynt to falle a-doun
>
> (9–13)

More playfully, the narrator of the *House of Fame* is in a state of confusion about the alleged causes, and terminology, of dreams (7–58), although his counterpart in the *Parliament of Fowls* is more sombre: 'to my bed I gan me for to dresse, | Fulfyld of thought and busy hevynesse' (88–9). At the beginning of the *Consolation of Philosophy*, influential on later dream visions although not strictly one itself, Boethius describes a contemplative and introverted condition (using Chaucer's translation, *Boece*): 'I, stille, recordede these thynges with myself' (I. prosa 1. 1–2),[31] while de Margival is 'du cuer pensif' (49: 'extremely pensive') before his dream occurs.[32]

There is a certain homogeneity among highly personalized accounts of the narrator's state prior to the onset of dreaming, but the inwardness of the narrator is ascribed to a wide variety of causes. That of the *Pearl*-poet is caused by grief. He stands before the grave of his young daughter:

---

[29] Russell, *English Dream Vision*, 36, 40, and 79; D. G. Hale, 'Dreams, Stress, and Interpretation in Chaucer and his Contemporaries', *JRMMRA* 9 (1988), 47–61: 47; see also Nolan, *Gothic Visionary Perspective*, 139–42.

[30] D. Alighieri, *The Divine Comedy*, i: *Inferno*, ed. and trans. J. D. Sinclair, rev. edn. (London, 1948); and see Russell, *English Dream Vision*, 17; Lynch, *High Medieval Dream Vision*, 147.

[31] See Russell, *English Dream Vision*, 11. The *Consolation* is used as a model in T. Usk, *The Testament of Love*, ed. W. W. Skeat, in his *The Complete Works of Geoffrey Chaucer*, vii: *Chaucerian and Other Pieces* (London, 1897), Prol. 26.

[32] Windeatt, *Chaucer's Dream Poetry*, 127.

> Bifore þat spot my honde I spennd
> For care ful colde þat to me caȝt;
> A deuelly dele in my hert denned . . .

$$(49-51)$$

The poet of *Wynnere and Wastoure* broods on the political and social state of Britain, recalling its origins in heroism and treachery, and describing his own mixed perception of the wit and trickery which obtains, wise words contending with sly, deceptive ones (1–30). In a prophetic mode, and apocalyptic mood, he sees the world turned upside-down, with the wisdom and experience of mature men despised in favour of the callow jabbering of the young. The sad contemplations of Boethius, too, are brought about by political circumstances: head of the civil service under the Gothic emperor Theodoric, he fell from favour and was imprisoned in Pavia—the occasion for his *Consolatio*—before being executed. The beginning of Chaucer's translation reads: 'Allas! I wepynge, am constreyned to bygynnen vers of sorwful matere, that whilom in florysschyng studie made delitable ditees' (I. metrum 1. 1–3).

The desires and frustrations of erotic love prompt numerous literary dreams. Guillaume de Machaut, in order to console himself and to fix his thoughts on the object of his affections, makes a determined resolve in the *Fonteinne amoureuse* to compose a cheerful and optimistic poem (1–12). The author of *Li Fablel dou Dieu d'amors* (mid-thirteenth century) describes the onset of his dream in these terms:

> Par i matin me gisoie en mon lit;
> D'amors pensoie, n'avoie autre delit;
> Quant el penser m'endormi i petit,
> Songai un songe dont tos li cuers me rist.

$$(9-12)$$

(One morning I was lying in my bed—I was thinking of love and had no other pleasure—when I fell asleep a little with my thoughts. I dreamed a dream which delighted my heart.)[33]

Jean de Condé (d. 1345) begins his *Messe des oisiaus*:

> En pensant a la douche joie
> Dont amans en espoir s'esjoie,
> Fui couchié une nuit de may
> Tout sans pesance et sans esmay.

---

[33] Ed. C. Oulmont, in *Les Débats du clerc et du chevalier dans la littéraire poétique du moyen-âge* (Paris, 1911); Windeatt, *Chaucer's Dream Poetry*, 85.

Si m'endormi sans point d'arrest
Et songai . . .

(1–6)

(While thinking of the sweet joy with which a lover cheers himself in his hope,
I went to bed one May evening, quite free from sorrow and care. I then went
straight off to sleep and I dreamed . . .).[34]

All too easily, though, the darker side of love breaks through, and
melancholy, that plague of the despondent lover, replaces forced cheer-
fulness. It is melancholy, rather than what le Goff calls 'the Christian
intellectual's feeling of guilt', which breeds these dreams.[35] As Kruger
demonstrates in Chapter 2, Chaucer provides an anatomy of it in the
Book of the Duchess. There, the dreamer is afflicted by the depressing
images which flood his brain: 'sorwful ymagynacioun | Ys alway hooly
in my mynde' (14–15). He is denatured, alienated from his own nature
and from the natural world: 'agaynes kynde | Hyt were to lyven in thys
wyse' (16–17); he has lost his vitality through 'melancolye', a sickness
which has 'sleyn my spirit of quyknesse' and prompted disturbing
fantasies (23–9). The narrator of the *House of Fame* identifies the
'melancolyous' (30) man as one prone to dream, a prognosis confirmed
by Machaut in the *Fonteinne amoureuse* (61–8) and the tormented
Froissart of the *Paradys d'Amours* (5–8).[36]

In dealing with the immediate cause of a narrator's preoccupation,
we are in effect discussing his receptivity.[37] Whether brooding on a
personal grief or a political crisis, or in a state of spiritual elevation or
frustrated love, his inwardness predisposes him to the experience of
dreaming. He has become susceptible and sensitized by intense preoccupation. This receptivity, crucial to the onset of dreaming, is embodied
in Langland's narrator, who 'In a somur sesoun whan softe was þe
sonne . . . Wente forth in þe world wondres to here' (C, Prol. 1 and 4).
Another way of thinking of the narrator's anxiety is as a route to
the dream threshold, a kind of searching or wandering which is

---

[34] J. de Condé, *'La Messe des oiseaux' et 'Le Dit des Jacobins et des Fremeneurs'*,
ed. J. Ribard, Textes Littéraires Français (Geneva, 1970); Windeatt, *Chaucer's Dream
Poetry*, 104.

[35] J. le Goff, 'Dreams in the Culture and Collective Psychology of the Medieval West',
in his *Time, Work, and Culture in the Middle Ages*, trans. A. Goldhammer (Chicago,
1980), 201.

[36] See W. Calin, *A Poet at the Fountain: Essays on the Narrative Verse of Guillaume de
Machaut* (Lexington, Ky., 1974), 148–9; Edwards, *Dream of Chaucer*, 68–9.

[37] Lynch, *High Medieval Dream Vision*, 69 and 148. Cf. Erickson, *Medieval Vision*,
33–5.

then represented in his physical circumstances: wandering through the countryside, sleepless in his bedchamber, walking by a forest or stream.

What difference, then, does it make when a narrator crosses the boundary from wakefulness to sleep? What is the significance of that moment? The first point to be made is that the boundary is not an absolute division but a party wall within the same house, a wall with a connecting door. One thinks here of the lover's moment of entry into the garden of delight in the *Rose*—through a door which connects an excluded, if idealized, world with a privileged one (*Romaunt*, 509–644). Which is to say that the dream world is not to be thought of as wholly different from waking experience, but in some measure a different account of it, although the connections are not always immediately obvious. They were clear enough to Macrobius, who found in that portion of Cicero's *De republica* on which he wrote his commentary the following statement: 'it frequently happens that our thoughts and conversations react upon us in dreams' ('fit enim fere ut cogitationes sermonesque nostri pariant aliquid in somno').[38] The idea resurfaces in, say, *Dives and Pauper*, written between 1405 and 1410, as well as in late fourteenth-century poetry.[39] In *Pearl*, the 'slepyng-slaʒte' of the dreamer reflects Pearl's death and resurrection, and foreshadows his own spiritual death and rebirth.[40] In the *Book of the Duchess*, Chaucer assumes the existence of a door connecting the rooms of wakefulness and sleep, while leaving the reader to puzzle out the nature of the relationship between the story of Ceyx and Alcyone (which the dreamer was reading before he dozed off) and the story of the Black Knight, which forms the subject of the dream (1324–34). In the *Parliament of Fowls* he is more forthright:

> The wery huntere, slepynge in his bed,
> To wode ayeyn his mynde goth anon;
> The juge dremeth how his plees been sped;
> The cartere dremeth how his cart is gon;

[38] Cicero, *Somnium Scipionis*, I. 4, in Macrobius, *Ambrosii Theodosii Macrobii Commentarii in Somnium Scipionis*, ed. J. Willis, Bibliotheca Scriptorum Graecorum et Romanorum Teubneriana (Leipzig, 1963), 156; trans. W. H. Stahl in Macrobius, *Commentary on the Dream of Scipio*, Records of Civilization: Sources and Studies 48 (New York, 1952), 70. See also Russell, *English Dream Vision*, 39.

[39] *Dives and Pauper*, I. xliii; ed. P. H. Barnum, vol. i, pt. 1, EETS os 275 (Oxford, 1976), 175, lines 12–16. This aspect of medieval dream theory endured: see Sir Thomas Browne, 'On Dreams' (before 1682), in *The Works of Sir Thomas Browne*, ed. G. Keynes, new edn., vol. iii (London, 1964), 230.

[40] Piehler, *Visionary Landscape*, 146.

The riche, of gold; the knyght fyght with his fon;
The syke met he drynketh of the tonne;
The lovere met he hath his lady wonne.

(99–105)

To insist too much on the interconnectedness of waking experience and the dream world might give the impression that the boundary between them is, after all, relatively insignificant. That is far from being the case.[41] Continuity there may be between the preoccupations of waking life and the dream content, but the latter is not simply an extension of the former: the dream, which by definition always has the dreamer at its centre, allows for a confrontation with the self and its preoccupations such that a process of self-realization may be achieved.[42] To put it another way: the boundary between wakefulness and sleeping divides us from ourselves. *Piers Plowman* is perhaps the most notable late medieval English example of a literary dream used to explore individual identity: once the narrator has fallen asleep, it is not long before the 'I' of the poem is being accused by Holy Church of being a 'dotede daffe' (C. I. 138) for failing to understand the rudiments of Christian doctrine.[43]

As in the case of *Piers Plowman*, to cross the boundary into the dream world is to enter territory which is authorized—authorized in the sense that it is populated by figures, like Holy Church, who have authority, who understand where they are, and authorized also because of the dream's sense of import. The narrator's existence, prior to the dream, may have lost its meaning, but within the dream it is full of enigmatic significance. The latent significance of dreams is sometimes reinforced by reference to appropriate authors. The *Rose* begins with a tribute to Macrobius, who took Scipio's dream seriously, and an affirmation of the prophetic nature of dreams (*Romaunt*, 1–20). The divine origin of biblical dreams gave this idea credence and currency.[44] Was it not to the

---

[41] For the orthodox Freudian view see H. Nagera *et al.*, *Basic Psychoanalytic Concepts on the Theory of Dreams*, Hampstead Clinic Psychoanalytic Library 2 (London, 1969), 15 and 40–2; but cf. R. de Becker, *The Understanding of Dreams, or the Machinations of the Night*, trans. M. Heron (London, 1968), 8 and 9.

[42] Spearing, *Medieval Dream-Poetry*, 5; Russell, *English Dream Vision*, 115; Browne, 'On Dreams', ed. Keynes, 232.

[43] Cf. J. H. Anderson, *The Growth of a Personal Voice:* Piers Plowman *and* The Faerie Queene (New Haven, 1976), 3; K. Brownlee, *Poetic Identity in Guillaume de Machaut* (Madison, Wis., 1984), *passim*.

[44] C. B. Hieatt, *The Realism of Dream Visions: The Poetic Exploitation of the Dream-Experience in Chaucer and his Contemporaries*, De Proprietatibus Litterarum, series

prophets themselves that God spoke, in visions and dreams? 'If there be among you a prophet of the Lord, I will appear to him in a vision, or I will speak to him in a dream' (Numbers 12: 6: 'Si quis fuerit inter vos propheta Domini, in visione apparebo ei, vel per somnium loquar ad illum').[45] Chaucer uses such precedents playfully to authorize the dream of the *Book of the Duchess*. His dream was so wonderful, says the narrator, that no one has the wit to interpret it:

> No, not Joseph, withoute drede,
> Of Egipte, he that redde so
> The Kynges metynge Pharao.

> (280–2)

Paradoxically, the constraints of authority within the dream world coincide with a loss of personal control and a sense of liberation. No longer responsible for his own actions (or inaction), the dreamer comes under the influence of powers beyond himself, to which he has no choice but to abandon himself. This is as true of the religious vision as it is of the secular dream: 'The word of the Lord came to Ezechiel the priest . . . and the hand of the Lord was there upon him' (Ezekiel 1: 3: 'factum est verbum Domini ad Ezechielem . . . et facta est super eum ibi manus Domini'). This signals the exertion of divine authority. As a result, the prophet is released into a privileged but autonomous world. The *Pearl*-poet, on falling asleep, has the sense of his soul's escaping from his body. His body remains on his daughter's grave-mound, but 'my spyryt þer sprang in space' (61). By means of the dream his spirit is released for adventure, but consequently he has lost his bearings: 'I ne wyste in þis worlde quere þat hit wace' (65). One critic sees this kind of surrender as a response to, or compensation for, the preoccupations of waking life.[46] That this is not always the case is intimated in the vision of Boethius, where his confrontation and dialogue with Lady Philosophy lead to a sense of existential liberation, however much he remains incarcerated in Theodric's prison. One thinks also of the *Book of the Duchess*, where a claustrophobic bedchamber is transformed in the dream to one engulfed

---

practica 2 (The Hague, 1967), 24; D. F. Hult, *Self-Fulfilling Prophecies: Readership and Authority in the First* Roman de la rose (Cambridge, 1986), 114–26. Cf. Lynn Thorndike, *A History of Magic and Experimental Science*, ii: *During the First Thirteen Centuries of Our Era* (New York, 1923), 154, 161–4, and 575–7.

[45] Peden, 'Macrobius', 59–60; Russell, *English Dream Vision*, ch. 2; Wolff, *Mirror of Conscience*, 13.

[46] Piehler, *Visionary Landscape*, 3.

in spring birdsong, set with dazzling, sun-filled windows, from which the dreamer is soon transported to join in a bustling hunt. In this he has no choice, but the sense of relief, of vitality, and sociability after his denatured, alienated, and claustrophobic waking existence is almost palpable.

Perhaps one of the most significant features of the boundary between waking and dreaming is its offer of a point of entry into new levels of perception otherwise inaccessible. According to Macrobius, who quotes Porphyry, 'All truth is concealed. Nevertheless, the soul, when it is partially disengaged from bodily functions during sleep, at times gazes and at times peers intently at the truth, but does not apprehend it' ('latet . . . omne verum. hoc tamen anima cum ab officiis corporis somno eius paululum libera est interdum aspicit, non numquam tendit aciem nec tamen pervenit').[47] Before the inner eye of Langland's dreamer there unfolds a vision of the universe—Tower of Truth, field full of folk, dale of death—which is nothing short of a marvel: 'merueylousliche me mette' (C, Prol. 8). He sees things normally hidden, and the sense of having broken through to a fundamental level of understanding is very strong. The dream makes possible perceptions which, while anchored in the dreamer's spiritual self, are also moral, social, and political.[48]

The dream threshold also transforms reality: the other world which the dreamer enters is both like and unlike the familiar one of waking experience. Having pondered social and political divisiveness, and having walked through an attractive landscape, the poet of *Wynnere and Wastoure* falls asleep to dream of a place—'Me thoghte I was in the werlde' (47)—which is a pleasant green expanse a mile wide in which two opposing armies face each other. The transformation of reality can mean an intensification of natural effects to the point where they become altogether different. The *Pearl*-poet finds himself walking among hills set with crystal cliffs, past trees with leaves like burnished silver, and grinding beneath his feet gravel made of pearls (73–84).

The grammar and syntax of the world beyond the borderland of sleep are also different.[49] The everyday is both transformed and laden with tantalizing meanings. With his eyes closed, the dreamer enters a world

---

[47] Macrobius, *Commentary on the Dream of Scipio*, i. 3, 18; ed. Willis, ii. 12; trans. Stahl, 92.

[48] Cf. *Mum and the Sothsegger*, ed. M. Day and R. Steele, EETS os 199 (Oxford, 1936), lines 871 ff.

[49] Spearing, *Medieval Dream-Poetry*, 10.

where meaning is nevertheless relayed in visual terms, but ones which may lack apparent coherence and stability.[50] Its language is symbolic: ideas are represented in associated images, in a more or less complex systematic way, to the point where the dream may become an allegory in its own right.[51] To the extent that a dream represents ideas, part of its function in providing a new level of understanding should be called analytical.[52] Whatever the subject-matter, the content of medieval literary dreams signals a turning inwards, accelerating and intensifying a process that may have begun before the dream. Dreams can only happen inside the mind. But they certainly do not reflect the kind of analysis which is entirely cerebral. Their processes include feeling as much as thought, free association as much as logic, images more than abstractions.

What do all these differences, either side of the dream boundary, add up to? One general answer might be that the onset of dreaming indicates a state of altered consciousness.[53] The state of altered consciousness which the dream boundary encloses is sometimes suggested by a quickening of the spirits or a sharpening and intensifying of sensual experience, as if the narrator, once inside the dream, is more fully alive, however inert his body may be. Guillaume de Lorris's lover dreams of taking an intense pleasure in the May birdsong (*Romaunt*, 100–8), and of being 'Joly and gay, ful of gladnesse' (109) as he walks by a stream, delighting in its appearance (110–31). Similarly, and as already noted, the narrator of the *Book of the Duchess*, who complains that 'Defaute of slep and hevynesse | Hath sleyn my spirit of quyknesse' (25–6), is seemingly regenerated by his dream, with its celestial May birdsong (291–320), flowery meadow, and burgeoning trees which harbour numerous deer, squirrels, and other animals (397–42).[54] In de Margival's *Dit de la panthère* (47–90) the immediate effect of the dream is, again, a sudden arrival in an idealized landscape full of wild vitality which contrasts with the civilized but withdrawn state of the narrator.[55]

---

[50] Wolff, *Mirror of Conscience*, 303.

[51] Cf. M. Zink, 'The Allegorical Poem as Interior Memoir', in *Images of Power: Medieval History/Discourse/Literature*, ed. K. Brownlee and S. G. Nichols, Yale French Studies 70 (New Haven, 1986), 100–26.

[52] Piehler, *Visionary Landscape*, 20; cf. Edwards, *Dream of Chaucer*, 2.

[53] Cf. W. C. Curry, *Chaucer and the Mediaeval Sciences*, rev. edn. (New York, 1960), 208, quoting Averroes.

[54] J. A. W. Bennett, *Chaucer's* Book of Fame: *An Exposition of 'The House of Fame'* (Oxford, 1968), 8–9.

[55] Windeatt, *Chaucer's Dream Poetry*, 127–8.

Yet such evidence of the exciting of physical awareness is not confined to the far side of the dream boundary. As we have seen in, say, the case of the *Parlement of the Thre Ages*, and in numerous other examples, the May setting, the birds, stream, forest, flowers, are almost *de rigueur* as a prelude to dreaming. In which case, are we to think of the dream boundary as a cause, or merely as a symptom, of altered consciousness?

Certainly in a number of cases the existence of the dream is crucial and important. Scipio's account of the universe is given credibility by Macrobius precisely because it derives from a dream—dreams being, on certain occasions such as this one, divinely inspired. A similar sense of authenticity attaches to the experience of the *Pearl*-poet's dreamer, not least because his revelation of another world (and of the continued existence in it of his beloved daughter) has biblical precedent, in Apocalypse itself. Langland, too, clearly attaches, and wants his audience to attach, great importance to the idea that dreams can be of divine origin.

In such cases, the dream is both cause *and* symptom: it provokes a special, intense kind of altered consciousness, in which the dreamer is made the recipient of God's word, while at the same time telling us that state of altered consciousness has been achieved.[56] There may be an analogy here with another indicator of altered consciousness: enchantment. The departure of a hero or heroine for faery (and their eventual return) similarly shows both that he or she has entered an altered state *and* that the altered state has been caused by the intervention of powers beyond the individual's immediate control. This, perhaps, is the secular equivalent of the causative dream, for the experiences reserved for faery are to do with the social order. One thinks of the seizing by faery forces of Herodis in the Middle English romance *Orfeo* (before 1330), when her adventure in the other world is a means of representing social response to mental disorder, or madness.[57] Other instances of literary dreams are more ambiguous as to whether the dream is to be seen as a cause or an effect of altered consciousness. Chaucer is notorious for keeping in play that very question: *are* dreams divinely inspired, or merely caused by bad digestion? But in many cases—perhaps the majority—the casual use, arbitrary placing, or indeed the absence of a

---

[56] Cf. Lynch, *High Medieval Dream Vision*, 55–6.

[57] *Sir Orfeo*, ed. A. J. Bliss, 2nd edn. (Oxford, 1966), lines 57–194. Cf. N. Frye, *The Secular Scripture: A Study of the Structure of Romance* (Cambridge, Mass., 1976), 102, and see pp. 53, 99, and 102–4. Note also how resistant the dream vision is to the exploration of serious mental disturbance in Thomas Hoccleve, *The Regiment of Princes*, ed. M. C. Seymour, in his *Selections from Hoccleve* (Oxford, 1981), lines 109–11.

dream boundary where one might be expected suggest that it should be read as a symptom of an altered state and nothing more, that the existence of a dream boundary is not in itself crucial to the meaning of the poem. It follows that the genre 'dream vision' is perhaps not as watertight as some writers have suggested.[58]

Let me illustrate this from some examples. Machaut's *Dit dou lyon* begins with the familiar spring setting: nature is in full throat. In a neat reversal of the usual scenario, the narrator wakes to birdsong, and recollects his lady-love. Prompted by the fine weather, music, and the beauty of nature, he rises from his bed to walk by a river which encloses a garden. Finding a boat, he crosses the river and so enters the garden. There are shades here of the *Rose*, and a dream-like quality to the events which unfold, but Machaut has dispensed with the dream boundary which might have marked the point of transition to a state of altered consciousness.[59] The *Dit dou lyon* might be compared with the anonymous *Fablel dou Dieu d'amors*, the opening of which contains many of the same elements, but with the inclusion of a dream boundary. The sequence is: lying in bed with thoughts of love, falls asleep and dreams; within dream arises in May to the sound of birdsong; walks in flowery meadow, through which runs a delightful stream; walks by the river until a garden, enclosed by a moat, comes into view; enters garden; observes that the garden belongs to Love and is accessible only to those of high birth (9–74).[60] It is difficult to see quite what Machaut lost by excluding the dream boundary, or what the author of the *Fablel* gained by including it.[61] In another poem, *Le Lay de franchise*, Deschamps studiously avoids a dream boundary when he might have been expected to include one: on a glorious May day the narrator dresses in green and sets off to the wood to gather blossom—a ritual which betokens his state of amorous sorrow. Thinking of his lady in terms of a flower, he crosses a heath to a manor, surrounded by a moat, where he observes other May rituals performed by aristocratic people.[62]

---

[58] Cf. Russell, *English Dream Vision*, 2 and 5.

[59] G. de Machaut, *Le Dit dou lyon*, ed. E. Hoepffner, in his *Œuvres de Guillaume de Machaut*, vol. ii, SATF (Paris, 1911), lines 1–188; Windeatt, *Chaucer's Dream Poetry*, 65–6. See C. B. Hieatt, '*Un Autre Forme*: Guillaume de Machaut and the Dream Vision Form', *ChauR* 14 (1979–80), 97–115.

[60] Windeatt, *Chaucer's Dream Poetry*, 85.

[61] Calin, *Poet at the Fountain*, 160; cf. G. de Machaut, *The Judgment of the King of Navarre*, ed. and trans. R. B. Palmer, Garland Library of Medieval Literature 45, ser. A (New York, 1988), lines 1–547.

[62] E. Deschamps, *Le Lay de franchise*, ed. le marquis de Queux de Saint-Hilaire, in *Œuvres complètes de Eustache Deschamps*, ed. Saint-Hilaire and G. Raynaud, vol. ii,

I am not suggesting that the dream boundary has become redundant, or been reduced to the status of an outworn convention, but that for certain poets it is one option among many for signifying a state of altered consciousness, and is probably reserved for signalling an intensification or deepening of that state. The dream vision is thus distinguished from the *chanson d'aventure*, with which it shares a number of generic markers: birdsong, the stream, the forest, the garden.[63] Many are by their nature images of threshold. Entry into the garden, as already noted, is crucial; so is crossing the stream or river; or being at the edge of the forest; or leaving a bedchamber.[64]

Earlier in this chapter, such situations were seen as preparatory to the experience of dreaming, signalling a state of readiness or receptivity before a state of altered consciousness should develop. It may be more accurate to see them as representing a series of boundaries, marking progressive stages of penetration of an altered state. They may culminate in the dream boundary, or the dream boundary may be an early indicator of altered consciousness, followed by others, or it may be entirely absent. That all depends on the priorities and choices of the author.

To see the dream boundary in this way, as one device among many for signifying a state of altered consciousness, helps to explain the apparently casual treatment of dreaming sometimes found in writers like Chaucer and Langland who might be expected to have been more careful. The F-version of Chaucer's Prologue to the *Legend of Good Women* describes the narrator worshipping the daisy in a paradisal spring landscape, before falling asleep in an arbour and dreaming of the God of Love (F197–209). In the revised G-version, the account of falling asleep in the arbour is advanced so that it precedes the description of the landscape (G89–103). This may be evidence not of revision for the sake of it, but of an awareness of the respective potency of the dream boundary and idealized nature as indicators of a changed state, and of the different effects and meanings to be achieved by virtue of their relative

---

SATF (Paris, 1880), lines 1–130; Windeatt, *Chaucer's Dream Poetry*, 152–4. Cf. J. Gower, *Confessio Amantis*, ed. J. A. W. Bennett, in his *Selections from John Gower* (Oxford, 1968), lines 93–137, where the onset of dreaming is again withheld, despite the usual indicators.

[63] Davidoff, *Beginning Well*, 36–46.

[64] At least one of these images, that of a river, was taken by medieval dream interpreters to indicate a range of meanings, from security to anxiety and impending danger. See S. R. Fischer, *The Complete Medieval Dreambook: A Multilingual, Alphabetical Somnia Danielis Collation* (Berne, 1982), 122–3.

positions. In the G-version, there follows a further intensification of other-worldly perceptions as the arrival of the God of Love is heralded by signifiers—flowers, birdsong—which almost suggest that the poet is experiencing a dream within a dream (G104–43).[65]

Then again there is the notorious case of one of Langland's dreams within a dream. In the B-version of *Piers Plowman* (XVI. 18–167), his account of the tree of Charity is enclosed by a dream boundary within an already existing dream. Whether this is credible or not is beside the point: the episode is a moment of intense visionary experience, vouchsafed by no less a person than Piers himself, a figure for Christ. It culminates in an account of Christ's suffering, death, and eventual triumph which brings tears to the eyes of the dreamer.[66] In the revised C-version, Langland's account of the personal effects of the Christian story is dropped. According to one editor, he decided to postpone the impression that the dreamer was, by this stage, 'fully prepared for the full revelation of Christ's sacrifice'.[67] Consequently, in the C-version Langland deleted the onset of an inner dream because the vision of the tree of Charity does not lead to an intensification of personal consciousness (although he inadvertently preserves the moment of waking from the inner dream). Here again, what might appear to be an arbitrary or even a muddled decision may point instead to a clear sense of the uses and effects of the dream boundary.[68]

A few words remain to be said about the boundary on the other side of the literary dream, beyond which lies the return to waking reality—but waking reality of a particular kind, because it is marked by a reflecting back on the content and meaning of the dream. The sense that dreams need to be composed (or reconstituted) before they can be understood is, naturally, an appealing idea to the authors of literary dreams, in that it provides them with a role to which they are eminently suited. The dependence of dream survival upon literary reconstruction is clear from Apocalypse onwards, when John is enjoined by God: 'What thou seest, write in a book and send to the seven churches which

[65] Cf. J. M. Gellrich, *The Idea of the Book in the Middle Ages: Language Theory, Mythology, and Fiction* (Ithaca, NY, 1985), 215.

[66] W. Langland, *The Vision of Piers Plowman: A Critical Edition of the B-Text*, ed. A. V. C. Schmidt (London, 1978). Subsequent citations from the B-text are from this edition. The complexities of effect are rehearsed in A. V. C. Schmidt, 'The Inner Dreams in *Piers Plowman*', *MÆ* 55 (1986), 24–40: 24–33.

[67] Ed. Pearsall, 301, note to XVIII. 179.

[68] See S. Kruger, 'Mirrors and the Trajectory of Vision in *Piers Plowman*', *Speculum*, 66 (1991), 74–95: 78–9 and 93–5.

are in Asia' (Apocalypse 1: 11: 'Quod vides, scribe in libro: et mitte septem Ecclesiis, quae sunt in Asia'). On waking from *his* dream Langland reaches for his writing implements: 'And y wakned þerwith and wroet as me mette' (C. XXI. 481). Chaucer's narrator is more self-conscious about the literary possibilities of a dream. At the end of the *Book of the Duchess* he resolves, over time, to 'put this sweven in ryme' (1332).

The afterlife of a dream is, naturally enough, a time when the validity or otherwise of the experience is opened to debate. This allows the author a considerable amount of latitude, or margin for error. It is an occasion when the latent ambiguities about the significance of dreams can be fully exploited.[69] Authors, it might be thought, have a vested interest in suggesting that 'their' dream was authentic and significant. This is certainly the case with Macrobius' commentary on the dream of Scipio, for in the third chapter he erects an extremely influential theory of dreams on the basis of what Scipio saw, and proceeds to evaluate the dream according to his various categories.[70] Langland, for his part, wants to muddy the water, to mingle the categories of personal and divine dreams in order to encourage his audience to take dreams seriously. Awaking on Malvern hills, he rehearses the stories of Daniel, Nebuchadnezzar, and Joseph (C. IX. 304–18). 'Sowngewarie', the interpretation of dreams, is not therefore something to be dismissed out of hand as superstitious nonsense, although it may be this, as the author of *Dives and Pauper* stresses (I. xliii–xlvi). Biblical precedent suggests that 'on meteles to stodie' is an instructive and crucial activity. Chaucer, as already noted, can leave his audience more room for manoeuvre— reminding it of various theories but leaving to them an assessment of the dream in the light of those possibilities of interpretation (see *HF* 12–58), or he might, as in the *Parliament of Fowls* (31) invoke a recognized authority such as Macrobius on which to pattern his own 'recalled' dream.

But the afterlife of a dream is not merely an arena in which an author can more or less conspicuously display his wealth of literary strategies. It is also a time when, without beating about the bush and rehearsing dream theory, he can register the impact of the dream as a revelation of truth, a clarification of perplexing thoughts. De Margival's narrator, in

---

[69] See Russell, *English Dream Vision*, 51 and ch. 2. For an additional anatomy of dream types see *Dives and Pauper*, I. xliii; ed. Barnum, vol. i, pt. 1, pp. 74–7.

[70] Macrobius, *Commentary*, 1. 3, 1–11; ed. Willis, ii. 8–11; trans. Stahl, 87–90.

his *Panthère d'Amours*, awakes from a painful dream, reconsiders it, and finds 'Riens . . . qui fust mensonge' (2197: 'nothing in it which was untrue').[71] What is more, it gives him new volition to labour faithfully in pursuit of his lady, in the hope of winning mercy. Oton de Grandson's dreamer in *Le Songe Saint Valentin* awakes with a more radical conviction: that love is not wrong (as he had formerly thought) but a fundamental bond between people and among animals, in short a natural thing, a God-given good. As experienced by human beings it can cause sorrow, but here the dreamer maintains his new-found perspective by expressing sympathy and compassion for those who suffer through love. He ends with a prayer to the God of Love that the hope, fidelity, and loyalty of lovers should be rewarded (314–449).[72]

It is not always thus.[73] Far from waking with a new sense of calm understanding, Langland's dreamer is prone to awake more puzzled and agitated then when he began. The *visio* ends with him troubled and worried by the concluding scene of his second dream, when Piers receives a controversial and enigmatic pardon from Truth. It causes an argument between Piers and a priest and, in two versions of the poem, is torn up by Piers himself. The sound of their argument wakes Langland's dreamer, who finds himself 'Meteles and moneyles on Maluerne hulles | Musynge on this meteles' (C. IX. 297–8). Similarly, the effect of a later dream is to drive him further into himself, ever more preoccupied and distracted with problems which, at the outset, he had not dreamt of, and which now appear to control his form of life:

> And I awakede þerwith, witteles ner-hande,
> And as a freke þat fay were forth can y walken
> In manere of a mendenaunt mony ȝer aftur.
> And many tymes of this meteles moche thouhte y hadde . . .
>
> (C. XV. 2–5)

Langland's narrator cannot always escape the therapeutic effects of dreams. Having witnessed in sleep the defeat of Satan by Christ with triumphant commentary by Righteousness, Peace, Truth, Mercy, and Love, he awakes from the carolling of these damsels to the ringing

---

[71] Windeatt, *Chaucer's Dream Poetry*, 132.

[72] Ed. A. Piaget, in his *Oton de Grandson: Sa vie et ses poésies*, Mémoires et Documents Publiés par la Société d'Histoire de la Suisse Romande, ser. 3, vol. i (Lausanne, 1941); Windeatt, *Chaucer's Dream Poetry*, 123–4.

[73] Hale, 'Dreams, Stress, and Interpretation', 53.

of bells on Easter morning, and calls Kit his wife and Calote his daughter so that they might go to church and honour the cross on which Christ died (C. XX. 470–8). Thus can the afterlife of a dream see doubted values reaffirmed, or readjusted, if only after a tortuous process of self-examination. Here, as in other cases, the dreamer is changed from the state he was in before the dream began.[74] He is put back in touch with himself or (as it might be) with nature. He is no longer alienated but integrated and resocialized. If formerly lost, he now has a sense of direction. In short his identity in relation to society has been reconstructed. In his dream he suffers a sense of dislocation, and his surroundings are de-familiarized, so that he emerges with a fresh acuity of perception.[75]

If the dream framework was one device among many for indicating a state of altered consciousness, it was nevertheless strongly favoured by English poets in the second half of the fourteenth century. It provided them with an instrument of radical analysis and evaluation. For, unlike other, less potent, indicators of transition, the dream enabled writers to explore the roots both of the self and of society. In some measure, the literary dream is the meeting-place of both, being at once intensely private and expansively public, providing a means whereby the outer world can be read through the inner. Dreams, by their nature, are able to express a sense of fragmentation, a loss of continuity between the self and the outer world, since they operate through striking juxtaposition, distortion, displacement, condensation, and apparent incoherence.[76] A dream is therefore well suited to the representation and analysis of alienation, of a sense of lost authority, or of a searching for connections that have become hidden, tenuous, or problematic.

Into what explanatory historical framework might we put the literary mechanism of the dream vision? From the evidence so far adduced, it would be plausible to see the remarkable concentration of literary dreams in the second half of the fourteenth century as a response to those economic, social, political, and religious conditions which were likely to produce a sense of fragmentation, of lost identity, of questionable authority. One might speculate on the social impact of severe

[74] Cf. Russell, *English Dream Vision*, 136.
[75] Cf. Froissart, *Paradis d'Amours*, ed. Dembowski, lines 1696–1723; Windeatt, *Chaucer's Dream Poetry*, 56–7.
[76] See D. Brewer, 'Escape from the Mimetic Fallacy', in id. (ed.), *Studies in Medieval English Romances: Some New Approaches* (Cambridge, 1988), 6–7; Nagera, *Basic Psychoanalytic Concepts*, 54–5.

depopulation caused by recurrent plague, of prolonged war, of schism, revolt, and heresy, and their likely effects on the sensibilities of poets.[77] We might therefore understand the widespread use of the dream vision in these terms: society itself was in a state where boundaries were breaking down under the pressure of severe, recurrent, and frequent crisis. What the dream vision provided was a radical means of representing, and reflecting upon, both those experiences and the pervasive sense thereby produced of being in a state of transition.[78]

To proceed further, in an unquestioning manner, along this speculative path, runs the risk of recreating precisely that kind of inadequate historicizing pinpointed in the opening paragraphs of this essay. For instance, it would be tempting, especially in the case of a writer like Langland, to take an issue such as authority and demonstrate the closeness of its social, religious, and literary manifestations. But to do so would privilege one kind of text at the expense of others, and the conclusions reached would not necessarily fit other dream visions by his contemporaries.[79] Nor would it advance an answer to the present question: why this genre at this time? The subject of authority is hardly one that depended for its poetic treatment on the dream vision.

We must return, therefore, to what is distinctive about the genre, namely its capacity, as identified earlier, to indicate a state of altered consciousness. Is it possible to clarify or redefine that general term? It would be difficult to improve upon the word used by Kruger: the state of altered consciousness which the dream vision signals and explores is precisely that of 'betweenness'. It is as if the author of a dream vision is saying: 'I want to focus on the state of being between sleep and wakefulness, death and life, inertia and excitation, natural and artificial states, experience and authority, salvation and damnation, being lost and finding direction, solitude and sociability, private and public, male and female, health and sickness, constraint and liberation, alienation and integration.' Of course, the middle ground which the dream vision thus opens up is by its nature constantly shifting, elusive, open to renegotiation.

The experience of betweenness is what the dream vision, distinctively, allows poets to express and explore. That experience, we might

<hr />

[77] Cf. C. Muscatine, *Poetry and Crisis in the Age of Chaucer*, University of Notre Dame Ward-Phillips Lectures in English Language and Literature 4 (Notre Dame, Ind., 1972), ch. 1.

[78] Cf. P. E. Dutton, *The Politics of Dreaming in the Carolingian Empire*, Regents Studies in Medieval Culture (Lincoln, Nebr., 1994).

[79] On Chaucer's more elliptical approach in *HF* and *LGW* see Gellrich, *Idea of the Book*, chs. 5 and 6; cf. Delany, *Skeptical Fideism*, 46–7 and 118–22.

reasonably assume, derives from the extraordinary circumstances found in English society in the second half of the fourteenth century. What we now need is a subtle instrument of analysis, founded in a theoretical approach, in order to test that assumption—one which will provide the fullest possible historical context for differing representations of betweenness across a wide range of texts. Now the condition of betweenness, or liminality, is a cultural phenomenon well known to anthropologists, and it is in their discipline, as Lynch has recognized, that the theoretical structure exists for a more thorough historicizing of the dream vision. There are various theories of liminality, but one particularly appropriate to the present enquiry was developed by Victor and Edith Turner.[80] Its focus was pilgrimage—a cultural practice well known in the Middle Ages, but also one which not infrequently appears as a motif within the dream vision.[81]

The recurrent representation of pilgrimage within dream visions is due in part to the complex figurative status which pilgrimage enjoyed in the Western Christian tradition. It signalled the alienation of the soul from God, and its desire to progress towards salvation.[82] The dream

[80] See J. R. Andreas, 'Festive Liminality in Chaucerian Comedy', *ChauN* 1/1 (1979), 3–6: 3; E. Turner, 'The Literary Roots of Victor Turner's Anthropology', in K. M. Ashley (ed.), *Victor Turner and the Construction of Cultural Criticism: Between Literature and Anthropology* (Bloomington, Ind., 1990), 163–9; T. Pison, 'Liminality in *The Canterbury Tales*', *Genre*, 10 (1977), 157–71; F. B. Jonassen, 'The Inn, the Cathedral, and the Pilgrimage of *The Canterbury Tales*', in S. G. Fein, D. Raybin, and P. C. Braeger (eds.), *Rebels and Rivals: The Contestive Spirit in* The Canterbury Tales, Studies in Medieval Culture 29 (Kalamazoo, Mich., 1991), 1–35: 4–8; and also B. Geremek, 'The Marginal Man', in J. Le Goff (ed.), *Medieval Callings*, trans. L. G. Cochrane (Chicago, 1987), 347–73.

[81] *Piers Plowman* is one notable, if complex, example. See also G. de Deguileville, *The Pilgrimage of the Lyfe of the Manhode: Translated Anonymously into Prose from the First Recension of Guillaume de Deguileville's Poem* Le Pèlerinage de la vie humaine, ed. A. Henry, vol. i, EETS os 288 (Oxford, 1985), pt. 1, lines 1–146, pp. 1–4; and for commentary L. R. Muir, *Literature and Society in Medieval France: The Mirror and its Image 1100–1500*, New Studies in Medieval History (Basingstoke, 1985), 172–5; S. K. Hagen, *Allegorical Remembrance: A Study of* The Pilgrimage of the Life of Man *as a Medieval Treatise on Seeing and Remembering* (Athens, Ga., 1990), 112–17; S. Wright, 'Deguileville's *Pèlerinage de Vie Humaine* as "Contrepartie Edifiante" of the *Roman de la Rose*', *PQ* 68 (1989), 399–422. See also the beginning of *The Pilgrimage of the Soul: A Critical Edition of the Middle English Dream Vision*, ed. R. P. McGerr, vol. i, Garland Medieval Texts 16 (New York, 1990), bk. 1, lines 1–20, from a Middle English translation (*c.*1413) of the second part of Guillaume's trilogy, written in 1355. For a brief discussion of other dream pilgrimages in the French tradition, see S. A. Barney, 'Allegorical Visions', in J. A. Alford (ed.), *A Companion to* Piers Plowman (Berkeley and Los Angeles, 1988), 117–33: 126–8.

[82] G. B. Ladner, '*Homo Viator*: Mediaeval Ideas on Alienation and Order', *Speculum*, 42 (1967), 233–59; F. C. Gardiner, *The Pilgrimage of Desire: A Study of Theme and Genre in Medieval Literature* (Leiden, 1971), ch. 1.

vision, on the other hand, given its biblical status as a mode of communication with God, is an appropriate context in which to address such matters. Conversely, the practice of pilgrimage is not infrequently bound up with visionary experiences, notably when a saint appears in a dream to perform a miracle far removed from his or her shrine, or when a vision of the saint itself prompts a pilgrimage.[83] Thus pilgrimage and dream have complementary potentials: the one, pilgrimage, is ideally an exteriorized mysticism; the other, dream vision, may be an interiorized pilgrimage, with an urge to mirror and effect spiritual transformation through self-examination.[84]

Given the possible, generic, interpenetrations of pilgrimage and dream vision, the anthropological approach developed by Turner and Turner would seem to provide a promising model for analysing both cultural phenomena. Drawing on the work of van Gennep, they describe how liminality is experienced in the course of a rite of passage.[85] The rite has three phases: separation; limen, or margin; and aggregation:

The first phase comprises symbolic behavior signifying the detachment of the individual or group, either from an earlier fixed point in the social structure or from a relatively stable set of cultural conditions . . . during the intervening liminal phase, the state of the ritual subject . . . becomes ambiguous, he passes through a realm or dimension that has few or none of the attributes of the past or the coming state, he is betwixt and between all familiar lines of classification; in the third phase the passage is consummated, and the subject returns to classified secular or mundane social life.[86]

[83] Cf. B. Ward, *Miracles and the Medieval Mind: Theory, Record and Event 1000–1215* (London, 1982), 97; and see J. Sumption, *Pilgrimage: An Image of Mediaeval Religion* (London, 1975), 16–17 and 26–7.

[84] V. and E. Turner, *Image and Pilgrimage in Christian Culture: Anthropological Perspectives*, Lectures on the History of Religions Sponsored by the American Council of Learned Societies, NS 11 (New York, 1978), 7; Lynch, *High Medieval Dream Vision*, 48; Nolan, *Gothic Visionary Perspective*, ch. 4; S. Stanbury, *Seeing the* Gawain-*Poet: Description and the Act of Perception*, Middle Ages ser. (Philadelphia, 1991), 12–13; S. Stakel, 'Structural Convergence of Pilgrimage and Dream-Vision in Christine de Pizan', in B. N. Sargent-Baur (ed.), *Journeys Toward God: Pilgrimage and Crusade*, Studies in Medieval Culture 30 (Kalamazoo, Mich., 1992), 195–203.

[85] A. van Gennep, *The Rites of Passage* [1908], trans. M. B. Vizedom and G. L. Caffee (Chicago, 1960).

[86] Turner and Turner, *Image and Pilgrimage*, 2. See also E. Leach, *Culture and Communication. The Logic by which Symbols are Connected: An Introduction to the Use of Structuralist Analysis in Social Anthropology*, Themes in the Social Sciences (Cambridge, 1976), 77–9.

The application of a liminoid structure to the dream vision would seem fairly straightforward.[87] Separation would correspond with the alienated and solitary state of the dreamer; limen to the dream experience itself; aggregation to the afterlife of dreaming. This order of analysis has been proposed by Lynch.[88] But the correspondences are more subtle. For the dream vision, like the pilgrimage, is from the anthropological viewpoint initiation to, not through, a threshold. In other words, what appeared to be marginal, peripheral, a state of transition, both into and out of the dream, is on reflection central, essential. An acceptance of the state of being liminal, between heaven and hell, is a crucial movement towards spiritual enlightenment; the realization that one occupies disputed territory, between the conflicting claims of individual identity and those of society at large, is a step in the direction of both intellectual expansion and social reintegration.

According to Turner's account, the pilgrim is an initiand who experiences a new and more profound mode of existence.[89] Pilgrimage frees the participants from the secular world, and intensifies their piety. The act of piety expressed through pilgrimage reaches its apogee at the pilgrim's destination, usually a shrine within a holy place, which represents in a particularly powerful way the basic components of the faith. Although the pilgrim then returns to everyday life, the belief remains that he or she has made a significant spiritual advance.

Pilgrimage has many features in common with the liminality attributed more generally to rites of passage. First, there is a deliberate rejection of social norms and structures. Differences of status are ignored or inverted, anonymity is preferred, dress and behaviour tend towards simplicity, possessions count for little. Within the pilgrimage group a sense of *communitas* develops which itself levels social difference and offers an alternative to conventional structures. This is especially marked when the impulse to pilgrimage is a response to crisis, to an impending

---

[87] See V. Turner, 'Liminal to Liminoid, in Play, Flow, and Ritual: An Essay in Comparative Symbology', in his *From Ritual to Theatre: The Human Seriousness of Play* (New York, 1982), 20–60.

[88] Lynch, *High Medieval Dream Vision*, 47–8.

[89] What follows is based on Turner and Turner, *Image and Pilgrimage*, 8, 9, 14, 15, and 34; V. Turner, *The Forest of Symbols: Aspects of Ndembu Ritual* (Ithaca, NY, 1967), ch. 4; id., *The Ritual Process: Structure and Anti-Structure*, The Lewis Henry Morgan Lectures, 1966 (Chicago, 1969), chs. 3 and 4; id., 'Liminal to Liminoid', 24–30; id., *Dramas, Fields, and Metaphors: Symbolic Action in Human Society*, Symbol, Myth, and Ritual ser. (Ithaca, NY, 1974), ch. 5; and id., 'Pilgrimage and *Communitas*', SMiss 23 (1974), 305–27.

or perceived fracturing of the social structure. The reconfiguration of normal social relations leads to a novel, challenging, and sometimes playful and comic, juxtaposition of incongruous components.

Second, not only the group but also the individual embraces self-awareness and reconstruction. That process may be associated with death and rebirth, with entering darkness and emerging into light, with anonymity, with a sense of freedom, with deliberate privation, which may include poverty, nakedness, ordeal, submissiveness, and humility. The initiand is also driven inwards to consider the general meaning but also the personal significance of those religious and cultural values normally taken for granted. As a result the individual, through personal learning and transformation, evaluates subjective experience within its institutionalized context, to the point of becoming critical of both. What eventually emerges is an integral person and purpose from the multiple personae and roles which formerly obtained. Finally, there are dislocations of place and space. The leaving of familiar territory is characterized as a departure for the unknown, for a wilderness, which itself figures spiritual and intellectual waywardness. At the same time, stasis is exchanged for movement, which in turn reflects the whole process of self-realization.

Such categories of analysis have tremendous potential for describing and understanding the workings and priorities of the dream vision, but they also have limitations, and it is therefore important to proceed with some caution. Attractive and applicable though Turner's theory may be, its abstracting, generalizing, and universalizing tendencies need to be resisted, and are open to question and qualification. For instance, if one thinks of later fourteenth-century England, then the ideal model of pilgrimage advanced by Turner would seem to be in retreat, either through its incorporation into institutional practices, or through its abuse, or by virtue of the attacks made upon pilgrimage by reformers such as the Lollards. Again, it would be difficult to demonstrate that a pilgrimage narrative like the unfinished *Canterbury Tales*, with its affinity to the dream vision, or the perpetually self-examining *Piers Plowman*, ever arrive, through the motif of pilgrimage, at a stable, transcendent moment of personal and social reintegration. Each work is more adequately characterized as offering a pluralism, a variety of unreconciled points of view, subsumed under the common experience of pilgrimage. The nature, intention, and objective of that pilgrimage vary from voice to voice and from persona to persona and from character to character so that there are as many Canterburys, or Truths, as there are pilgrims. What both works offer in their representation of pilgrimage is—and here I quote from a recent critique of Turner's thesis—'a *realm of competing discourses*'.[90]

On the other hand, Turner's theory of liminality, precisely because it is so wide-ranging, provides a means of studying the 'betweenness' so extensively and subtly represented by dream visions in a wider social and historical context. For liminality cannot be studied in isolation from its social context. It is seen by anthropologists to apply to all phases of decisive cultural change, in which the previous orderings of thought and behaviour are subject to revision and criticism; when hitherto unprecedented modes of ordering relations between ideas and people become possible and desirable.[91] Theories of liminality thus have great potential for understanding the nature of the English dream vision in the later fourteenth century and for plotting its affiliations with the cultural moment from which it sprang.[92] It offers a framework within which to consider decisive cultural changes and responses to it, be they social, political, religious, or literary.

[90]   J. Eade and M. J. Sallnow, Introduction to ead. (eds.), *Contesting the Sacred: The Anthropology of Christian Pilgrimage* (London, 1991); but cf. Turner, *Dramas, Fields, and Metaphors*, 198, quoting Lewis.

[91]   Turner and Turner, *Image and Pilgrimage*, 2; Turner, *Ritual Process*, 148 and 153–4.

[92]   Turner, *Ritual Process*, 42, offers a brief comment on the importance of dream symbolism to the instigators of *communitas*, using the example of St Francis.

2. Medical and Moral Authority in the Late Medieval Dream

Steven Kruger

I. Dreams and Disease: Henryson's Testament of Cresseid

Cresseid's dream in Robert Henryson's *Testament of Cresseid* is closely, indeed causally, linked to her illness, faithfully predicting and enacting disease. Awaking from her vision and taking up a mirror, the once 'fair' (42, 78) Cresseid discovers that she has become, as the closing words of the dream explicitly predict, 'lyke ane lazarous' (343).[1] The dream's uncanny truth would seem to signal first and foremost its supernatural quality. Henryson describes the dream in terms that clearly associate it with divinely inspired experience; it is 'ane extasie' occurring while Cresseid is 'Ravischit in spreit' (141–2).[2] The first image of the dream evokes the love and harmony that bind the cosmos: Cupid rings 'ane siluer bell, | Quhilk men micht heir fra heuin vnto hell' (144–5), and in so doing calls 'The seuen Planetis' together (147). '[A]ll seuin' are 'deificait' (288), participating in 'deuyne sapience' (289), and their actions clearly express a moral judgement arrived at in the realm of

---

[1] Henryson, *Testament of Cresseid*, in *The Poems*, ed. Fox. On the connection between dreams and mirrors see Kruger, *Dreaming in the Middle Ages*, 136–9; id., 'Mirrors and the Trajectory of Vision'.

[2] *MED* gives only one meaning for *extasie*, which appears to be a new word in late 14th-cent. English: 'Elation, ecstasy'. Note the religious situation of the first quotation given, from Wyclif's Bible, Deeds [Acts] 3: 10 (immediately after the healing of a cripple): 'Thei weren fulfillid with wondryng and exstasie, that is, leesynge of mynde of resoun and lettyng of tunge.' For *ravishen*, *MED* gives various meanings available to Henryson, including (for 'ben ravished') 'to be carried up (into heaven, the stars, clouds, etc.)' and 'to drive someone into a state of stress; transport (sb. into an ecstasy, a vision, contemplation, etc.)'. On the meaning of *ravish* in relation to dreams, see also E. Wilson, 'The "Gostly Drem" in *Pearl*', *NM* 69 (1968), 90–101. As Wilson suggests, *ravish* is used in works like *The Chastising of God's Children* to describe both spiritual and intellectual vision (in the Augustinian scheme of corporeal, spiritual, and intellectual vision) and to refer specifically to the dreams and visions of saints Paul, John, and Peter. *MED, ravishen* 3(c), gives a variety of such instances.

divinity. Cresseid's sin—'To change in filth all thy feminitie' (80)—is compensated for by the 'change' of her disease: in Saturn's words, 'I change thy mirth into melancholy' (316). The 'spottis' (339) of leprosy brought by the dream surely express a moral judgement on Cresseid's 'spotted' behaviour—'with fleschlie lust sa maculait' (81).

Simultaneously, however, the dream is deeply implicated in the 'natural', in the realm of the body—and not just because it results in physical disease. The seven gods of the dream are not fully transcendent deities but rather the planets whose 'power' extends to 'all thing *generabill*' (148; my emphasis). Indeed, Henryson emphasizes not only the stately and godly qualities of these figures but also their physicality, their status as astronomical forces affecting, for instance, 'Wedder and wind, and coursis variabill' (150). Their power, according to medieval medical discourse, would extend as well to the realm of health and sickness[3] and, strikingly, 'Mercurius', chosen by the other gods 'To be foirspeikar in the parliament' (266) of the dream, is depicted not only as rhetorician (240, 269) and 'poeit' (245) but also as a physician strongly reminiscent of Chaucer's Doctour of Phisik:[4]

> Boxis he bair with fine electuairis,
> And sugerit syropis for digestioun,
> Spycis belangand to the pothecairis,
> With mony hailsum sweit confectioun,
> Doctour in phisick, clad in ane skarlot goun,
> And furrit weill, as sic ane aucht to be;
> Honest and gude, and not ane word culd lie.

$$(246-52)$$

It is Mercury who chooses Saturn and Cynthia (300) to respond to Cupid's complaint against Cresseid, and it is these deputies who pronounce a detailed and relentlessly physical punishment for her: 'In all hir lyfe with pane to be opprest, | And torment sair, with seiknes incurabill, | And to all louers to be abhominabill' (306–8). Laying 'ane frostie wand' (311) on Cresseid's head, Saturn declares:

---

[3] For introductory comments on medical astrology, see N. G. Siraisi, *Medieval and Early Renaissance Medicine: An Introduction to Knowledge and Practice* (Chicago, 1990), 67–8, 111, 123, 128–9, 134–6, 149, and 152. On the importance of astronomical phenomena for dreaming, see T. Gregory, 'I sogni e gli astri', in id. (ed.), *I sogni nel medioevo*, Seminario Internazionale, Rome, 2–4 Oct. 1983 (Rome, 1985), 111–48.

[4] See esp. the following details in Chaucer's GP portrait of the Physician: 'With us ther was a Doctour of Phisik' (411); 'Ful redy hadde he his apothecaries | To sende hym drogges and his letuaries' (425–6); 'of greet norissyng and digestible' (437); 'In sangwyn and in pers he clad was al, | Lyned with taffata and with sendal' (439–40).

Thy greit fairnes and all thy bewtie gay,
Thy wantoun blude, and eik thy goldin hair,
Heir I exclude fra the for evermair.

I change thy mirth into melancholy,
Quhilk is the mother of all pensiuenes;
Thy moisture and thy heit in cald and dry;
Thyne insolence, thy play and wantones,
To greit diseis; thy pomp and thy riches
In mortall neid; and greit penuritie
Thow suffer sall, and as ane beggar die.

(313–22)

Cynthia, the Moon, then passes her own 'sentence diffinityue' (333) on Cresseid:

Fra heit of bodie here I the depryue,
And to thy seiknes sall be na recure,
Bot in dolour thy dayis to indure.

Thy cristall ene mingit with blude I mak,
Thy voice sa cleir, vnplesand hoir and hace,
Thy lustie lyre ouirspred with spottis blak,
And lumpis haw appeirand in thy face:
Quhair thow cummis, ilk man sall fle the place.
This sall thow go begging fra hous to hous
With cop and clapper lyke ane lazarous.

(334–43)

The physical symptoms here presented in the dream—the spots, lumps, and hoarse voice—closely match medieval medical descriptions of leprosy.[5] The association of the disease with the cold and dry of melancholy, and of the melancholy planet Saturn,[6] is especially striking.

One might indeed read Cresseid's dream in a wholly physical, medicalized way. After all, in late medieval Aristotelian and medical traditions dreams were understood as capable of revealing the symptoms of

---

[5] See S. N. Brody, *The Disease of the Soul: Leprosy in Medieval Literature* (Ithaca, NY, 1974), 49–51, 173–7; J. Parr, 'Cresseid's Leprosy Again', *MLN* 60 (1945), 487–91.

[6] Curry, *Chaucer and the Mediaeval Sciences*, 8; see also M. Fattori, 'Sogni e temperamenti', in Gregory (ed.), *I sogni nel medioevo*, 105; M. W. Stearns, 'Robert Henryson and the Leper Cresseid', *MLN* 59 (1944), 265–9: 268–9. On the significance of the topos of 'Saturn and his children' for the later Middle Ages, and more specifically for Chaucer in *CT*, see P. Brown and A. Butcher, *The Age of Saturn: Literature and History in the Canterbury Tales* (Oxford, 1991).

a disease before these presented themselves to waking consciousness. In Aristotle's words, 'all beginnings are small' and 'the beginnings of disease and other bodily affections will be small, and these necessarily show themselves more in sleep than in the waking state'.[7] Moreover, melancholy disorders were thought to result in a particularly rich dream life.[8] In its connection to melancholy, leprosy leads its sufferers to be 'afraid in sleep' and to experience 'horrible dreams'; as the surgeon Guy de Chauliac (d. 1368) claims, lepers 'have heavy and grievous dreams'.[9] In addition, like all of the bodily humours, melancholy conditions particular kinds of dream image: 'the operation of black bile is signified when one sees while asleep many things tinted with a dark colour, and [when one sees] blackness and fears and tremblings' ('Cumque multa fusco colore tincta, atque nigredinem et timores ac pavores in somno aliquis aspicit, bilis nigrae operatio significatur').[10] Henryson's Saturn, whose 'lyre was lyke the leid' (155), and Cynthia, 'Of colour blak . . . Haw as the leid, of colour nathing cleir' (255, 257), are certainly melancholic dream images. Cynthia herself exhibits the symptoms of leprosy—

---

[7] Aristotle, *Parva naturalia*, ed. and trans. W. S. Hett, rev. edn; Loeb Classical Library (London, 1964), 463a; *Aristotle's Psychology: A Treatise on the Principle of Life* (De anima *and* Parva naturalia), trans. W. A. Hammond (London, 1902), 249. A Latin translation of Aristotle's *De somno et vigilia*, *De somniis*, and *De divinatione per somnum*, from the *Parva naturalia*, was available by the early 13th cent., and later in a revised version (*c.*1260–70) by William of Moerbeke. See S. D. Wingate, *The Mediaeval Latin Versions of the Aristotelian Scientific Corpus, with Special Reference to the Biological Works* (London, 1931), 48–52, 92–3; B. G. Dod, 'Aristoteles latinus', in N. Kretzmann, A. Kenny, J. Pinborg, and E. Stump (eds.), *The Cambridge History of Later Medieval Philosophy: From the Rediscovery of Aristotle to the Disintegration of Scholasticism, 1100–1600* (Cambridge, 1982), 47, 49, 50–1, 63–4, 76; M.-T. d'Alverny, 'Translations and Translators', in R. L. Benson and G. Constable (eds.), *Renaissance and Renewal in the Twelfth Century* (Cambridge, Mass., 1982), 436. The medieval Latin versions are available in the edition of H. J. Drossaart Lulofs: *De somno et vigilia liber, adiectis veteribus translationibus et Theodori Metochitae commentario* (Leiden, 1943), and *De insomniis et De divinatione per somnum: A new Edition of the Greek Text with the Latin Translations*, 2 vols. (Leiden, 1947).

[8] See e.g. Vincent of Beauvais, *Speculum naturale* (Douai, 1624; repr. Graz, 1964), bk. 26, ch. 35, col. 1862, where 'a cold and dry complexion, as when melancholy is dominant' ('complexio frigida et sicca, sicut melancholia dominans') is identified as one of the four principal causes of the motion of dream images. See also ibid., bk. 26, ch. 59, col. 1875.

[9] Both passages are cited in Brody, *Disease of the Soul*, 51. The first is from an anonymous 13th-cent. description of leprosy.

[10] G. Hoffmeister, 'Rasis' Traumlehre: Traumbücher des Spätmittelalters', *AK* 51 (1969), 137–59: 150. Rasis's *Liber ad Almansorem* was translated into Latin in the second half of the 12th cent.; see d'Alverny, 'Translations and Translators', 453; D. Jacquart and C. Thomasset, *Sexuality and Medicine in the Middle Ages*, trans. M. Adamson (Princeton, 1988), 22.

'Hir gyte was gray and full of spottis blak' (260)[11]—and Saturn explicitly
wields the power of black bile, the cold and dry humour: 'I change thy
mirth into melancholy . . . Thy moisture and thy heit in cald and dry'
(316, 318). The whole of Cresseid's dream might thus be read as arising
out of melancholic humour occasioned by incipient leprosy.

But it would, I think, be wrong to make Cresseid's dream into a purely
physical phenomenon. Cresseid does not simply fall ill, but becomes
sick because of her transgression of certain natural and at the same time
moral boundaries. Her illness is explicitly linked both to her blasphem-
ing of Cupid and Venus (274) and to 'hir leuing vnclene and lecherous'
(285). The dream involves not just the body, and it shows the pagan gods
not just in their natural, astronomical roles; it also depicts a celestial
realm where these gods are 'Participant of deuyne sapience' (289).
Simultaneously cosmic or transcendent and physical or mundane, the
dream in Henryson merges a religious, moralizing language with a medical, physicalizing one. These two discourses strengthen one another:
the medical details of the dream make moral punishment not only a
transcendent, divine decision but also the natural consequence of
'unnatural' behaviour, while the celestial qualities of the dream intimately tie a mundane physical event, Cresseid's illness, to the judgements
of 'deuyne sapience'. Moral ideology is thus 'naturalized' even as the
language of natural science takes on the colouring of transcendence.

II. The Medical Transformation of Medieval Dream Theory

In the later Middle Ages, the dream was a locus where such a merging or
crossing of medical and moral discourses was especially apt to occur,
and the conflation of the two was facilitated by certain important
changes in ideas about dreaming, by what I will call the 'somatizing' of
dream theory. Although, throughout the medieval period, somatic
causes of dreams were recognized, the twelfth- and thirteenth-century
introduction of new medical and scientific texts to the Latin West gave
the body and bodily process a new prominence in European dream
theory. Thus, the notion that dream images reflect humoral complexion
became more and more common as medical texts exerted their influence

[11] Cf. the 'spottis blak' (339) with which Cynthia curses Cresseid. The echo is noted in
Brody, *Disease of the Soul*, 50 n. 49, who also cites other critics. On Cynthia's specific role
in the generation of leprosy, see Parr, 'Cresseid's Leprosy Again'.

on medieval culture.[12] This notion was found in Rasis's *Liber ad Alman-sorem* and Avicenna's *Canon* (both translated into Latin in the second half of the twelfth century),[13] as well as in such newly available non-medical writers as Algazali and Averroes.[14] Avicenna presented the idea in a particularly prominent place, in the first book of the *Canon* as part of a general discussion of the medical signs that indicate which of the humours is dominant ('de signis dominii cuiuslibet humorum').[15] Here, Avicenna discusses as a group a whole range of somatic 'signa' for sanguine, phlegmatic, choleric, and melancholic temperaments: the patient's general physique; skin colour; hairiness; the state of the mouth, tongue, nostrils, pulse, urine, faeces; muscle tone; the presence of abnormal phenomena like vomiting or headache; and the quality of dreams. The rule of sanguine humour is signified 'when a man sees in [his] dreams red things, or much blood coming out of his own body, or [sees] himself swimming in blood, and the like' ('cum homo in somniis res videt rubeas aut sanguinem multum ex suo corpore exire aut se in sanguine natare et similia'). A phlegmatic temperament is demonstrated by 'dreams in which waters and rivers and snows and rains and cold are seen' ('somnia in quibus vide[n]tur aque et flumina et niues et pluuie et frigus'). Red or yellow choler is signified when one dreams of 'fires and yellow banners', 'burning or the heat of a bath or of the sun', or when one sees 'things which are not yellow [as] yellow' ('somnia in quibus videntur ignes et vexilla citrina et videre res que non sunt citrine citrinas et videre incensionem aut calorem balnei aut solis aut his similia'). And finally, 'the dreams [that signify the rule of black bile] create terror out of shadows and torture and black things and terrors' ('somnia terrorem facientia ex tenebris et cruciatu et rebus nigris et terroribus').[16]

[12] See Fattori, 'Sogni e temperamenti'; G. Fioravanti, 'La "scientia somnialis" di Boezio di Dacia', *Atti della Accademia delle Scienze di Torino*, ii: *Classe di scienze morali, storiche e filologiche*, 101 (1966–7), 329–69: 347–50.

[13] Jacquart and Thomasset, *Sexuality and Medicine*, 22; d'Alverny, 'Translations and Translators', 453 and 459. See also n. 10 above (on Rasis) and nn. 15 and 16 below (on Avicenna).

[14] For the humoral material in Algazali, see *Algazel's Metaphysics: A Mediaeval Translation*, ed. J. T. Muckle (Toronto, 1933), pars IIᵃ, tractatus V. 6 (pp. 190–1). On the translation of Algazali, see d'Alverny, 'Translations and Translators', 444–6. On Averroes' use of the humoral topos, see Fioravanti, '"Scientia somnialis"', 348.

[15] Avicenna, *Liber canonis* (Venice, 1507; repr. Hildesheim, 1964), bk. 1, *fen* 2, doctrine 3, ch. 7 (fo. 42ᵛ). See also O. C. Gruner, *A Treatise on the Canon of Medicine of Avicenna, Incorporating a Translation of the First Book* (London, 1930; repr. New York, 1973), 277.

[16] Avicenna, *Liber canonis*, bk. 1, *fen* 2, doctrine 3, ch. 7 (fos. 42ᵛ–43ʳ). See also Gruner, *Treatise on the Canon*, 277.

Such humoral material quickly became widespread in Latin dream theory, appearing in the twelfth century, for instance, in Pascalis Romanus' *Liber thesauri occulti* (*c*.1165)[17] and the Cistercian *De spiritu et anima*,[18] and then, during the thirteenth and fourteenth centuries, in writers as diverse as Michael Scot,[19] Albertus Magnus,[20] Vincent of Beauvais,[21] Boethius of Dacia,[22] Arnald of Villanova,[23] William of Aragon,[24] Robert Holkot,[25] and Geoffrey Chaucer.[26]

The dependence of dreams upon the humours may, as Chaucer's Pertelote suggests, provide a useful key for reading dream images, but

---

[17] Pascalis' work probably predates the Latin translation of Avicenna and Rasis, but since Pascalis is himself a translator, at least from the Greek (see C. H. Haskins, *Studies in Mediaeval Culture* (Oxford, 1929), 169), he probably had access to certain as yet untranslated Galenic works. See S. Collin-Roset, 'Le *Liber thesauri occulti* de Pascalis Romanus (un traité d'interprétation des songes du XIIᵉ siècle)', *AHDLMA* 30 (1963), 111–98: 126. For the humoral material see, in Collin-Roset's edition, bk. 1, ch. 1 (pp. 143–4).

[18] The *De spiritu et anima* was often wrongly ascribed to Augustine. For the humoral material, see *De spiritu et anima*, PL 40, ch. 25, trans. E. Leiva and B. Ward in *Three Treatises on Man: A Cistercian Anthropology*, ed. B. McGinn (Kalamazoo, Mich., 1977), 179–288: 221.

[19] Michael Scot flourished in the first half of the 13th cent.; see d'Alverny, 'Translations and Translators', 455–7. On the humoral material from Scot's *De secretis naturae*, see Fioravanti, '"Scientia somnialis"', 348.

[20] Albertus Magnus lived *c*.1193–1280. For the humoral material, see the *Summa de creaturis*, in *Opera omnia*, ed. A. Borgnet, 38 vols. (Paris, 1890–9), vol. xxxv, question 50, article 1 (pp. 435–6).

[21] Vincent of Beauvais wrote in the mid-13th cent. For the humoral material, see the *Speculum naturale*, bk. 26, ch. 54, cols. 1872–3, borrowed by Vincent from Albertus Magnus, *Summa de creaturis*. P. Aiken, 'Vincent of Beauvais and Dame Pertelote's Knowledge of Medicine', *Speculum*, 10 (1935), 281–7, sees Vincent as an important source for Chaucer's medically informed view of dreaming in NPT.

[22] Boethius of Dacia flourished in Paris in the 1270s. For the humoral material, see Boethius of Dacia, *De somniis*, in *Opera*, vol. vi, pt. 2, ed. N. G. Green-Pederson, Corpus Philosophorum Danicorum Medii Aevi (Copenhagen, 1976), 388–90, trans. J. F. Wippel in *On the Supreme Good, On the Eternity of the World, On Dreams* (Toronto, 1987), 74–6. See Fioravanti, '"Scientia somnialis"', for a full discussion of Boethius' treatment of dreaming.

[23] Arnald of Villanova died *c*.1311. In his discussion of humoral material in the *Praxis medicinalis*, he cites e.g. Avicenna: see Fattori's discussion in 'Sogni e temperamenti', 102–4.

[24] William of Aragon flourished *c*.1330. For the humoral material, see R. A. Pack, 'De pronosticatione sompniorum libellus Guillelmo de Aragonia adscriptus', *AHDLMA* 33 (1966), 237–92: 268–9.

[25] Holkot wrote the *Lectiones* on the Book of Wisdom *c*.1334–6. For the humoral material, see R. Holkot, *In librum sapientiae regis Salomonis praelectiones CCXIII* (Basle, 1586), *lectio* 103 (p. 350), and *lectio* 202 (p. 666). R. A. Pratt, 'Some Latin Sources of the Nonnes Preest on Dreams', *Speculum*, 52 (1977), 538–70, proposes that Holkot was an important source for the dream-lore of NPT.

[26] See Chaucer, NPT 2923–69.

the importance of medical treatments of dreaming goes beyond their introduction of a 'colour-coded' system for interpreting dreams. The connection between dreams and the humours, along with other newly introduced medical material, is most important as it indicates a new way of looking at dreams, an intensified concern with dream process, with how precisely dreams and their images come into being. We see this in Avicenna's inclusion of dream material within his more general treatment of bodily functions and the Galenic humours. We also see it in more and more elaborate attempts, influenced by both medical writings and the newly rediscovered Aristotelian corpus, to explain the presentation of dreams in relation to the most basic of bodily processes—heating, cooling, dissipation and gathering of energies, digestion, the movement of vapours and spirits among the organs and faculties of the body. To quote briefly from one extensive treatment of this sort, by Vincent of Beauvais:

The movement [of images in a dream] descends from the locus of the fantasy, and touches the common sense, and returns to the fantasy. Truly, when there is evaporation from the place of digestion to the brain, a thin blood is elevated, and descends to the interior of the animal head [i.e. the head as locus of the animal spirit], upon which the animal spirit goes forth, carrying images from the locus of the fantasy to the organ of the common sense. When these [images] move the common sense, a dream arises, and the form brought down from the fantasy to the common sense seems to be perceived.

([H]ic motus descendit a loco phantastico, et tangit sensum communem, ac reuertitur ad phantasiam. Cum enim euaporatio fit a loco digestionis ad cerebrum, sanguis subtilis eleuatur, ac descendit ad interius capitis animalis, cum quo progreditur animalis spiritus simulachra deferens a loco phantasiae ad organum sensus communis. Quae cum mouent sensum communem fit somnium, et videtur sentiri forma delata a phantasia ad communem sensum.)[27]

We say moreover that dreams appear more frequently at the end of sleep . . . because . . . at its beginning, the digestive heat is strengthened, and one finds the food mixed up, the pure with the impure. And therefore it brings a disturbed evaporation up into the head, in which images cannot well result. But at the end [of sleep], when the more impure blood sinks downward, and only the thin [blood] rises upward, then the animal spirit is purified, and images begin to result in dreams.

(Nos autem dicimus quod in fine dormitionis frequentius apparent somnia . . . quia . . . calor digestiuus confortatur in principio, et inuenit cibum permixtum

---

[27] Vincent of Beauvais, *Speculum naturale*, bk. 26, ch. 34, cols. 1861–2. Vincent here depends upon Albertus Magnus, *Summa de creaturis*, question 46 (p. 421).

purum cum impuro. Ideoque turbatum euaporationem sic eleuat ad caput, in qua non bene resultant imagines. At in fine cum impurior sanguis residet deorsum, et subtilis tantum eleuatur sursum, tunc purificatur spiritus animalis, et incipiunt resultare simulacra insomnijs.)[28]

Where an early dream theorist like Gregory the Great (d. 604) asserts that dreams arise 'from the fullness or emptiness of the stomach',[29] but without explaining the processes leading from stomach to dream, or where Macrobius (fourth to fifth century) asserts a connection between the *insomnium* and 'eating or drinking', 'hunger or thirst',[30] but again without giving any more detailed description of internal process, a twelfth-century, medically aware writer like Pascalis Romanus, adapting and elaborating Macrobius, explicates the *insomnium* and *visum* by means of an elaborate psychosomatics. Thus, to counter the 'common opinion' that the *incubus* (a sub-species of Macrobius' *visum*) 'is a small being in the likeness of a satyr and that it presses sleepers at night in such a way that it almost kills them by suffocation', Pascalis deploys a complex medical explanation:

there is a certain blood in the human body that does not run about through the veins nor through any other fixed routes, but is in the heart or around the heart. And when one sleeps lying on the left side or even supine,[31] this blood, by a certain abundance of humours, runs down to that same part and chokes the heart; and it [the heart] is so close to the left side that it cannot [then] be opened or closed [i.e. beat]. For the heart, since it is always the seat of the spirit, is naturally in motion nor does it wish to be obstructed. When, however, the heart is so choked by blood and humours that it cannot freely open and close itself nor be in its natural motion, the humours become heavy in the sleeper, so that he thinks that he is holding up a whole house or some other mass.

---

[28] Vincent of Beauvais, *Speculum naturale*, bk. 26, ch. 47, col. 1868. Vincent here depends upon Albertus Magnus, *Summa de creaturis*, question 47 (p. 427).

[29] Gregory the Great, *Dialogues*, bk. IV, ch. 50, sect. 2, and *Moralia in Job*, bk. VIII, ch. 24, sect. 42. For the Latin texts, see *Dialogues*, ed. A. de Vogüé, Sources Chrétiennes 251, 260, 265 (Paris, 1978–80); *Moralia in Iob*, ed. M. Adriaen, Corpus Christianorum, Series Latina 143, 143A, 143B (Turnholt, 1979–85). For English versions, see *Dialogues*, trans. O. J. Zimmerman, The Fathers of the Church: A New Translation 39 (New York, 1959); *Morals on the Book of Job*, 3 vols., A Library of Fathers of the Holy Catholic Church, translated by members of the English church (Oxford, 1844–50).

[30] Macrobius, *Commentary on the Dream of Scipio*, trans. Stahl, 1. 3. 4 (p. 88).

[31] Medical writers often consider the position of the body during sleep to influence the digestive process, and hence potentially the quality of dreams. See e.g. Avicenna, *The Poem on Medicine*, trans. H. C. Krueger (Springfield, Ill., 1963), 57; M. Savonorola, *Libreto de tutte le cosse che se magnano: Un opera di dietetica del sec. XV*, ed. J. Nystedt (Stockholm, 1988), 188–9.

(quidam sanguis est in corpore humano, qui non discurrit per venas neque per aliquos certos meatus, sed est in corde vel circa cor. Hic itaque sanguis quando aliquis dormit, jacens super latus sinistrum vel etiam resupinus, quedam habunda[n]tia humorum ad eandem partem decurrit corque suffocat; itaque est proximum sinistro lateri quod non potest aperiri vel claudi. Nam cor, quia sedes est semper spiritus, est in motu naturaliter nec vult impediri. Cum autem cor ita suffocatum est a sanguine et humoribus, quod non potest se libere aperire et claudere nec esse in suo motu naturali, gravantur humores in dormiente, ut putet se totam domum vel aliquam molem sustinere.)[32]

As I have suggested elsewhere, such late medieval shifts in dream theory did not reconstruct dreaming as a simply somatic phenomenon: the mainstream of medieval dream theory never reached the position of Aristotle's *Parva naturalia*, where the dream would be wholly confined to the realm of the physical.[33] Writers like Vincent, Pascalis, and Albertus Magnus embraced the possibility of both mundane and transcendent dreams: dreams naturally arise from our bodies, but that does not mean that they cannot also be caused or shaped from outside the body—by the planets, by angels and demons, even directly by God. Later medieval dream theorists tended to preserve the complexity of dream types that, from late antiquity on, consistently characterized European dream theory. But with the new medical emphasis on dream process came an essentially new way of regarding that complexity. Rather than assume that each distinct dream type involves a distinct mechanism of action— meaningless dreams arising from within the dreamer, meaningful dreams from outer, transcendent forces (as in Gregory the Great)—at least some late medieval dream theorists began to treat all dreams as involving similar internal processes. This is a possibility anticipated in Augustine's comments on dreaming in both the *De Genesi ad litteram* and *De cura pro mortuis gerenda* (fourth to fifth century), but not there explored in any detail in terms of the psychosomatics of the dream.[34] Writers like Albert and Vincent, however, began in elaborate ways to suggest that common processes unite all dream experience. Thus,

[32] Collin-Roset, '*Liber thesauri occulti*', bk. 1, ch. 10 (pp. 158–9). I quote my own translation of the passage from *Dreaming in the Middle Ages*, 71, with slight modifications.

[33] Kruger, *Dreaming in the Middle Ages*, 83–122.

[34] See Augustine, *De Genesi ad litteram libri duodecim*, ed. J. Zycha, Corpus Scriptorum Ecclesiasticorum Latinorum, vol. 28, sect. 3; pt. 1 (Prague, 1894), bk. 12, trans. J. H. Taylor as *The Literal Meaning of Genesis*, 2 vols., Ancient Christian Writers: The Works of the Fathers in Translation 42 (New York, 1982), and *De cura pro mortuis gerenda*, PL 40, cols. 591–610, trans. H. Browne as *On Care to Be Had for the Dead*, A Select Library of the Nicene and Post-Nicene Fathers of the Christian Church 3 (Buffalo, 1887), 537–51.

Albert, in explaining how heavenly movements might cause dreams that predict the future, developed a complex system that brought internal and external forces together on the common ground of the dream. In part the clarity and truth-value of dreams depend upon the strength of the light (*lumen*), motion (*motus*), or form (*forma*) being transmitted from the heavens; but human process also plays a crucial role in producing these dreams, even those that most clearly reveal some celestial truth:

the celestial forms sent to us, touching our bodies, move them strongly, and imprint their virtue [on them]. . . . The imaginative soul receives this movement according to the mode which is possible for it, and this [mode] is according to the forms of the imagination [that is, the soul receives the celestial movement in images].

(formae coelitus evectae ad nos, corpora nostra tangentes fortissime movent, et suas imprimunt virtutes. . . . [A]nima . . . imaginativa . . . recipit motum secundum modum possibilem sibi, et hoc est ad formas imaginationis.)[35]

Similarly, both Albert and Vincent feel called upon to explain the mechanism by which angels, given a nature essentially different from the human, might nonetheless communicate with human beings through dreams:

Truly all dreams exist in corporeal similitudes. . . . Therefore no dreams arise from such pure and simple intellects as belong to angels. We, however, say that, although in the angels forms may be simple, nevertheless, since an angel and [its] intelligence are substances working on human souls, as the philosophers say: those forms are simple in them [the angels], but are received by the soul or souls as particular and corporeal, and this is the solution of Alpharabius. It may also be said that intelligence pours into [the human being] a simple thought, for which thought, certainly, the imagination [then] forms images.

(Omnia vero somnia sunt in corporalibus similitudinibus. . . . Nulla ergo somnia sunt a puris et simplicibus intellectibus quales sunt Angelorum. Nos autem dicimus quod licet in Angelis sint formae simplices, tamen quia Angelus et intelligentia sunt substantiae in animas humanas agentes, vt dicunt philosophi: Formae illae sunt in eis simplices, recipiuntur ab anima vel animabus, vt particulares et corporales, et haec est solutio Alpharabij. Posset etiam dici quod intelligentia simplicem intellectum infundit, cui scilicet intellectui imaginatio format imagines.)[36]

---

[35] Albertus Magnus, Commentary on Aristotle's *De divinatione per somnum*, in *Opera omnia*, ix, 190. Gregory, 'I sogni e gli astri', 121–33, discusses Albert's system. Using Albert's theory as a base, William of Aragon elaborated a similar treatment of dreaming; see Pack, 'De pronosticatione sompniorum'.

[36] Vincent of Beauvais, *Speculum naturale*, bk. 26, ch. 57, col. 1874; Vincent borrows here from Albertus Magnus, *Summa de creaturis*, question 51 (pp. 442–3).

Albert and Vincent are not satisfied simply with asserting that angels have the power to send dreams to human beings; they also want to understand how such dreams might operate given what they know about angels and about the workings of the dream process in the faculty of imagination.

In my view, then, the most important consequence of the new somatic treatment of dreaming is in the ways it enables a bringing together of different kinds of dream—internally and externally motivated, celestial and mundane, angelic, demonic, and human—on the common ground of one unitary dream process involving certain universal psychosomatic elements. This later medieval somatic unification of dreaming might, I think, have significant implications for our reading of late medieval dream narrative. Recognizing the somatic possibilities of the dream may move us away from the simple allegorizing and spiritualizing tendencies of much dream-vision criticism. The dreamer has a body that plays an important part in determining the content and form of his or her dreams, and the progress of the dream may productively be read not just as an itinerary of spiritual ascent but as the effect and record of certain physiological and psychosomatic processes.

In my previous work on the implications of medieval dream theory for reading dream narrative, I have proposed that ideas of the dream's 'doubleness' and 'middleness'—its consistent connection to and navigation between a transcendent realm of spirit and an earthly realm of body—enabled the development of the 'middle vision', a literary genre balancing the mundane and the celestial: 'Poems of this tradition simultaneously evoke opposed ideas about the nature of dreaming, and, by doing so, situate themselves to explore areas of betweenness—the realms that lie between the divine and the mundane, the true and the false, the good and the bad.'[37] As Spearing has recognized, in the complexity of late medieval dream types lies the possibility of a simultaneous deployment of opposed types that will create a consistent, self-conscious ambivalence:

The dream in *The Book of the Duchess*, then, could be classified as a *somnium naturale*, a *somnium animale*, or a *somnium coeleste*. . . . Seen in one way, the

---

[37] Kruger, *Dreaming in the Middle Ages*, 129. See also p. 135, where I suggest that Chaucer's *BD* in particular participates in the 'sustained ambiguity of the middle vision'; my current consideration of *BD* represents a partial rethinking of that suggestion. See also Kruger, 'Mirrors and the Trajectory of Vision'; id., 'Imagination and the Complex Movement of Chaucer's *House of Fame*', *ChauR* 28 (1993–4), 117–34, for readings that emphasize the ambivalence of the dream vision's movement.

dream is a heavenly vision, conveying the truth in a symbolic form. . . . At the same time, the merely psychological explanation of the dream would provide suggestions for the organization of the dream-poem as an intricate late-medieval work of art. In later dream-poems Chaucer will make these issues explicit and generalize them, so that the uncertainty about the status of dreams can be used as a way of discussing the status of the poem as such.[38]

And as Lynch suggests, 'the substitution of one mode of knowing for another' in the later Middle Ages enabled, in Chaucer's poetry at least, a 'dialogism' that Lynch would deny to the earlier 'high medieval dream vision': 'The dream vision genre would become, in Bakhtin's terms, "novelized" . . . as generic conventions would come to reflect a significantly different set of assumptions, ones that allowed for a more real pluralism, that permitted, even demanded, multiple expressions of a truth whose unity was difficult or impossible of apprehension.'[39]

While I do not wish here to take back my earlier formulation, or to deny the power of readings of dream poetry like Spearing's and Lynch's that emphasize ambiguity and plurality, I do wish to rethink such positions in the light of what I am here proposing about the 'somatizing' of later medieval dream theory. Given the late medieval focus on a certain unitary process through which mundane and transcendent dream causes would both operate, one might see the dream's doubleness working not so much via a tension or balance of higher and lower terms as through an addition or superimposition of them. That is, as I have suggested about the *Testament of Cresseid*, we might see the dream as a place where moral or spiritualizing and somatic or naturalizing discourses, rather than being played off against each other, come together in mutual reinforcement. Perhaps the dream that Chaucer includes in the frame of his *Book of the Duchess*, Alcyone's dream of her dead husband Ceyx, dramatizes just such a bringing together of somatic and spiritual power. Brought on through her prayer to the gods and through their responding action—that is, brought on by forces that transcend the dreamer's body—Alcyone's dream is nonetheless most striking for its strong physicality: Ceyx's actual body, not some simulacrum, is caught up into the dream, appearing to Alcyone in the flesh.

---

[38] Spearing, *Medieval Dream-Poetry*, 61.

[39] K. L. Lynch, 'The *Book of the Duchess* as a Philosophical Vision', *Genre*, 21 (1988), 279–305: 282–3. For Lynch's treatment of the earlier dream-vision tradition, see her *High Medieval Dream Vision*.

III.   The Movement of Correction in Chaucer's Book of the Duchess

Chaucer's *Book of the Duchess* evokes bodily illness in a variety of ways.[40] As an elegy, it concerns itself repeatedly, if often obliquely, with death: the real death of Blanche, Duchess of Lancaster, during the plague of 1368;[41] the death of 'White', Blanche's fictional counterpart; the deaths of Ceyx and Alcyone in the Ovidian story Chaucer reshapes by metamorphosing metamorphosis into death; and the deaths from 'sorrowful' illness feared for both the poem's narrator and the knight of his dream:

> For nature wolde nat suffyse
> To noon erthly creature
> Nat longe tyme to endure
> Withoute slep and be in sorwe.
> And I ne may, ne nyght ne morwe,
> Slepe; and thus melancolye
> And drede I have for to dye.
>
> (18–24)
>
> Hit was gret wonder that Nature
> Myght suffre any creature
> To have such sorwe and be not ded.
>
> (467–9)

Although Chaucer suppresses 'any reference to plague . . . in favour of a more generalized and abstract allusion to death', as Butterfield has recently argued, the *Book of the Duchess* may nonetheless be productively read in relation to the 'politics of plague'.[42] And the poem explicitly and insistently concerns itself with melancholic illness occasioned

---

[40]   I am concerned here to pursue a reading of *BD* that, in foregrounding the body, resists the critical tendency noted by L. O. Fradenburg, ' "Voice Memorial": Loss and Reparation in Chaucer's Poetry', *Exemplaria*, 2 (1990), 169–202, to abandon the particular and embodied, often identified with the 'female' or 'feminine', 'in favor of some form of transcendence' (185), a move that replicates the elegiac impulse to pass beyond grief for the individual and to assert a transcendent authority that makes loss make sense.

[41]   For the argument that Blanche's death occurred in 1368 rather than 1369, as previously believed, see J. J. N. Palmer, 'The Historical Context of the *Book of the Duchess*: A Revision', *ChauR* 8 (1973–4), 253–61; S. Ferris, 'John Stow and the Tomb of Blanche the Duchess', *ChauR* 18 (1983–4), 92–3.

[42]   A. Butterfield, 'Pastoral and the Politics of Plague', *SAC* 16 (1994), 3–27: 22. P. P. Buckler, 'Love and Death in Chaucer's *The Book of the Duchess*', in J. S. Mink and J. D. Ward (eds.), *Joinings and Disjoinings: The Significance of Marital Status in Literature* (Bowling Green, Oh., 1991), 6–18, also places *BD* in the context of the Black Death.

by love and by loss. The poem's tripartite structure—focused first on the narrator, then on Alcyone, and finally on the knight—depends upon a triple reiteration of melancholia.[43]

The narrator, while he denies knowledge of the cause of the 'sick-nesse' (36) that he has 'suffred this eight yeer' (37)—'Myselven can not telle why | The sothe' (34–5)—presents a remarkably detailed symp-tomatology, anatomizing in particular the physiological dysfunction of the brain under the influence of sleeplessness. Both the imaginative and estimative faculties are disturbed,[44] with *imaginatio* working overtime (14–15) to present 'Suche fantasies' (28) that the narrator, his *aestimatio* confounded, is unable to judge 'what is best to doo' (29), unable even to distinguish 'Joye' from 'sorowe' (10):

> I have so many an ydel thoght
> Purely for defaute of slep
> That, by my trouthe, I take no kep
> Of nothing, how hyt cometh or gooth,
> Ne me nys nothyng leef nor looth.
> Al is ylyche good to me—
> Joye or sorowe, wherso hyt be—
> For I have felynge in nothyng,
> But as yt were a mased thyng,
> Alway in poynt to falle a-doun;
> For sorwful ymagynacioun
> Ys alway hooly in my mynde.
>
> (4–15)

Despite his estimative disturbance, the narrator is able to recognize the 'sorrowful' nature of his own situation (14, 21) and to identify his

---

[43] The importance of the 'triptych' structure of the poem has been emphasized, for instance, in D. C. Baker, 'Imagery and Structure in Chaucer's *Book of the Duchess*', *SN* 30 (1958), 17–26, and H. Phillips, 'Structure and Consolation in the *Book of the Duchess*', *ChauR* 16 (1981–2), 107–18.

[44] On *imaginatio* and *aestimatio* and their interrelation, see E. R. Harvey, *The Inward Wits* (London, 1975), esp. pp. 44–6; M. W. Bundy, *The Theory of Imagination in Classical and Mediaeval Thought*, University of Illinois Studies in Language and Literature 12/2–3 (Urbana, Ill., 1927); V. A. Kolve, *Chaucer and the Imagery of Narrative: The First Five Canterbury Tales* (Stanford, 1984), esp. pp. 20–4. Imagination, working with the *sensus communis*, receives and retains images from the five senses; estimation judges the *intentiones* that inhere in images, and it informs the perceiver about the hostility or harm-lessness of the things perceived.

On what he calls the 'psychology of perception and cognition' in *BD*, see D. Burnley, 'Some Terminology of Perception in the *Book of the Duchess*', *ELN* 23 (1986), 15–22; J. S. Neaman, 'Brain Physiology and Poetics in *The Book of the Duchess*', *RPL* 3 (1980), 101–13; Lynch, '*Book of the Duchess*', 288.

sleeplessness as unnatural, 'agaynes kynde' (16), and, therefore, perilous; but awareness of his endangered position does not help him escape from malaise. Rather, it leads, in a kind of vicious circle, to further 'melancolye' (23) and 'drede' (24), to a 'hevynesse' that, combined with 'Defaute of slep' (25), robs his 'spirit' of 'quyknesse' (26). He lives devoid of vitality: 'I have lost al lustyhede' (27).

The symptoms that the narrator thus describes, and their circular reinforcement, are clearly associated, in medieval medical works, with a superabundance of melancholic humour.[45] As Klibansky, Panofsky, and Saxl point out, Constantinus Africanus, translating Isḥâq ben 'Amrân, portrays melancholy illness 'as "motions disturbed by black bile with fear, anxiety, and nervousness", that is to say, as a physically-conditioned sickness of the soul which could attack all three "virtutes ordinativae"—imagination, reason, and memory—and thence, reacting on the body, cause sleeplessness, loss of weight, and disorder of all the natural functions'.[46] Melancholy, as the cold and dry humour, is particularly conducive to the formation of strong impressions in the imagination, impressions that, as in lovesickness, might then be obsessively considered and reconsidered.[47] The narrator's obsessive depiction of his own obsessive illness fits just such a pattern. And the larger movement of the *Book of the Duchess* can be described as a repeated, circular return to the question of melancholy.[48]

Thus the story of Ceyx and Alcyone, read by the narrator for diversion as he lies sleepless in bed, directly echoes his melancholic illness. Alcyone responds to the disappearance of Ceyx with 'wonder' (78; compare line 1); she is sorrowful (85, 95, 98, 100, 104, 202, 203, 210, 213; compare lines 10, 14, 21); her physical and mental capacities are

---

[45] On melancholy in *BD*, see esp. J. M. Hill, '*The Book of the Duchess*, Melancholy, and that Eight-Year Sickness', *ChauR* 9 (1974–5), 35–50; C. F. Heffernan, 'That Dog Again: *Melancholia Canina* and Chaucer's *Book of the Duchess*', *MP* 84 (1986), 185–90.

[46] R. Klibansky, E. Panofsky, and F. Saxl, *Saturn and Melancholy: Studies in the History of Natural Philosophy, Religion, and Art* (London, 1964), 83. See also p. 92, where Klibansky *et al.* suggest that, in scholastic works, melancholy's effects often were—as in Chaucer—associated specifically with imaginative and estimative dysfunction. The reported symptoms of melancholy remain quite stable at least into the Renaissance: see R. Burton, *The Anatomy of Melancholy*, ed. H. Jackson (New York, 1977), First Partition, 382–429, and the 'synopsis' on pp. 128–9.

[47] See e.g. the opening of Gerard of Berry's *Glosses on the Viaticum*, in M. F. Wack, *Lovesickness in the Middle Ages: The Viaticum and its Commentaries* (Philadelphia, 1990), 198–9.

[48] M. B. Herzog, 'The *Book of the Duchess*: The Vision of the Artist as a Young Dreamer', *ChauR* 22 (1987–8), 269–81: 270–1.

disturbed—she swoons (103, 123, 215), refuses to eat (92), is 'forwaked' (126), 'wery' (127), 'ful nygh wood' (104). Just as the narrator suggests that 'there is phisicien but oon | That may me hele' (39–40), so Alcyone 'Ne . . . koude no reed but oon' (105). And as though recognizing the points of contact between his own situation and Alcyone's, the narrator responds to her story strongly and sympathetically, feeling 'such pittee and such rowthe' that he 'ferde the worse al the morwe | Aftir to thenken on hir sorwe' (97, 99–100). Indeed, the outcome of Alcyone's illness, her sudden death, presents a limit, the worst-case scenario, for the narrator's own illness, enacting the death he fears for himself.

Significantly, of course, Alcyone's illness, like the narrator's, eventuates in a dream linked to both body and divinity, a dream that reveals the truth but at the same time is closely connected to Alcyone's psychosomatic distress.[49] Here, the somatic connections of the dream are emphasized not only by the literal bringing of Ceyx's body to Alcyone's bedside but also by certain clearly melancholic features of the dream situation. Although it is Juno and her 'messager' (133) who respond most directly to Alcyone's prayer for 'grace to slepe and mete | In my slep som certeyn sweven | Wherthourgh that I may knowen even | Whether my lord be quyk or ded' (118–21), the divinity immediately responsible for the dream is Morpheus, the ruler of a 'derke' (155), barren (155–9), chthonic realm, 'ygrave . . . wonder depe' (164–5), pervaded by a 'dedly slepynge soun' (162), 'as derk | As helle-pit overal aboute' (170–1). This dark underworld, from which Alcyone's revelatory dream arises, is inhabited by creatures (potential dreams) who, frozen in lethargy, echo in their attitudes Alcyone's own despondent poses: 'Somme henge her chyn upon hir brest' (174; compare 'she heng doun the hed', 122); 'And somme lay naked in her bed' (176; compare 'And broghten hir in bed al naked', 125).

The narrator's own dream stands in a similarly intimate connection to his illness, and particularly to the state of melancholy. As Heffernan has suggested, Chaucer's depiction of the fawning 'whelp' (389) in the dream may evoke medical accounts of 'melancholia canina' or 'lycanthropia'.[50] It is this whelp which guides the dreamer through a bright landscape to a

---

[49] The truthful nature of the dream is perhaps emphasized by the time at which it occurs—'Ryght even a quarter before day' (198). Dreams arising not long before dawn were thought to be more likely to reveal the truth since, by that time, digestion was largely complete. See the passage cited from Vincent of Beauvais, *Speculum naturale*, bk. 26, ch. 47, col. 1868, above. See also Kruger, *Dreaming in the Middle Ages*, 72, 99, 106; C. Speroni, 'Dante's Prophetic Morning-Dreams', *SP* 45 (1948), 50–9.

[50] Heffernan, 'That Dog Again'.

wood of melancholic dream images—'things tinted with a dark color',[51] 'hit was shadewe overal under' (426)—where the dreamer discovers the knight 'clothed al in blak' (457) lamenting his lost love 'White'.

The knight of course suffers from an illness similar to that of both the narrator and Alcyone: 'he heng hys hed adoun' (461) repeats the gesture of Alcyone and of the inhabitants of the land of Sleep; and his 'compleynte' (464), with its 'dedly sorwful soun' (462), echoes the 'dedly slepynge soun' (162) of Morpheus' cave. Like the narrator's illness, the knight's is here anatomized in some physiological detail:

> Whan he had mad thus his complaynte,
> Hys sorwful hert gan faste faynte
> And his spirites wexen dede;
> The blood was fled for pure drede
> Doun to hys herte, to make hym warm—
> For wel hyt feled the herte had harm—
> To wite eke why hyt was adrad
> By kynde, and for to make hyt glad,
> For hit ys membre principal
> Of the body; and that made al
> Hys hewe chaunge and wexe grene
> And pale, for ther noo blood ys sene
> In no maner lym of hys.
>
> (487–99)[52]

Although here the focus is on disturbances of the heart rather than the head, a mental fixation like the narrator's is also detailed:

> he spak noght,
> But argued with his owne thoght,
> And in hys wyt disputed faste
> Why and how hys lyf myght laste;
> Hym thoughte hys sorwes were so smerte
> And lay so colde upon hys herte.
> So, throgh hys sorwe and hevy thoght,
> Made hym that he herde me noght;
> For he had wel nygh lost hys mynde,[53]
> Thogh Pan, that men clepeth god of kynde,
> Were for hys sorwes never so wroth.
>
> (503–13)

---

[51] Hoffmeister, 'Rasis' Traumlehre', 150.

[52] Cf. J. E. Grennen, 'Hert-Huntyng in the Book of the Duchess', MLQ 25 (1964), 131–9: 139.

[53] Note the close parallel here to Alcyone's near-madness (104).

In their ensuing conversation, both the narrator and the knight explicitly note the knight's ailment:

> by my trouthe, to make yow hool
> I wol do al my power hool.
> And telleth me of your sorwes smerte;
> Paraunter hyt may ese youre herte,
> That semeth ful sek under your syde.

(553–7)

> May noght make my sorwes slyde,
> Nought al the remedyes of Ovyde,
> Ne Orpheus, god of melodye,
> Ne Dedalus with his playes slye;
> Ne hele me may no phisicien,
> Noght Ypocras ne Galyen.

(567–72)

The *Book of the Duchess* thus focuses attention unremittingly upon the realm of body and bodily illness, but to what end? Certainly, Chaucer's medically resonant dream operates differently from Henryson's. In the *Testament of Cresseid*, after all, the dream serves to diagnose and produce illness while, in the *Book of the Duchess*, illness is the poem's starting-point. As I will suggest, however, Chaucer's poem stands with Henryson's in its use of the dream as a ground for the conflation of somatic and spiritual concerns. In Henryson, moral correction occurs through a dream that disfigures the sexualized female body as a way of taming it. The gods' moral judgement, that Cresseid has turned 'feminitie' into 'filth', is made real—and physically so—in the transformation of her body through disease; where moral 'filth' is at first metaphorical, the dream brings together somatic and spiritual realms in order to literalize moral failure as 'filthy' illness. Chaucer's poem relies upon a similar, but inverse, movement. Here, illness is not diagnosed or discovered through the dream; rather, the dream promises, at least in part, to provide a remedy for illness. Although the narrator, having gestured towards the only 'phisicien' that might heal him (39–40), denies that any remedy is near at hand—'That wil not be mot nede be left' (42)—the movement to reading, and from reading to sleep, is, as Olson has pointed out, a therapeutic one.[54] The primary symptom of the

---

[54] G. Olson, *Literature as Recreation in the Later Middle Ages* (Ithaca, NY, 1982), 85–9.

narrator's illness, his insomnia, is, after all, relieved, and we might reasonably expect the dream that ensues to continue a therapeutic movement. Moreover, as I will suggest, the dream of the *Book of the Duchess* is not simply somatic but rather an intervention in bodily illness supported by the moral force of the dream's traditional transcendent connections. While Henryson depicts a moral correction that operates through the dream's somatic force, Chaucer's dream moves towards a correction of physical illness that depends, in its notion of somatic health, upon certain moral imperatives.

Alcyone's dream may here be taken as at least a partial model for the narrator's. The Ovidian dream as Chaucer retells it works towards a cure of Alcyone by demanding that she moderate her 'excessive' reaction to Ceyx's absence: 'Let be your sorwful lyf, | For in your sorwe there lyth no red' (202–3). The dream operates through the body of Ceyx, and its primary goal is a relief of Alcyone's bodily and psychological distress. At the same time, all that is somatic in the dream depends upon the action of the gods, and its argument, intended to return Alcyone to bodily health, is directed towards spiritual correction, demanding a detachment from body, a recognition of the limitations of earthly happiness: 'I am but ded' (204); 'To lytel while oure blysse lasteth!' (211). The return to somatic health depends somewhat paradoxically upon a rejection of body, a reordering of spirit that will allow Alcyone to resume an ordered life in the world. While the correction needed for the narrator's return to health is even more complex, it too ultimately involves a simultaneous movement towards reordering the body and letting it go.

Of course, Alcyone's dream fails to achieve its therapeutic goal: rather than move her out of illness, the confirmation of Ceyx's death intensifies 'sorwe' (213) and leads to a swift death. Still, the dream does attempt a certain simultaneously somatic and spiritual correction. And while it fails to cure Alcyone, it does participate in a larger therapeutic trajectory for the narrator. The decision 'To rede and drive the night away' (49) is the narrator's first step out of a circular obsession with his own illness, and the thoughts and actions that the account of Alcyone's dream puts into motion—the playful prayer to Morpheus or Juno 'Or som wight elles' (242–4)—lead immediately to a falling asleep that doubtless represents a first step in the cure of insomniac illness: 'I had be dolven everydel | And ded, ryght thurgh defaute of slep, | Yif I ne had red and take kep | Of this tale next before' (222–5).

With the Alcyone story, then, a forward movement begins for the narrator, countering the poem's initial, melancholic circularities. While those circularities are reiterated in a variety of ways—melancholic ill-ness reappears in the dream; the hunt, broken off, returns at the dream's conclusion; the knight's self-revelation proceeds by fits and starts, struc-tured by a triple reiteration of its refrain, 'Thou wost ful lytel what thou menest; | I have lost more than thow wenest' (743–4, 1137–8, 1305–6); the awakened dreamer promises 'to put this sweven in ryme' (1332) and thus, as the poem ends, recalls its beginning—they are now complicated by a linear movement that strongly promises escape from repetitive, obsessive illness. The sleepless narrator has, after all, finally fallen asleep to dream his 'wonderful', 'ynly swete . . . sweven' (276–7).

The description of the dream as 'ynly swete' neatly evokes, as does the narrator's reference to Macrobius (284), the dream's traditional double-ness. On the one hand, 'ynly swete' might allude to an understanding of dreams as allegorically significant, composed of the *chaf* of images and the enclosed ('ynly'), nourishing ('swete') *fruyt* of hidden signifi-cance, containing, like meaningful fictions, an instructive core beneath an entertaining surface.[55] At the same time, given the narrator's warn-ings about the difficulty of 'reading' this particular dream (277–89), we might be steered away from searching for hidden significance and instead be tempted to see 'ynly swete' as pointing towards the dream's somatic connections: in so far as it is medically therapeutic, working against the internal disturbances of melancholy, the dream is 'inwardly sweet'. My point here is that the poem does not demand from us a deci-sion that the dream should fit either one or the other of these possibil-ities; rather, it might function both as (morally or spiritually) instructive and as (somatically) corrective.

That the dream stands in some sense counter to its frame—both the narrator's self-description and the account of Alcyone and her own, not successfully therapeutic, dream—is clear from its opening moments. To enter this dream is to move from darkness to light and from passivity to activity, from a night of sleeplessness to a morning awakening.[56] The

[55] J. I. Wimsatt, '*The Book of the Duchess*: Secular Elegy or Religious Vision?', in J. P. Hermann and J. J. Burke, Jr. (eds.), *Signs and Symbols in Chaucer's Poetry* (University, Ala., 1981), 113–29, makes a similar suggestion at p. 118.

[56] On the contrast of night and day in the poem, see Baker, 'Imagery and Structure'. On the contrast between activity and passivity, see L. J. Kiser, 'Sleep, Dreams, and Poetry in Chaucer's *Book of the Duchess*', PLL 19 (1983), 3–12. On the changes that occur in mov-ing into the dream—including changes in the narrator himself—see e.g. J. R. Kreuzer, 'The Dreamer in the *Book of the Duchess*', PMLA 66 (1951), 543–7: 544–5; B. H. Bronson, '*The Book of the Duchess* Re-opened', PMLA 67 (1952), 863–81: 870–1; W. H. Clemen, *Chaucer's Early Poetry*, trans. C. A. M. Sym (London, 1963), 39; G. R. Crampton,

scenes of the preamble—the undescribed bedchambers of the narrator and Alcyone, the briefly sketched tempest in which Ceyx perishes, and the sterile realm of Sleep—are replaced by a brightly decorated bed-room and flourishing springtime landscape.[57] The passive, almost para-lysed, narrator remains enclosed within his chamber during the poem's preamble, but in the dream he quickly abandons his room, moving out into the world to participate in its activities. Where, before the dream, the narrator's encounter with 'kynde' or 'nature' occurs only in the adversarial experience of illness ('agaynes kynde | Hyt were to lyven in thys wyse', 16–17), and in reading stories meant 'to be in minde, | While men loved the lawe of kinde' (55–6), the dream dramatizes a movement into greater and greater proximity with the natural. Beginning in the enclosed bedchamber where birdsong and sunlight and clear air can be experienced only indirectly, filtered through elaborately decorated windows and walls, the narrator moves first into the social, ritual, and still adversarial encounter with nature that the hunt represents and then, led by the whelp, more directly into the natural landscape:[58]

> And I hym folwed, and hyt forth wente
> Doun by a floury grene wente
> Ful thikke of gras, ful softe and swete,
> With floures fele, faire under fete,
> And litel used; hyt semed thus,
> For both Flora and Zephirus,
> They two that make floures growe,
> Had mad her dwellynge ther, I trowe . . .
>
> (397–404)

'Transitions and Meaning in *The Book of the Duchess*', *JEGP* 62 (1963), 486–500: 490; B. F. Huppé and D. W. Robertson, Jr., *Fruyt and Chaf: Studies in Chaucer's Allegories* (Prince-ton, 1963), 44–5; J. B. Severs, 'Chaucer's Self-Portrait in the *Book of the Duchess*', *PQ* 43 (1964), 27–39: 34–5; R. Delasanta, 'Christian Affirmation in *The Book of the Duchess*', *PMLA* 84 (1969), 245–51: 248–50; R. A. Peck, 'Theme and Number in Chaucer's *Book of the Duchess*', in A. Fowler (ed.), *Silent Poetry: Essays in Numerological Analysis* (London, 1970), 73–115: 78–9 and 93; J. Winny, *Chaucer's Dream-Poems* (New York, 1973), 53 and 71–3; R. R. Edwards, 'The *Book of the Duchess* and the Beginnings of Chaucer's Narra-tive', *NLH* 13 (1982), 189–204: 194–5; A. Taylor, 'Epic Motifs in Chaucer's "Tale of Ceyx and Alcyone"', *Helios*, 14 (1987), 39–45: 42. M. Stevens, 'Narrative Focus in *The Book of the Duchess*: A Critical Revaluation', *AM* 7 (1966), 16–32: 18–19, however, denies that the dreamer undergoes any real change in the course of the poem; J. N. Brown, 'Narrative Focus and Function in *The Book of the Duchess*', *MSE* 2 (1969–70), 71–9, concurs.

[57] See Baker, 'Imagery and Structure'; D. Walker, 'Narrative Inconclusiveness and Consolatory Dialectic in the *Book of the Duchess*', *ChauR* 18 (1983–4), 1–17.

[58] Several critics have emphasized the thematic importance of 'kynde' for the poem. See R. M. Lumiansky, 'The Bereaved Narrator in Chaucer's *Book of the Duchess*', *TSE* 9

The movement that the dream thus institutes can be consistently read in somatic terms. Initiated in a momentary escape from melancholy when, stimulated by the account of Alcyone's dream, the narrator playfully prays for sleep, the dream itself opens in a landscape far from melancholic. But the dream does not represent simply a reversal or denial of illness. Rather, the bright opening of the dream leads into a movement of discovery whose goal is a return to melancholy that will not be simply circular but will, rather, move the narrator towards an understanding, and correction, of his illness. The dreamer moves out of his bedchamber, into the hunt for a 'hert' that, on the literal level, may fail, but that succeeds in returning the narrator to the 'hert' of his own distress. Led back into a landscape of melancholy ('hit was shadewe overal under', 426) that is simultaneously the landscape of natural phenomena, the narrator discovers first abundant 'herts' that have eluded the literal hunt (427) and then the knight and his grieving 'hert' (488).[59] Although this forward movement leads circularly back to a dark landscape at the centre of which is the lamenting knight, the figure who arrives at that landscape stands in a position very different from that which he occupies at the poem's opening. In the person of his dreaming self, the narrator now stands separate from himself as the subject of illness.[60] Rather than experience the psychic confusions of melancholia from the inside—as at the

(1959), 5–17; L. Eldredge, 'The Structure of the *Book of the Duchess*', *RUO* 39 (1969), 132–51; L. V. Sadler, 'Chaucer's *The Book of the Duchess* and the "Law of Kinde"', *AM* 11 (1970), 51–74; R. B. Burlin, *Chaucerian Fiction* (Princeton, 1977), 59–74; J. M. Fyler, 'Irony and the Age of Gold in the *Book of the Duchess*', *Speculum*, 52 (1977), 314–28; R. D. Dilorenzo, 'Wonder and Words: Paganism, Christianity, and Consolation in Chaucer's *Book of the Duchess*', *UTQ* 52 (1982), 20–39.

[59] On the complex wordplay around the *hert*, and for various readings of the significance of literal and figurative hunts in the poem, see Grennen, '*Hert-Huntyng*'; M. A. Carson, 'Easing of the "Hert" in the *Book of the Duchess*', *ChauR* 1 (1966–7), 157–60; Delasanta, 'Christian Affirmation', 250–1; D. Luisi, 'The Hunt Motif in *The Book of the Duchess*', *ES* 52 (1971), 309–11; A. L. Kellogg, *Chaucer, Langland, Arthur: Essays in Middle English Literature* (New Brunswick, NJ, 1972), ch. 7; M. Thiébaux, *The Stag of Love: The Chase in Medieval Literature* (Ithaca, NY, 1974), 115–27; J. Leyerle, 'The Heart and the Chain', in L. D. Benson (ed.), *The Learned and the Lewed: Studies in Chaucer and Medieval Literature*, Harvard English Studies 5 (Cambridge, Mass., 1974), 113–45: 114–18; R. A. Shoaf, 'Stalking the Sorrowful H(e)art: Penitential Lore and the Hunt Scene in Chaucer's *The Book of the Duchess*', *JEGP* 78 (1979), 313–24; S. P. Prior, '*Routhe and Hert-Huntyng* in the *Book of the Duchess*', *JEGP* 85 (1986), 3–19; D. Scott-Macnab, 'A Re-examination of Octovyen's Hunt in *The Book of the Duchess*', *MÆ* 56 (1987), 183–99.

[60] Readings that posit the knight as the dreamer's surrogate largely follow Bronson, '*Book of the Duchess* Re-opened'. For one recent elaboration of such a reading, see R. W. Hanning, 'Chaucer's First Ovid: Metamorphosis and Poetic Tradition in *The Book of the Duchess* and *The House of Fame*', in L. A. Arrathoon (ed.), *Chaucer and the Craft of Fiction* (Rochester, Mich., 1986), 121–63: 122–41.

beginning of the poem—he is now able to project his obsessive involvement in illness outward, on to the (imagined) person of the knight, and to assess this objectification of his illness 'objectively'. Thus, in observing the knight, the narrator moves to delineate, in addition to the symptoms of mental disturbance experienced from within and described at the poem's opening, the illness's full observable effects on body and heart. In the fiction that the dream presents, the narrator is no longer the passive sufferer of melancholy but rather a figure who, like Boethius' Lady Philosophy or like the *confabulator* of medical tradition,[61] may actively lead the knight to expose the causes of his illness and thus pursue its cure (547–57). The dialogue between the narrator and the knight indeed plots out a trajectory of discovery: the knight's initial lyric and allegorical expositions (and avoidances) of his situation give way to a more and more literal, historical account of loss.[62]

Moreover, the dream, especially in its emphasis on a movement from passivity to activity and from the 'agaynes kynde' to the 'natural', is not purely somatic, but also has a certain ideological, moralizing force. The narrator's illness is meaningful not just because it affects one individual's body and threatens his death but also because it potentially disrupts larger social structures thought to be both naturally and divinely instituted. More particularly, the narrator's melancholic illness disturbs his participation in 'properly' gendered and sexualized behaviour, and the dream operates not just to calm somatic disturbance but also to correct the narrator's gender and sexual identifications. That correction gains particular force from the dream's double positioning as an experience able to heighten both somatic and spiritual awareness. On the one hand, because of the dream's transcendent associations, the movement of somatic realignment can take on moral significance; on the other, the moralizing understanding of what is proper to the male body is underpinned by the dream's privileged access to the realm of nature.

[61] For Boethian readings of *BD*, see D. W. Robertson, Jr., 'The Historical Setting of Chaucer's *Book of the Duchess*', in J. Mahoney and J. E. Keller (eds.), *Mediaeval Studies in Honor of Urban Tigner Holmes, Jr.*, University of North Carolina Studies in the Romance Languages and Literatures 56 (Chapel Hill, NC, 1965), 169–95; C. P. R. Tisdale, 'Boethian "Hert-Huntyng": The Elegiac Pattern of *The Book of the Duchess*', *ABR* 24 (1973), 365–80; M. D. Cherniss, *Boethian Apocalypse: Studies in Middle English Vision Poetry* (Norman, Okla., 1987), 169–91. See Olson, *Literature as Recreation*, 88, on the narrator as the Black Knight's *confabulator*.

[62] On the interplay of the literal and the figurative in the poem, see A. C. Spearing, 'Literal and Figurative in *The Book of the Duchess*', *SAC: Proceedings*, 1 (1984), 165–71, in part a response to D. Aers, 'Chaucer's *Book of the Duchess*: An Art to Consume Art', *DUJ* NS 38 (1977), 201–5.

The corrective movement instituted by the dream, in so far as this is moral in its thrust, gains the force of what is understood to be natural to the human body and, in so far as it is somatic, that movement is supported by the dream's supposed access to moral truth.

One of the most striking qualities of the narrator's opening description of his illness is its absence of explicit references to gender and sexuality. In the poem's first forty-three lines, the speaker could equally well be male or female. When the narrator refers to a male attendant reaching him a book ('he it me tok', 48), we may conclude that the narrator is himself a man, but we should consider, in a poet who would later consistently impersonate feminine voices, the possibility that, at the poem's outset, a certain gender undefinedness or ambiguity is intended. Indeed, melancholic illness, in its challenges to the correct 'estimative' functioning of the mind and in the danger it therefore poses that an unworthy object might be elevated to a place of prominence in the subject's (obsessive) thinking and desire, always threatens a certain overthrowing of mental hierarchy figured as gender hierarchy, the dominance of (masculine) reason over (feminine) impulse. In other words, melancholic illness, for the male subject, threatens feminization. As Wack has suggested for lovesickness, in a formulation that can, I believe, be extended more generally to melancholia:

The patient considers [the beloved woman] better, more noble, and more desirable than other women, even though this may not objectively be the case. The overestimation of her desirability immobilizes the lover's mental faculties in meditation on her mental image. . . . there is a loss of inner control and governance in the noble subject, a degradation of the mental faculties expressed in the infantilization or feminization of the lover's body and behaviour.[63]

The narrator's passivity, his inability to overcome the 'fantastic' operations of his mind, despite his awareness of the dangers these pose for him, coupled with Chaucer's initial reticence about the narrator's gender, contribute to an opening portrait in which proper masculinity, at least by its absence, is an issue.[64]

The poem's opening is similarly, indeed more strikingly, reticent when it comes to the narrator's positioning as a romantic or sexual subject. Of course, critics beginning with Sypherd have often, and

---

[63] Wack, *Lovesickness*, 72.

[64] Cf. E. T. Hansen, *Chaucer and the Fictions of Gender* (Berkeley and Los Angeles, 1992), 61; G. Margherita, *The Romance of Origins: Language and Sexual Difference in Middle English Literature* (Philadelphia, 1994), 94–9.

rightly, taken the details of the eight years' sickness (36–7) and 'phisicien but oon' (39) as conventions of love poetry that might point towards the narrator's implication in melancholic *love*sickness.[65] What seems to me most striking about such details, however, is not their resonance with the poetry of courtly love but rather their failure to specify for themselves any precise field of reference. Certainly, they allow for Sypherd's reading but, as a whole series of opposing critical readings would suggest, they also leave themselves open to non-romantic—Boethian or theological—interpretations. Here, the narrator is not lovesick but bereaved, and perhaps spiritually endangered.[66] One might, indeed, point out that, in Chaucer's own corpus of writing, the figure of the 'phisicien' refers not only to the beloved woman of romance traditions (as when, in the *Book of the Duchess* itself, the knight refers to White as 'my lyves leche' (920) or when Criseyde is depicted as Troilus' 'leche', *TC* II. 571, 1066, 1582), but also to Lady Philosophy ('fisycien', *Bo* I. prosa 3. 4, and 'leche', *Bo* I. prosa 4. 5; IV. prosa 2. 129), the Virgin Mary ('my soules leche', *ABC* 133–4), Christ ('oure soules leche', PardT 916), and God ('oure lyves leche', SumT 1892).

Chaucer seems in fact purposely to have excluded from the poem's opening passage any explicit reference to love or lovesickness. The opening lines of the *Book of the Duchess* are strongly indebted to the opening of Froissart's *Paradys d'Amours*:[67]

---

[65] W. O. Sypherd, 'Chaucer's Eight Years' Sickness', *MLN* 20 (1905), 240–3. Those who, with Sypherd, assess the narrator's predicament as that of a lover include G. L. Kittredge, *Chaucer and his Poetry* (1915; Cambridge, Mass., 1967), 39–40; J. L. Lowes, 'The Loveres Maladye of Hereos', *MP* 11 (1914), 491–546: 544; id., *Geoffrey Chaucer and the Development of his Genius* (Boston, Mass., 1934), 117–18; M. W. Stearns, 'A Note on Chaucer's Attitude Toward Love', *Speculum*, 17 (1942), 570–4; R. S. Loomis, 'Chaucer's Eight Years' Sickness', *MLN* 59 (1944), 178–80; M. Galway, 'Chaucer's Hopeless Love', *MLN* 60 (1945), 431–9; K. Malone, *Chapters on Chaucer* (Baltimore, 1951), 23–4; Bronson, '*Book of the Duchess* Re-opened', 869; D. Bethurum, 'Chaucer's Point of View as Narrator in the Love Poems', *PMLA* 74 (1959), 511–20: 513; Hieatt, *Realism of Dream Visions*, 68; Spearing, *Medieval Dream-Poetry*, 52 and 59; P. C. Boardman, 'Courtly Language and the Strategy of Consolation in the *Book of the Duchess*', *ELH* 44 (1977), 567–79: 570–1; Fyler, 'Irony and the Age of Gold', 315; A. Butterfield, 'Lyric and Elegy in The *Book of the Duchess*', *MÆ* 60 (1991), 33–60: 48–9; J. J. Anderson, 'The Narrators in the *Book of the Duchess* and the *Parlement of Foules*', *ChauR* 26 (1991–2), 219–34: 220–1. Cf. J. Lawlor, 'The Pattern of Consolation in The *Book of the Duchess*', *Speculum*, 31 (1956), 626–48.

[66] See Lumiansky, 'Bereaved Narrator', 17; D. W. Robertson, Jr., *A Preface to Chaucer* (Princeton, 1962), 464; id., 'Historical Setting', 189; Huppé and Robertson, *Fruyt and Chaf*, 33; Delasanta, 'Christian Affirmation', 246–8; Cherniss, *Boethian Apocalypse*, 171; Wimsatt, 'Secular Elegy or Religious Vision?', 113–14; C. Donnelly, 'Challenging the Conventions of Dream Vision in The *Book of the Duchess*', *PQ* 66 (1987), 421–35: 425.

[67] For a general discussion of the French sources of *BD* see J. Wimsatt, *Chaucer and the French Love Poets: The Literary Background of the Book of the Duchess* (Chapel Hill,

Je sui de moi en grant mervelle
Coument tant vifs, car moult je velle,
Et on ne poroit en vellant
Trouver de moi plus travellant,
Car bien sachiés que par vellier
Me viennent souvent travellier
Pensees et merancolies
Qui me sont ens au coer liies.
Et pas ne les puis desliier,
Car ne voel la belle oubliier
Pour quelle amour en ce travel
Je sui entrés et tant je vel.[68]

(I can only be amazed that I am still alive, when I am lying awake so much. And one cannot find a sleepless person more tormented than myself, for as you well know, whilst I am lying awake sad thoughts and melancholy often come to torment me. They bind my heart so tightly, and I cannot loosen them, for I do not want to forget the fair one, for love of whom I entered into this torment and suffer such sleeplessness.)[69]

The opening of Froissart's poem operates by first sketching the narrator's melancholic illness and then, in lines 10–12, defining the cause of that illness—love for a beautiful woman ('la belle'). In Chaucer, the account of illness is maintained and elaborated, but its (hetero)sexual cause is never specified.[70] And beyond the non-specification of the narrator's illness as the feminizing but still heterosexual malady of lovesickness, the narrator's language also perhaps implies connections to a certain non-normative, non-procreative, 'perverse' sexuality. His illness is explicitly associated with what is 'agaynes kynde', and while this phrase might have a broad range of implications, like the 'phisicien but oon' pointing in several different directions at once, one of its strong and specific resonances would be with moralizing discourses directed at

NC, 1968). For further discussion of Chaucer's relation to Froissart and the *Paradys d'Amours*, see G. L. Kittredge, 'Chaucer and Froissart (with a discussion of the date of the Méliador)', *EStn* 26 (1899), 321–36; J. B. Severs, 'The Sources of "The Book of the Duchess"', *MS* 25 (1963), 355–62: 355–7; Fyler, 'Irony and the Age of Gold', 314–15; B. Nolan, 'The Art of Expropriation: Chaucer's Narrator in *The Book of the Duchess*', in D. M. Rose (ed.), *New Perspectives in Chaucer Criticism* (Norman, Okla., 1981), 203–22: 204–5 and 207–11; Edwards, '*Book of the Duchess*', 190–1 (see also Edwards, *Dream of Chaucer*, 68–70); Donnelly, 'Challenging the Conventions', 424–5; Russell, *English Dream Vision*, 146–7.

[68] Ed. Dembowski, lines 1–12.   [69] Windeatt, *Chaucer's Dream Poetry*, 41.

[70] Cf. Nolan, 'Art of Expropriation', 205; Donnelly, 'Challenging the Conventions', 424–5.

sexual behaviour 'contra naturam'.[71] Indeed, the knight of the narrator's dream will later speculate that his devotion to (heterosexual) love (see line 774) came to him 'kyndely' (778).

In part the Alcyone episode serves to specify, and heterosexualize, what is unspecified, and even potentially 'queer', in the narrator's initial (non-)sexual stance. Alcyone's situation brings together both the romantic and metaphysical (Boethian/theological) possibilities hinted at, but not specified, in the description of the narrator's illness: Alcyone is both lover, longing for the absent beloved, and bereaved spouse in need of philosophical or theological consolation. And in the Ovidian story, both love and bereavement are specified as heterosexual. In so far as we identify the narrator with Alcyone—and the poem gives us strong reasons to do so—we may retrospectively recast the narrator's distress as itself heterosexual.

The dream frame thus begins a process of sculpting the narrator's initially amorphous illness into a recognizable and conventional form— the form of heterosexual desire and loss—and it is this very movement, the narrator's identification with Alcyone leading to his (playful) reiteration of her falling asleep, that initiates the larger curative or therapeutic movement of the poem. Correction of the narrator's illness begins with a displaced, heterosexualizing specification of it. But just as the Alcyone episode leaves much unresolved regarding the possibility of a cure for the narrator's own melancholy—Alcyone after all dies in response to the dream sent to assist her—it also fails fully to resolve the problems of gender and sexuality raised by the narrator's illness. The heterosexualizing of the narrator through a certain identification with Alcyone only serves to intensify the problem of gender identification.[72] Specifying the narrator's melancholy illness as romantic and heterosexual involves the cross-identification of narrator with ancient 'quene' (65). If the Alcyone episode serves to allay anxieties raised by Chaucer's

---

[71]   The phrase goes back, in the Christian tradition, to the New Testament (Romans 1: 26–7). It is used in the Middle Ages by such writers as Peter Damian; see *Liber Gomorrhianus*, PL 145, col. 161: 'Vitium . . . contra naturam velut cancer ita serpit, ut sacrorum hominum ordines attingat.' The fullest literary development of the implications of 'unnatural' sexuality occurs in Alain de Lille's dream vision, *De planctu naturae*, trans. J. J. Sheridan as *The Plaint of Nature* (Toronto, 1980). For a discussion of medieval ideas about sexuality and the '(un)natural', see J. Boswell, *Christianity, Social Tolerance, and Homosexuality: Gay People in Western Europe from the Beginning of the Christian Era to the Fourteenth Century* (Chicago, 1980), ch. 11.

[72]   Cf. Hansen, *Chaucer and the Fictions of Gender*, 66; Margherita, *Romance of Origins*, 95–6; R. Rambuss, '"Processe of Tyme": History, Consolation, and Apocalypse in the *Book of the Duchess*', *Exemplaria*, 2 (1990), 659–83: 670.

refusal clearly to attach his narrator to a particular sexualized position, it only serves to reinforce questions we might have about the narrator's 'masculinity'. (Gender-crossing also occurs in the Ovidian story in Chaucer's replacement of Juno's traditional female messenger, Iris, with an unnamed male messenger, whom some critics have identified as Mercury, 'the deity known for his ability to change gender when he pleased'.[73])

The Alcyone episode thus begins, but fails fully to carry through, a corrective specification of the narrator's position in relation to gender and sexuality. The work of the dream—as it moves the narrator out of stasis and passivity, into contact with a natural world, and finally into confrontation with the knight who externalizes his illness—is more rigorously to secure the narrator's heterosexual and 'masculine' identity. Indeed, the very same movement that works towards a correction of somatic disturbance operates to gender and sexualize the narrator. The movement out of the obsessive stasis of melancholy illness is a movement of masculinization, replacing traditionally feminine passivity with masculine activity. The entry into the conventional landscape of spring, where the 'sorwes' of 'wynter' (411–12) have been forgotten through the procreative force of Nature—'al the woode was waxen grene | Swetnesse of dew had mad hyt waxe' (414–15)—is both a movement out of the cold and dry of melancholy, away from the 'agaynes kynde' of illness, and a movement out of the non-heterosexualized, non-procreative position of the poem's opening, away from the 'agaynes kynde' of sexuality.

The bedchamber in which the dream begins is decorated with fictions that gesture both towards the masculine pursuit of war and towards the heterosexual and romantic:

> For hooly al the story of Troye
> Was in the glasynge ywroght thus,
> Of Ector and of kyng Priamus,
> Of Achilles and of Kyng Lamedon,
> And eke of Medea and of Jason,
> Of Paris, Eleyne, and of Lavyne.
> And alle the walles with colours fyne
> Were peynted, bothe text and glose,
> Of al the Romaunce of the Rose.
>
> (326–34)

[73] C. A. N. Martin, 'Mercurial Translation in the *Book of the Duchess*', *ChauR* 28 (1993–4), 95–116: 98. See also Kellogg, *Chaucer, Langland, Arthur*, 84–5.

The action that ensues in the dream serves to bring the narrator into both the realm of masculine pursuit and the courtly love landscape of 'the Rose'. As the dreamer moves from his bedchamber to the hunt forming outside, he enters a realm simultaneously masculine and heterosexualized. The hunt is of course a conventional figure of the pursuit of courtly love[74] and, as is emphasized strongly in Chaucer's poem, it is at the same time a realm of male homosociality.[75] Countering the narrator's strong identification with Alcyone is his eager entry here into a flurry of masculine movement: 'I herde goynge bothe up and doun | Men, hors, houndes, and other thyng; | And al men speken of huntyng' (348–50); 'Ther overtok y a gret route | Of huntes and eke of foresteres, | With many relayes and lymeres, | And hyed hem to the forest faste | And I with hem' (360–4); 'Every man dide ryght anoon | As to huntynge fil to doon' (374–5).

As with the Alcyone episode, the hunt is cut short. But from here the narrator is propelled (via the whelp) to the 'hert' of the poem, his encounter with the knight. In part this movement, in which the 'hert' the narrator himself hunts down is revealed to be not a beloved woman but the sick 'hert' of the knight, works against the heterosexualizing thrust of the dream. As Hansen points out, 'the mysterious, liminally male stranger encountered by the questing dreamer', the lovesick and hence feminized knight, 'may be said to occupy a position filled elsewhere in romance by fairy ladies'.[76] At the same time, however, the encounter with the knight certainly continues the movement into male homosociality that the hunt institutes. And after the initial shock of having the presumed object of the hunt, the (courtly, female) 'hert', turn out to be instead the (courtly, male) 'hert' of the bereaved lover, the process of heterosexualization pursued, if incompletely, in both the Alcyone episode and the hunt, continues—and this time in a much more elaborated and complete manner. The potential homoeroticism of the meeting between narrator and knight (and hunted 'hert') is deflected, as so often, into a male homosociality that operates to secure a bond between men through the (fantasmatic) heterosexual exchange of women.[77] Here, the body of

[74] See Thiébaux, *Stag of Love*.
[75] See E. K. Sedgwick, *Between Men: English Literature and Male Homosocial Desire* (New York, 1985).
[76] Hansen, *Chaucer and the Fictions of Gender*, 61.
[77] Cf. M. Ellmann, 'Blanche', in J. Hawthorn (ed.), *Criticism and Critical Theory* (London, 1984), 99–110; Hansen, *Chaucer and the Fictions of Gender*, 59; Margherita, *Romance of Origins*, 86; J. Ferster, *Chaucer on Interpretation* (Cambridge, 1985), 69.

the dead woman, White, fictively (re)created within the male–male dialogue, is evoked to serve as an object of transfer between the two men. Her evocation, on the one hand, explains the mourning knight's illness, and presumably moves towards its cure; at the same time, it fixes the sexually questionable narrator's interest on the matter of courtly heterosexuality. The conversation between knight and dreamer provides a guide to the world of courtly love—tracing the process by which the (male) lover falls in love with, suffers for, approaches, is rebuffed by, reapproaches, serves, and finally is bereft of, the beloved lady.

Like the story of Alcyone, the knight's story, as it unfolds, condenses the lovesickness of a pining lover with the grief of mourning, and it makes both of these heterosexual. Again, as in the Alcyone episode, in so far as we draw connections of identification between the knight and the narrator, we have here a specification and heterosexualization of the narrator's initially undefined, amorphous illness. Indeed, the narrator's concluding gesture in his dialogue with the knight is one of sympathetic identification: 'Is that youre los? Be God, hyt ys routhe!' (1310). And this seems to be precisely the required gesture to complete the movement of the dream. The frustrated and momentarily forgotten hunt with which the dream began is here reinvoked and judged conclusive: 'And with that word ryght anoon | They gan to strake forth; al was doon, | For that tyme, the hert-huntyng' (1311–13). And the forceful movement that the conclusion of the hunt then institutes—gesturing towards the public sphere of masculine action ('this kyng | Gan homwarde for to ryde', 1314–15) at the same time that it cryptically encodes, in its destination ('A long castel with walles white, | Be Seynt Johan, on a ryche hil', 1318–19), the heterosexual relation of John of Gaunt and Blanche of Lancaster that presumably motivates the whole poem[78]—reemphasizes the distance between the end-point of the dream and the poem's opening, with its hermetic bedchamber and its gender and sexual amorphousness.

The dream of the *Book of the Duchess* thus works to masculinize and heterosexualize the body of its ailing narrator. The correction of soma that the dream enacts—the tailoring of an at first amorphously defined body and its equally amorphous illness to certain naturalized designs of gender and sexuality—should not, however, be read as suggesting a full cure for the dreamer's illness nor even a neat solution to the poem's

---

[78] See F. Tupper, 'Chaucer and Richmond', *MLN* 31 (1916), 250–2; id., 'Chaucer and Lancaster', *MLN* 32 (1917), 54.

gender and sexual complications. After all, the movement I have just described, while it allows the hunt to be declared complete, and while it suggests that the dreamer no longer remains in his initial, paralysed, position, still leaves him in sympathetic identification with the ailing figure of the knight. This is a figure who, paradoxically, serves to bring the narrator closer to masculine and heterosexual positions at the same time that he enacts illness—and specifically the feminized illness—of the courtly lover who, perhaps improperly, over-values the beloved object of desire (as the dreamer suggests to the knight, 'I leve yow wel, that trewely | Yow thoghte that she was the beste | And to beholde the alder-fayreste, | Whoso had loked hir with your eyen', 1048–51).

While the knight's self-revelation in the courtly narrative of 'White' may operate therapeutically, the full therapeutic demand—that he detach himself from the lost object of desire, that he recognize (in Ceyx's consolatory words) that 'in . . . sorwe there lyth no red' (203), that he pursue the Boethian movement towards consolation hinted at repeatedly in the dialogue between knight and narrator ('But ther is no man alyve her | Wolde for a fers make this woo!', 740–1), that he transcend, leave behind, attachments to the body and the bodily—remains unmet. The complex medieval Christian ideology of body—one that embraces a 'proper' (masculine) gendering and heterosexual positioning of the male body—also recognizes that a truly masculine attitude towards body pushes beyond embodiment, towards spiritual transcendence. For that ideology, a movement like that of Henryson's *Testament of Cresseid* is relatively easy to endorse since here a too great immersion in body is punished by bodily illness. But the inverse movement, a movement out of illness into bodily health, must be complex, because it must recognize the priority, the greater 'healthiness', of certain bodily positions over others at the same time that it warns of the dangers of body as an inferior partner in the make-up of human beings, and a partner often identified with the female. Implicit in the path towards the masculinization and heterosexualization of the amorphous, ailing body of the poem's narrator is the understanding that the masculine, heterosexual body, while the body proper for a man, is itself a temporary position, and one that the truly masculine Christian will move beyond, striving for a 'virile', disinterested detachment from body. Alongside the strong thrust towards correcting the gender and sexual positioning of the dreamer operates the dreamer's own urging that the knight should recognize the deceptive and fleeting nature of bodily attachments. Chaucer thus represents the dream as not just bringing together medical and moral discourses to enforce a certain somatic correction that is at the same time a correction of gender and sexuality, but also adding to this already complex mixture the recognition of an imperative to transcend soma. At the same time that the dream maps out a therapeutic movement towards the correction of body, it suggests that the proper valuation of body and bodily desire might necessitate a rejection of body altogether. But the poem carries through this particular double movement only to a certain point; the hunt is complete only 'for that tyme'. At the conclusion of the *Book of the Duchess*, circularity reasserts itself. The narrator promises to write his dream down, and that promise reminds us that the moment of writing, the present tense of the poem's opening, while posterior to the dream, represents the dreamer as apparently unaffected by his successful falling asleep and the dream's corrective action.[79] Indeed, it is the morning after the dream that he 'fares the worse' (99) in sympathetic response to reading of Alcyone's distress and death.

The rejection of body is a position that no one in Chaucer's poem, with the exception of the dead Ceyx as he speaks the words of the gods—not Alcyone, not the knight, not the narrator or his dreaming self (despite that self's attempts to voice certain consolatory Boethian ideas)—is able fully to attain. At the core of the poem's final irresolution are certain unresolved, perhaps unresolvable, questions that, indeed, Chaucer would return to repeatedly in his poetic career, most notably in the poems of the Marriage Group: How to participate in love without falling into a feminized position? How to (hetero)sexualize the body without overvaluing it? How to mandate sexual desire and at the same time devalue that desire? While, as I have suggested, the dream, with its access to both spirit and soma, is an appropriate place to raise such questions, and while the dream of the *Book of the Duchess* does effectively work through certain complex issues about the body and its proper positioning, ending with a strong movement out of the landscape of melancholy and a certain 'straightening' of gender and sexual anomalies, it also reasserts, in its final circularity, the problems of body and melancholy illness, suggesting that the correction and (re)valuation of soma must, for embodied human beings who are also spiritual subjects, be worked through over and over again.

[79] Cf. Bronson, '*Book of the Duchess* Re-opened', 868.

3. Interpreting Dreams: Reflections on Freud, Milton, and Chaucer

DAVID AERS

> First, because he himself desires total knowledge: his aim is nothing less than the *complete elucidation* of Dora, despite his insistence on the fragmentary nature of the material. . . . such a desire for total, absolute knowledge exposes a fundamental assumption in Freud's epistemology.[1]

There is now available a substantial scholarly literature on medieval dream theory and literary dream visions, some of it combining extremely skilful analysis of texts with admirable reconstructions of relevant cultural and philosophic histories.[2] The concerns of the present essay, however, are somewhat marginal to the preoccupations of this scholarship. They are reflections on forms of power and the roles of gender in the interpretation of dreams, and it is hoped that they might encourage work along some of the lines sketched out here. Such work would need to engage with a wide range of medieval and early modern genres and institutions of discourse, pursuing historical enquiries into changes and continuities in the interpretation of dreams, together with enquiries into the various conditions and consequences of these continuities and changes. At the very least such studies would contribute to our understanding of the histories of the subject and of hermeneutics in European cultures. They might also encourage our rethinking of

---

[1] T. Moi, 'Representations of Patriarchy: Sexuality and Epistemology in Freud's *Dora*', in C. Bernheimer and C. Kahane (eds.), *In Dora's Case: Freud, Hysteria, Feminism* (London, 1985), 194.

[2] See esp. Delany, *Chaucer's House of Fame*; Spearing, *Medieval Dream-Poetry*; Lynch, *High Medieval Dream Vision*; Russell, *English Dream Vision*; Kruger, *Dreaming in the Middle Ages*. Also of interest are M. Weidhorn, *Dreams in Seventeenth-Century English Literature* (The Hague, 1970); N. Smith, *Perfection Proclaimed: Language and Literature in English Radical Religion 1640–1660* (Oxford, 1989), ch. 2; D. Régnier-Bohler, 'Imagining the Self', in P. Ariès and G. Duby (eds.), *A History of Private Life,* ii: *Revelations of the Medieval World*, trans. A. Goldhammer (Cambridge, Mass., 1988), 311–94: 385–91.

conventional periodizations together with the narratives and ideologies they tend to assume.[3]

The text I have chosen to address here is not *The Interpretation of Dreams* (1900), but 'Fragment of an Analysis of a Case of Hysteria ("Dora")' (1905), one of Freud's best-known case histories.[4] Here he claims that while 'the technique of interpreting dreams may be easily learnt from the instructions and examples' already given in *The Interpretation of Dreams* (39), the present case history shows how the technique 'can be turned to account for the discovery of the hidden and repressed parts of mental life' (155). His statement takes up the dominant metaphors in the preface to the study, metaphors which represent the interpreter as the discoverer, the 'conscientious archaeologist' who can 'bring to the light of day after their long burial the priceless though mutilated relics of antiquity' (41). He also presents himself as the good translator, one who has 'learnt how to translate the language of dreams into the forms of expression of our own thought-language', thus opening out a path of 'knowledge' that is 'essential for the psychoanalyst' (44). Indeed, 'the technique of dream-interpretation', he writes, 'is similar to that of psychoanalysis' (155). In this particular exercise of interpretation, however, we should recall that the producer of the dream text, Dora, herself ended the treatment. In doing so she was perhaps seeking to show Freud that she was actually other than a text and other than those 'priceless though mutilated relics of antiquity' that the archaeological interpreter described himself as having brought to light.[5] Be that as it may, what I shall attend to here is the exchanges between female dreamer and male interpreter together with the modes of interpretation favoured by the interpreter. My main concerns are encapsulated in the following terms: social relations, power, gender, and allegory. I will briefly illustrate a way of understanding Freud's hermeneutical strategies before moving to a meditation on their

---

[3] See D. Aers, 'A Whisper in the Ear of Early Modernists; or, Reflections on Literary Critics Writing the "History of the Subject"', in id. (ed.), *Culture and History: Essays on English Communities, Identities and Writing 1350–1600* (Hemel Hempstead, 1992), 177–202; L. Patterson, 'On the Margins of the Post-modern', *Speculum*, 65 (1990), 87–108.

[4] The text used here, and cited in the essay by page number, is from S. Freud, *Case Histories I: 'Dora' and 'Little Hans'*, trans. A. and J. Strachey, ed. A. Richards, The Pelican Freud Library 8 (Harmondsworth, 1977). For the history of Freud's writing up of the case, see the editor's introduction, pp. 31–4.

[5] The literature on this case is, not surprisingly, immense; for an excellent introduction to it, see Bernheimer and Kahane (eds.), *In Dora's Case*. See now P. J. Mahony, *Freud's Dora* (New Haven, 1996).

relationship to earlier interpretations of dreams in texts that explicitly present themselves as 'literary'.[6]

Dora's arrival at the modern, secularized confessional[7] was not voluntary. The 18-year-old girl had been brought by her father who wanted Freud to ' "talk" Dora out of her belief' that he was having an affair with a family friend, a belief that was well founded (150, and see pp. 52, 57). As Freud notes, 'he handed her over to me for psychotherapeutic treatment' (49). The exchanges between Dora and Freud, including the exchanges around her dreams, thus take place in a context where relations of political power are clear: Dora inconveniently resists her father's will and so is handed over to a male interpreter who at once agrees with the father that the young woman is 'unmistakably neurotic' (49). It is particularly striking in this context that not once does the interpreter invite Dora to tell him how she feels about being used as an unwilling exchange object between men. Indeed, he never makes the relations of power here a topic for mutual exploration. His failure sets the framework both for Freud's treatment of Dora and for the concerns of this essay.

In the 'analysis of a case of hysteria' it emerged that Dora's father disliked Dora's mother and had been nursed during a long illness by a family friend, Frau K. Dora was very fond of the K.s' two children, intimate with their parents, and shows desire for Frau K. which Freud, at the time of analysis, could not acknowledge.[8] Frau K.'s nursing of Dora's father became a long affair. At the age of 14 Dora experienced an extremely disturbing event. Herr K. manipulated arrangements with his wife and clerks so that he was alone at his office where the young adolescent was to meet up with Frau K. and her husband. Herr K. pulled down the shutters of the room when Dora arrived and 'suddenly clasped the girl to him and pressed a kiss upon her lips' (58–9). Freud's comment here is as appalling as it is revealing: 'This was surely just the situation to call up a

---

[6]   For a reading of Freud's work as itself an example of 'modernist fiction' see S. Marcus, 'Freud and Dora: Story, History, Case History', in Bernheimer and Kahane (eds.), *In Dora's Case*, 56–91. This is not, of course, how Freud represents his own putatively scientific work.

[7]   See M. Foucault, *The History of Sexuality*, i: *An Introduction*, trans. R. Hurley (Harmondsworth, 1981), 62–7.

[8]   See esp. Freud, 'Dora', 95–8, 146 n., and 162 n.: 'I failed to discover in time and to inform the patient that her homosexual (gynaecophilic) love for Frau K. was the strongest unconscious current in her mental life.' Or, in a different register: 'These masculine or, more properly speaking, *gynaecophilic* currents of feeling are to be regarded as typical of the unconscious erotic life of hysterical girls' (98). Some might like to compare the play by H. Cixous, *Portrait de Dora* (Paris, 1976).

distinct feeling of sexual excitement in a girl of fourteen who had never before been approached.' He writes this before he relates that 'Dora had at that moment a violent feeling of disgust, tore herself free from the man, and hurried past him to the staircase and from there to the street door.' Freud goes on, however, to insist that Dora's resistance to Herr K.'s sexual attack is an unequivocal sign of sickness: 'the behaviour of this child [sic] of fourteen was already entirely and completely hysterical. I should without question consider a person hysterical in whom an occasion for sexual excitement elicited feelings that were preponderantly or exclusively unpleasurable' (59). His gloss systematically occludes issues of power and violence; it also occludes betrayal of trust, the complex network of family relations, and Dora's feelings for Frau K. It is hardly surprising that the role of the interpreter and his collusion with sexual assault should not be problematized.[9] Far from any such critical self-reflexivity, Freud continues to assert that any 'healthy girl in such circumstances' would 'certainly' have felt 'genital sensation' rather than the 'disgust' Dora recounted so unequivocally (60). The interpreter's gloss on what he calls 'the little scene' (59) rejects any form of resistance: 'I have formed in my own mind the following reconstruction of the scene. I believe that during the man's passionate embrace she felt not merely his kiss upon her lips but also the pressure of his erect member against her body.' The gloss asserts that Dora has 'repressed' this perception, displacing it by 'the unpleasurable feeling which is proper to the tract of mucous membrane at the entrance to the alimentary canal— that is by disgust' (60). The mode of commentary is one that has abandoned any pretence of dialogue. Dora's voice is silenced and her own account of the event, let alone of her feelings, denied or, rather, subsumed and superseded in the exegete's imperialistic discourse.

Dora's cough, which began when she was a child (51–2) is assimilated to this sexual assault and Dora's reactions. Freud treats her 'disgust' at Herr K.'s attack as a 'symptom': 'The pressure of the erect member [a product of the exegete's fantasy, we recall] probably led to an analogous change in the corresponding female organ, the clitoris; and the excitation of this second erotogenic zone was referred by a process of displacement to the simultaneous pressure against the thorax and became

[9] In Lacan's view, Freud is driven and blinded by an unconscious identification with Herr K.: see J. Lacan, 'Intervention on Transference', in Bernheimer and Kahane (eds.), *In Dora's Case*, 92–104. This reading sidelines both Freud's dissolution of the exegete's power and Freud's collusion with sexual assault, whether by Herr K. or anyone else, as is made clear in the quotations I have given from p. 59 of 'Dora'.

fixed there' (61). Dora's coughing, having been linked with an alleged clitoral excitement (the invention of the gloss), is in turn led back to her thumb-sucking in childhood, now read as a figure for 'sucking at the male organ' (85). Freud acknowledges that Dora rejected this interpret-ation, but her rejection is itself easily assimilated by the allegorist: 'To be sure, she would not hear of going so far as this in recognizing her own thoughts' because for a 'symptom' to emerge 'it was essential that she should not be completely clear on the subject' (81). The resistance of Dora's text to the interpreter's assumptions confirms the need for the interpreter's allegorical modes and, of course, their veracity. About this Freud is emphatic in a footnote added in 1923: 'an exclamation on the part of the patient of "I didn't think that", or "I didn't think of that" . . . can be translated point-blank into: "Yes, I was unconscious of that"' (92 n. 1). Or, addressing Dora's case particularly, '"No" signifies the desired "Yes"' (93, and see pp. 104–6). In the glossing of texts this may be called Nietzschean reading: between human beings, if acted out, it takes us into the domain of rape.

The interpretation of Dora's two dreams takes place in this context and pursues the exegetical modes described above (99–152). The first dream contained a sequence in which Dora's house is on fire and her mother wants to delay leaving until she has saved her jewel-case. Dora's father objects to this: 'I refuse to let myself and my two children be burnt for the sake of your jewel-case' (99). Freud focuses on the jewel-case, telling Dora he is sure she had thought she would herself 'accept it with pleasure'. Dora replied 'I don't know' (104). Freud's comment on this answer is extremely revealing both about his hermeneutic presuppos-itions and the ancestry of his discourse: 'The regular formula with which she confessed to anything that had been repressed' (104 n. 1, and see p. 112). He takes up the jewel-case: 'Perhaps you do not know that "jewel-case" [*Schmuck-kästchen*] is a favourite expression . . . for the female genitals.' This allegorical move leads on to the triumphant observation that 'The meaning of the dream is now becoming even clearer.' Freud informs Dora that her mother was the former rival for her father's affections and 'you were ready to give your father what your mother withheld from him' (105).[10] So the allegorical mode works remorselessly to confirm the already known universal truths of the Oedipal triangle.

[10] He also tells her that she is 'ready to give Herr K. what his wife withholds from him' (Freud, 'Dora', 106).

Objects outside the dream continue to function as allegorical images working in the same way as the jewel-case. So when Dora arrives wearing 'a small reticule' of a kind that 'had just come into fashion' it turns out to be an allegorical image confirming the interpreter's views that Dora was repressing memories of masturbation, 'probably in childhood' (112, and see pp. 110–19 and 91 n. 1). Watching her playing with this object, he 'explained to her the nature of a "symptomatic act"' (113). This object, he assures his reader, has a meaning which 'fits in quite extraordinary well' with his reading of Dora's 'unconscious'. In fact it is 'very easy to interpret'. Dora's reticule 'was nothing but a representation of the genitals', and her playing with it an announcement that she would like 'to masturbate' (113–14).[11]

I will take leave of Freud's text by considering one further example of his interpretative strategies, this time from his treatment of Dora's second dream. It is explicitly about Dora's rebellion against her parents and about the death of her father, a death which, in the dream, enables her to return home, finding her mother and others already at the cemetery (133–4). During the journey home she 'went to the station' but, having great difficulty finding it, she 'saw a thick wood before me which I went into' (133). Freud traces certain components of the dream to a painting Dora recalls seeing the day before she had the dream. In it there was a thick wood and, in the background, nymphs (138–9). Hearing this, Freud notes that immediately 'a certain suspicion of mine became a certainty' (139). The exegesis continues in familiar mode. The dream's station and the dream's cemetery 'represent the female genitals', an allegory now confirmed by the painting. In the latter the thick wood represents 'pubic hair' while the nymphs represent 'the labia minora, which lie in the background of the "thick wood"'.[12] Putting allegorical iconography into narrative movement, the exegete finds the dream revealing 'a phantasy of defloration, the phantasy of a man seeking to force an entrance into the female genitals' (139–40). Dora's own language, iconography, cultural networks, and readings are totally irrelevant to this exegesis and its metaphysical assumptions. Dora is textualized and glossed: 'I informed Dora of the conclusions I had reached' (140). Given the flow of power and the strategies of reading it is not surprising that Freud never asks about the role of his own fantasy and will to dominion

---

[11] For examples of this allegorical mode working to sustain different metaphysics, see D. Aers, *Piers Plowman and Christian Allegory* (London, 1975), 20–42.

[12] Freud also writes that the term 'nymphs' is occasionally used by 'physicians' to refer to 'the labia minora' (Freud, 'Dora', 139).

in his interpretation. His mode again eschews dialogue, preferring the techniques of the inquisitor with a schedule of suspicions, and a search to construe clues which will confirm them. Dora's termination of the analysis is taken as a sign of resistance to the heroic discoverer, 'an unmistakable act of vengeance on her part' against a man who 'conjures up the most evil of those half-tamed demons that inhabit the human breast, and seeks to wrestle with them'. Allegorical exegete, confessor, inquisitor, and exorcist, such a man should hardly 'expect to come through the struggle unscathed' (150). As for Dora, whether she was scathed or unscathed by her encounter with Freud's 'phallocentric' epistemology[13] and his exegetical methods, that Freud does not ask.

From Freud I move back two and a half centuries to a moment in the great epic of a revolutionary Protestant poet. Near the beginning of Book V of *Paradise Lost* Eve has a dream.[14] She finds it exciting and confusing. She also finds it frightening because it figures forth resentments and aspirations she had not known before the dream, but ones she recognizes, however ambivalently, as her own. But before Milton has Eve recount her dream he depicts Adam. He focuses on the man's 'pure digestion', his 'temperate vapours' and the 'light sleep' from which he wakes with the dawn and the 'matin song' of birds (V. 1–8). This gives us an image of carnality ordered in the temperate life, one that foreshadows Raphael's speculations about humanity's potential spiritualization, ascending the scale of being (V. 491–500). The image provides a sharp contrast to that of the woman the poet moves on to describe. Eve has neither seen the (symbolic?) dawn nor heard nature's 'matin song': she still lies 'unwakened', 'With tresses discomposed, and glowing cheek, | As through unquiet rest' (V. 10–11). Overflowing with love and wonder at her beauty, Adam anticipates the words of the bridegroom in the Song of Songs and calls his wife to join him in work which is simultaneously a celebration of the creation. But Eve's discomposed hair and cheeks are of course signs of her disturbance. Her carnality is apparently not as well ordered as her husband's. This much, then, Milton conveys before he lets Eve tell her dream.

It is typical of Milton's work that, while he evokes supernatural causes for the dream, he carefully separates this suggestion from his description of the human experience. He does so by placing it in another book and by making its effects thoroughly ambiguous. We recall how

[13] Moi, 'Representation of Patriarchy', 198.
[14] *Paradise Lost*, V. 28–92: all references are to *The Poems of John Milton*, ed. J. Carey and A. Fowler (London, 1968).

Ithuriel and Zephon found Satan 'Squat like a toad, close at the ear of Eve', trying to influence her 'fancy', trying to conjure up 'phantasms and dreams', or to 'taint' the spirits that ascend to the brain (IV. 799–809). There we received no hint as to whether Satan's intrusions could have any effects on the sinless human. And now, in the next book, the earlier episode is not even mentioned by the narrator. It is certainly not offered as a determinate causal explanation for the dream's contents. These are located within Eve's inchoate feelings, ones systematically recapitulated in the Fall (Book IX). Here I will have to ignore the extraordinary density of the dream's poetry, with its seemingly endless connections to other parts of the poem, focusing instead on the interactions among dream, female dreamer, and male interpreter.

When the 'discomposed' woman wakes she recounts her dream to the man. It is a dream of astonishing complexity, one that includes some startling theological implications. For unfallen Eve discloses her pleasures in the transgressions of the law she has been taught to obey, just as she discloses their fearfulness and the relief she feels at emerging from her fantasies unscathed. Yet despite this complex and contradictory set of feelings it never occurs to Adam that he should ask Eve what this dream means to her, to her experience of life with Adam in Eden, under the law. (Perhaps it never occurred to Milton either—but how closely he identifies with Adam here we certainly cannot tell.)

Instead of opening an exploratory dialogue with Eve, Adam informs her of his reactions and his fears, immediately moving into an analysis of the dream. He opts for theologico-moral concepts and, more extensively, psycho-physiological abstractions. Most tellingly, the form he chooses is a monologue. It concludes with an assertion that 'what in sleep thou didst abhor to dream, | Waking thou never wilt consent to do' (V. 94–121). In this decisive move the interpreter concludes his scientific discourse by setting aside a crucial element in Eve's own account of her dream—namely, her pleasure. True enough, she felt 'damp horror' when the angel plucked the forbidden fruit. But she felt a lot else besides 'horror', as she has made perfectly explicit—feelings that included 'quickened appetite', exhilarating flight, and wonder at her 'high exaltation'. There is actually no reason to think she did not eat the forbidden fruit, for she says 'I, methought, | Could not but taste'. All this part of Eve's narrative Adam sets aside. When he has finished his own commentary neither he nor the author invites Eve's responses to his own reading. We thus encounter a monologism that leaves no spaces for

Eve's voice, her feelings, and her particular experiences, experiences quite as distinct from Adam's as Dora's were from Freud's. It is an interpretative mode which reinforces received divisions of power and authority around the construction of gender.

It seems to confirm the contrast between Eve's creation and Adam's creation which *Paradise Lost* elaborates so inventively (IV. 440–91 and VIII. 250–441). Eve, we recollect, is there associated with flowers, waters, a cave, lying down, the Narcissus myth, and a self-delight in which she initially rejects the heterosexual choice for which she is destined. Indeed, not until she has actually been 'seized' by Adam does she submit to the correct position of adoring self-subjection, only then commenting on how far she is 'excelled by manly grace' (IV. 477–91) and pitying Adam for having to put up with such an inferior companion (IV. 440–9).[15] Apparently she has no glimmering of God, of spiritual life, or even of intellectual power, all of which are heavily emphasized in the story of Adam's creation in Book VIII. Despite this, however, the poet has created the dream as a space in which the resentments and compensatory ambitions of the subordinated and patronized woman can and do find a voice. That this voice should be interpreted by her husband to produce a reading that gratifies his desire, already sanctified by his God (VIII. 399–402, 449–51), is not surprising. After all, neither Adam nor Milton, despite his writings on divorce and his defence of polygamy, shares the resistance to the disciplines of Protestant and patriarchal marriage so sharply articulated by Mary Astell in her *Reflections upon Marriage* (London, 1706).[16] It may be more surprising, and perhaps instructive, to find the twentieth-century founder of psychoanalysis and its interpretation of dreams developing the silencing strategies of *Paradise Lost* under the guise of intrepid scientific discovery, enlightenment, and emancipation.

I now move back into fourteenth-century culture to consider how Chaucer addressed problems analogous to those I have raised in relation to the interpretation of dreams, power, and gender in work by Milton

---

[15] See the outstanding essay by M. Nyquist, 'The Genesis of Gendered Subjectivity in the Divorce Tracts and in *Paradise Lost*', in M. Nyquist and M. W. Ferguson (eds.), *Re-membering Milton: Essays on the Texts and Traditions* (New York, 1987), 99–127; see also D. Aers and R. Hodge, '"Rational burning": Milton on Sex and Marriage', *MiltonS* 12 (1979), 3–33.

[16] See Nyquist's comments in her 'Genesis of Gendered Subjectivity', 123–34 and 127 n. 35; together with Christopher Hill, 'Marriage, Divorce and Polygamy', ch. 9 of his *Milton and the English Revolution* (London, 1977).

and Freud. Such a move invites charges of gross 'anachronism', charges that I am constructing cross-cultural analogies which must, necessarily, dissolve different, incommensurable horizons into one unhistorical continuum. Nobody concerned to respect the differences between diverse traditions of enquiry and forms of life, to resist imperialistic drives in the interpretation of other cultures and texts, could fail to take seriously the issues raised by such charges. She or he will strive to establish, as far as possible, a critical dialogue between rival traditions and cultural assumptions. But there is today another issue that also needs attention. It is a fact that many early modernists and some medievalists assume an a priori and profoundly unhistorical cluster of beliefs about the complete 'alterity' of medieval culture, an 'alterity' formed by an allegedly decisive rupture in European culture around Shakespeare's time. I have challenged this common paradigm elsewhere, exemplifying some of its effects on current histories of 'the subject' written by literary scholars, and also in a recent revisionist historiography of the transition from 'traditional religion' to Reformation Christianity in England.[17] While I have no wish to obliterate cultural differences I also have no wish to assume differences even if they enhance the possibilities of familiar and powerful narratives concerning the history of 'modernity'. In accord with some of this book's aims, I seek to encourage further work across conventional period divisions, work on continuities as well as changes and, perhaps especially, on changes that might be other than those predicted in the historical narratives we inherit. Such work will at least make us far more alert to ways in which current periodizations and their legitimizing narratives may shape our accounts of medieval and early modern Europe. And this awareness may encourage us to ask further questions whose answers may need not only interdisciplinary work but also work that moves across standard periodizations.

Chaucer's Wife of Bath offers us an insight which those who reflect on dream interpretation would do well to recall. She tells stories about her dreams as part of a strategy for luring the male who is to become her fifth husband (WBP 575–84). For her, then, the dream text is a complex social act, and the putative inner world from which it emerges actually determined by current social relations, expectations, and designs. The dream text is an act of communication in a sense markedly different from the ones maintained by Freud. For her, current relationships between

[17] See n. 3 above, and D. Aers, 'Altars of Power: Reflections on Eamon Duffy's *Stripping of the Altars*', *LitHist*, 3rd ser. 3 (1994), 90–105.

speaker and audience are decisive in shaping the text.[18] One can imagine what Freud might have made of this dream text:

> And eek I seyde I mette of hym al nyght,
> He wolde han slayn me as I lay upright,
> And al my bed was ful of verray blood.
>
> (577–9)

But the Wife of Bath offers her own allegorical exegesis, 'as me was taught', one that is very much part of the relationships with both her audiences (Jankyn and the Canterbury pilgrims): 'blood bitokeneth gold' (581). Having given this interpretation she goes on to observe that the dream has no existence independent of her own text. On the contrary, it is a form of fiction complete with exegetical commentary and social purposes, all of which she has inherited, she says, from 'my dames loore' (582–4; see also lines 575–6). The sequence almost invites any potential interpreter, whether Jankyn or Freud, to occupy the position of a knower who has the ability to track a road to the dreamer's hidden inner world, a road the dreamer herself cannot follow without an exegete's help. The invitation turns out to be both lure and trap, a gamesome lesson for those who might think that dream texts have hidden foundations accessible only to heroic and allegorizing archaeologists.

Chaucer's treatment of the interpretation of dreams in the Nun's Priest's Tale is also both complex and full of laughter. Once again the poet suggests that dream texts and their interpretations are appropriately approached through attention to the social relations within which they are produced. We learn about the dense social relations in the enclosed yard before we read Chauntecleer's account of his dream (2821–87). We also learn that Chauntecleer's voice is peerless, his appearance dazzling, his position as ruler of seven females absolute and absolutely self-interested (2850–68). It is in this setting that the governor, the 'gentil cok' (2865) wakes up groaning. His beloved Pertelote asks him what troubles him and his response is a story of a frightening dream (2888–907). Here Chaucer stages an exchange between a male dreamer/narrator and a female interpreter. Is hers the response to Chauntecleer's prayer that God should interpret his dream 'aright' (2896)?

---

[18]   She, and Chaucer, would have much sympathy with the account of language and the inner world offered by V. N. Volosinov [M. Bakhtin], *Marxism and the Philosophy of Language* (Cambridge, Mass., 1986), 86.

Her initial reaction belongs to her own sense of social order and cultural norms, including the norms of class and gender in that order. She had already shown disapproval at the cock's signs of vulnerability (2888–91), and her invocation of the concept of 'shame' is now elaborated in a response which includes the will to ensure that Chauntecleer maintains the official code of a chivalric honourman.[19] She warns him that the confession of fear his dream has elicited will cost him her heart and all her love (2908–20). So the poet suggests how the act of listening is shaped by the listener's interests in maintaining dominant codes: her own role as 'faire damoyselle Pertelote', a courtly paragon (2869–75), is bound up with a chivalric framework which prescribes how males should meet dangers. She does not leave matters here, however, but turns to the interpretation of dreams, a designedly therapeutic turn (2921–69). She argues that all dreams are the immediate effect of bodily misfunction, and proceeds to apply this theory to the particular balance of humours in the dreamer. Far from needing a divine interpreter, a fearless archaeologist, a new Hermes, the male merely needs laxatives, 'To purge yow bynethe and eek above'. She prescribes herbal remedies, kindly offers to find them for her husband, and instructs him, 'Pekke hem up right as they growe and ete hem yn' (2942–67). The language here itself offers hilarious desublimation of dream interpretations which assume that dreams are the royal road to some transcendental region, whether the divine mind or its modern secularized descendant, the Unconscious. Pertelote insists that dreams neither merit the work of interpretation nor deserve to be met with anxiety (2921, 2969).

The cock, unlike Dora or Eve, is not silenced by the interlocutor. Far from it, his task is to reassert his masculine identity, to reject the position of being subject to the female's voice (2970–3156). He does so by moving into a distinctively clerical register—multisyllabic words, many abstractions, subordinate clauses embedded in long sentences (for example lines 2970–81)—a seemingly endless accumulation of written authorities allegedly greater than any the female could invoke, and the production of exempla to maintain his argument. Chaucer is revealing some of the ways in which scholastic language and arguments about the interpretation of dreams may be bound up with struggles for power, in the domestic realm and beyond. That is why the actual content of the cock's argument, his 'proof' about the significance of dreams, turns out to be of absolutely no interest to the speaker himself. Having

[19] See M. James, *English Politics and the Concept of Honour* (Oxford, 1978).

accumulated massive support for claims that 'many' (3109) dreams offer a privileged path to supernatural knowledge, having argued that his own dream should be treated not as the symptom of a need for laxatives but as a portentous indication of imminent adversity, and having vehemently rejected his wife's prescription of herbal laxatives as poisons he will defy (3151–6), he abandons the topic completely. This is perfectly understandable, since he has achieved his most pressing goal: namely, to reassert the power which Pertelote's materialist and disrespectful discourse has challenged. Once the female is silenced under his deluge of words and authorities he feels free to court her in a courtly idiom which is itself a guarantee of masculine power and the social subordination of women. The cock's extensive disquisition on the interpretation of dreams has also purged his anxieties: 'he was namoore aferd' (3176). Reconfirmed in his masculine and chivalric identity he now defies dreams (just as his lady had exhorted him to do at line 3174). He summons his female subordinates (3173–4) and combines this recovery of governorship with the triumph of his sexuality over a female who is now as silent as Dora or Eve:

> He fethered Pertelote twenty tyme,
> And trad hire eke as ofte, er it was pryme.
> He looketh as it were a grym leoun,
> And on his toos he rometh up and doun;
> Hym deigned nat to sette his foot to grounde.
> He chukketh whan he hath a corn yfounde,
> And to hym rennen thanne his wyves alle.

> (3177–83)

Here, as elsewhere in the *Canterbury Tales*, Chaucer satirizes the norms of competitive masculinity which Chauntecleer so successfully recomposes. Unlike the Freudian and Miltonic works considered earlier, this medieval poem bestows critical attention on the strategies of power and gender in the making of dream interpretations. It evokes a lust for dominion both in theoretical articulations and in the theorist's sexuality. This seems to have been a will at work in Freud's interpretation of Dora and her dreams, although it was as unacknowledged by him as by Chauntecleer. It makes rather a nice irony in the face of the great enlightener's intrepid hermeneutics of suspicion, 'bringing to light what human beings keep hidden within them . . . making conscious the most hidden recesses of the mind' (114).

I conclude this chapter by briefly recalling how Chaucer also addressed the interpretation of dreams in *Troilus and Criseyde*.[20] For Pandarus dreams are incorrigibly indeterminate, and he insists that 'Ther woot no man aright what dremes mene' (V. 364; and see lines 362–78). However, no more consistent in this matter than in others, he is ready to interpret Troilus' dreams. He treats them as the product of melancholy (V. 360–2). But Pandarus' opportunistic pragmatism never has the last word (any more than any other position does), and the metaphysical assumptions shaping his outlook are not vindicated.

Troilus begins having dreams as soon as Criseyde is traded to the Greeks (V. 246–59). They bear witness to his sense of isolation and his acute anxiety at being cut off from the woman who has become the nurturing source of his life.[21] At once Troilus interprets his own dreams as signs that his death is impending (V. 316–22). As Criseyde's stay in the Greek camp lengthens he becomes more and more desperate, and is consumed by jealousy (V. 1208–435). In this state he has a big dream, one whose significance breaks through Pandarus' dogmatic horizons (V. 1233–44). Troilus dreams he walks into a forest to weep in mourning for his lost lover. Here he sees a boar with great tusks sleeping 'ayeyn the bryghte sonnes hete'. And, stunningly: 'by this bor, faste in his arms folde, | Lay, kyssyng ay, his lady bryght, Criseyde' (V. 1240–1). On waking he takes the dream as a divine disclosure confirming the suspicions of his jealousy (V. 1245–53). Pandarus seeks to reassure his friend by sticking to his arguments about the undecidability of dreams (V. 1275–8) while, once more, contradicting his own theory by offering an allegedly reliable interpretation. First he claims that dreams are only projections (V. 1280). Then he suggests that in fact the boar signifies not Criseyde's new lover but her old father; its sleep in the sun signifies his approaching death. Warming to the exegetical task he invents details which he then includes in his interpretation: he adds tears to the dreamer's Criseyde, tears that confirm his interpretation, showing that Criseyde 'kissying' the boar signifies mourning over the dying parent. He concludes with an exhortation to the dreamer: 'Thus sholdestow thi drem aright expounde' (V. 1288). What Chaucer gives us here is an image of the interpreter. Pandarus' theoretical scepticism readily gives way to an allegorization understandably designed to set aside extremely

[20] For his interpretation of dreams in the early works see Delany, *Chaucer's House of Fame*; Spearing, *Medieval Dream-Poetry*; Lynch, *High Medieval Dream Vision*, together with Chs. 1, 2, and 4 of the present book.

[21] See D. Aers, *Community, Gender, and Individual Identity: English Writing 1360–1430* (London, 1988), ch. 3.

painful experience. But at this point the time and the space for evasion have passed, and Pandarus' blind pragmatism can no longer offer even the illusions of comfort.

The poet then gives the interpretation of Troilus' dream to the prophetess Cassandra. Unlike Dora, Troilus makes his own approach to the interpreter, freely (V. 1450–519). Cassandra's interpretation is, not surprisingly, unlike Freud's allegorization of Dora's dream and the picture of a forest with nymphs. Cassandra's interpretation situates the dream in its subject's cultural and social traditions while it confirms Troilus' own feelings about the erotic significance of Criseyde's kissing. The prophetess locates the image of the boar in a genealogical and his-torical network that recollects Theban material, 'olde stories', particu-larly relevant to the fate of Troy (V. 1450–519).[22] Only after establishing a rich cultural context does she conclude that the boar in the dream is a heraldic emblem, one that 'bitokneth' Troilus' rival, Diomede (V. 1513). As for the kissing in the dream, 'This Diomede is inne, and thow art oute' (V. 1516–19). Not silenced, Troilus abuses the female interpreter and dismisses her as a 'fool of fantasie', a 'fals' exegete (V. 1520–33).

This sequence is an extremely moving one and it includes some inter-esting implications for reflections on dream interpretation. For what we see are the consequences of an interpretation that breaks away from the dialogic mode. Cassandra is certainly trying to use her grasp of cultural history and the collective unconscious of Trojans to unpack the way the dream offers Troilus insight into his present situation. Nevertheless, her skilful exposition entails a lecture which becomes an imposition on the dreamer. Her mode, inevitably, is alien to his own way of trying to articu-late his situation and the inner pain that dominates Book V. He now either has to become a passive receiver in the face of the expert, the kind of subject to which Freud tried to reduce Dora, or he has to rebel. So even an interpretation as relevant to the dreamer's own situation as Cassandra's is to that of Troilus will probably be counter-productive if it moves into a monologic mode, for this must seem to the narrator/dreamer an alien encrustation, an imposition. It is characteristic of Chaucer, the most dialogic of poets, to have produced approaches to the interpretation of dreams, in different genres, which cast a powerful critical light on the work of the most influential modern theorist and practitioner of dream interpretation.

---

[22] On Cassandra's allusions see the notes to V. 1450–1519 in the Riverside edition, pp. 1054–5; on the use of the Theban material in the poem see esp. L. Patterson, *Chaucer and the Subject of History* (Madison, Wis., 1991), ch. 2.

4. Baring Bottom: Shakespeare and the Chaucerian Dream Vision

KATHRYN L. LYNCH

A Midsummer Night's Dream contains only a single actual dream, at the end of the second act: Hermia's nightmare vision of the crawling serpent devouring her heart. Why, then, is the play titled as though the entire framework were structured as a dream? A partial answer to this question emerges from the quality of the midsummer and midnight frolic in the woods and from the characters' own interpretations of what has happened to them. *A Midsummer Night's Dream*'s central actions seem remarkably dream-like even as they claim the status of real events, and so the characters, especially Theseus, are inclined to dismiss them as illusions. Upon awakening, Lysander replies 'amazedly' (IV. i. 145);[1] Demetrius refers to his memories of the night as 'small and undistinguishable, | Like far-off mountains turned into clouds' (IV. i. 186–7); and Theseus coolly dismisses the lovers' accounts of their dream-like experiences as 'more strange than true' (V. i. 2). These judgements form part of a pattern of references to dreams as brief, mutable, and insubstantial (see, for example, I. i. 144), all of which are subject to the play's complex irony.

Despite Hippolyta's famous corrective to Theseus' scepticism ('But . . . all their minds transfigured so together . . . grows to something of great constancy', V. i. 23–6), Bottom's 'dream', the single vision not to result in a lasting and constant love, receives the only commentary that honours its visionary promise, and that commentary is itself a marvellously funny biblical parody. As Holland has pointed out, the dream in antique and medieval dream theory was an ambiguous event, sometimes the insignificant product of anxiety and preoccupation, but sometimes the messenger of profound truth, indeed a messenger who 'strikes back at those who mock it'.[2] *A Midsummer Night's Dream* reflects this

---

[1] All quotations from *A Midsummer Night's Dream* are taken from Peter Holland's edition.

[2] P. Holland, 'Dreaming the *Dream*', in P. Iselin and J.-P. Moreau (eds.), '*Le Songe d'une nuit d'été*' *et* '*La Duchesse de Malfi*', Trames: Actes des Journées

ambiguity. Although it seems to celebrate visionary possibilities, the play's fifth-act relapse into complacency underscores the problems of accommodating genuinely transformative experience to reductive categories. Thus the confusions among dream, vision, and 'reality' become an important part of the drama's meaning, similar to the layers of artifice dramatized by the doubling of roles and plots—confusions which make us ask just where the 'play' begins and ends. *A Midsummer Night's Dream* gains immeasurably from ways in which encounters that feel 'dreamed' in fact seem 'really' to have happened, while the 'dream' framework requires us to question categories of experience that would marginalize the truly visionary and transformative.

But Shakespeare is doing more here than simply drawing on contemporary dream theory and the lived experience of dreaming in order to make his points about the relationship between imagination and interpretation. For the Renaissance writer, that theory was mediated through a complex literary tradition that has received too little attention in discussions of this play, the tradition of medieval dream visions itself shaped by late antique and medieval theories of the psyche and of the role of the imagination in dreams. It will be my argument that Shakespeare was an astute reader of this tradition, especially as it was used in Chaucer's early poems, and that he parodies and revises the medieval dream-vision tradition in his play as surely as he plays with romance. He calls his drama a 'dream', despite its being anchored firmly in the world of real experience, at least partly to evoke this literary tradition.

As I have argued elsewhere, the dream vision in the high Middle Ages, the 'philosophical vision', was deeply invested in that age's project of demonstrating the continuity of nature and grace.[3] From the eleventh to

---

Shakespeare–Webster (Limoges, 1989), 9–27. Holland's introduction to his recent edition of *A Midsummer Night's Dream* also contains useful material relating contemporary dream theory to the play: see esp. pp. 3–16. See also D. P. Young, *Something of Great Constancy: The Art of 'A Midsummer Night's Dream'* (New Haven, 1966), 115–19; M. B. Garber, *Dream in Shakespeare: From Metaphor to Metamorphosis* (New Haven, 1974), 4–9.

[3] Although simplified here for reasons of space, this is essentially the argument of my book *High Medieval Dream Vision*. Alongside the philosophical vision, a tradition of love visions, primarily French, had also developed, and Chaucer owes a considerable debt to writers within this generic sub-group, especially Guillaume de Machaut, whose *Jugement dou roi de Navarre* provides one of the most important sources for Chaucer's comment on poetry in the *Legend*; see e.g. W. Calin, *The French Tradition and the Literature of Medieval England* (Toronto, 1994), esp. pp. 269–301. At the same time, Chaucer's poem is distinguished from Machaut's relatively self-enclosed interest in courtly behaviour and in his own personal fortunes as a poet by an explicitly declared interest in the relationship between experience and authority, as well as by a more sustained exploration of the nature of poetic metaphor, translation, and the uses of the classical past.

the thirteenth centuries, the dream served as an authenticating device, guaranteeing the objectivity and authority of the vision and offering a psychological model that put the dreamer/narrator's imagination in the service of philosophical reason as he ascended to truth. Analysis of early dream poems shows that the dreamer seems to stand as a kind of figure of the imagination in relation to a guide (or a series of guides) who offers advice associated with reason or intellect. Notable examples include the ladies Philosophia from Boethius' *De consolatione philosophiae*, Natura from Alain de Lille's *De planctu naturae*, Raison from the *Roman de la rose*, and Dante's Virgil. This structural device mimics the structure of the dreaming mind as it was understood at the time, in which imagination becomes more active and receptive during dreaming, while reason dozes, thus creating a sort of psychic vacuum. Into that vacuum the imprecations of an allegorical reason can easily be drawn to make a point about the necessity of disciplining imagination if its images are to reflect a higher truth. Occurring in a liminal state neither wholly of the body nor outside it, the dream was an ideal framework within which to address the question of how the sensuous faculty of imagination could be related to the higher, abstract, intellectual faculties. Along the same lines, medieval writers, following Macrobius,[4] were also attentive to the similarities among dream imagery, narrative, and the vivid fables of the poets. Dream visions could thus undertake a defence of poetry at the same time as they reflected upon the relationship between natural and divine truth.

By the later Middle Ages, when Chaucer was writing, the philosophical background was somewhat different, and so the dream vision came to reflect a different set of assumptions about the relationship between earthly and divine truth, about the likelihood that visionary imagery would reflect truth, and about what truth it would reflect. The philosophical 'realism' of the high Middle Ages had required an epistemology that afforded the individual person the ability to move from the literal, visible world, to the abstract, invisible truth beyond it; the dream vision had taken as its special subject that movement, narrated as the central event of a dream or vision. The later Middle Ages, while not sceptical about the existence or even availability of divine truth, had grown uneasy about the power of unaided human reason to take steps towards it. Philosophers in this later period were involved in reinterpreting the sequence of knowing that raised the images furnished by the faculty of

---

[4] See *Commentary on the Dream of Scipio*, 1. 2; trans. Stahl, 83–7.

imagination to an abstract truth apprehensible by the reason or intellect. New epistemological theories were proposed to supplement and then to supplant the theory of abstraction, an epistemology that had underwritten the earlier dream visions. Late medieval vision poems reflect this hesitation, this failure of confidence in the grand unifying schemata of the twelfth and thirteenth centuries, to which historians of philosophy have often given the name of 'nominalism'.[5] Chaucer's dream poems are a case in point. The uncertain and comic narrator, the absent or vanishing guide, the multiplying styles, images, and systems of understanding in Chaucer's dream visions, suggest the difficulties of a poet working with a lack of confidence in a form that had been used less than a century earlier, by Dante, to chart out the path from this world to the next.[6]

In addition to reflecting a hesitancy about the epistemological underpinnings of the genre, Chaucer's visionary practice, like that of his contemporary William Langland, also bespeaks his newly complicated attitude towards his own art, his sense that, if the imaginations of dreamers cannot be securely linked to objective truth, then neither can the imaginations of poets. Rather than being a defence of poetry, like that offered by Dante or implied by Alain de Lille, Chaucer's dream poems describe an uncompleted poetic quest. Sophisticated, convoluted, tonally complex, they chronicle his doubts, his false starts in seeking poetic material, his frustrations as an artist. And these were concerns that would have found a sympathetic ear in Shakespeare, whose own reading of Chaucer is likely to have been quite attentive to the medieval poet's generic sophistication and philosophical complexity. More so than at any time afterwards, the Renaissance saw Chaucer as an intellectual, learned, and philosophical writer. William Caxton, for example, called him 'that noble & grete philosopher Gefferey Chaucer', and Gabriel Harvey praised his learning, his 'Astronomie, philosophie, and other parts of profound or cunning art'.[7] There is no reason to suppose

---

[5] For several reasons, the term 'nominalism' is currently a vexed one in medieval studies: see the interesting series of essays by H. A. Oberman, W. J. Courtenay, C. T. Davis, and P. O. Kristeller, in C. Trinkaus and H. A. Oberman (eds.), *The Pursuit of Holiness in Late Medieval and Renaissance Religion* (Leiden, 1974), 3–66.

[6] See my '*Book of the Duchess* as a Philosophical Vision'; '*The Parliament of Fowls* and Late Medieval Voluntarism (Parts 1 and 2)', *ChauR* 25 (1990), 1–16, 85–95; and 'The Logic of the Dream Vision in Chaucer's *House of Fame*', in R. J. Utz (ed.), *Literary Nominalism and the Theory of Rereading Late Medieval Texts: A New Research Paradigm* (Lewiston, NY, 1995), 179–204.

[7] For the citations from Caxton and Harvey, see C. F. E. Spurgeon, *Five Hundred Years of Chaucer Criticism and Allusion, 1357–1900* (1925; repr. New York, 1960), i, 62, 128. See also Thompson, *Shakespeare's Chaucer*, 3–8.

that Shakespeare would have brought a different set of expectations to Chaucer's poems, or that he would have been inattentive to the philosophical implications of the dream vision, even if his reading in the medieval vision tradition went no further than Chaucer. Yet, directly or indirectly, he might well have known other classics of the genre. Langland, as well as Chaucer, was popular in the Renaissance, and translations of Boethius' *De consolatione* and of nearly 8,000 lines of the *Roman de la rose*, both attributed to Chaucer, appear in William Thynne's 1532 edition of his poetry. The form, moreover, influenced other Renaissance texts as diverse as Spenser's *Faerie Queene* and Bunyan's *Pilgrim's Progress*.

There is, indeed, ample reason to argue that in *A Midsummer Night's Dream* Shakespeare was drawing explicitly on the medieval dream vision. Chief among the features of Shakespeare's play that would have recalled the tradition are its preoccupation with the imagination and the proper relationship of that faculty to reason. *A Midsummer Night's Dream* can even be read as an extended meditation on the right relationship between reason and imagination, culminating in Theseus' famous lines on the problem: 'Lovers and madmen have such seething brains, | Such shaping fantasies, that apprehend | More than cool reason ever comprehends' (V. i. 4–6). References to the harmony of the mental faculties, to imagination, to the roughly synonymous 'fantasy' or 'fancy', and to its absent but desired compliance with reason and legitimated will, are frequent in this play—as in Theseus' stern command to Hermia, 'arm yourself | To fit your fancies to your father's will' (I. i. 118), or in Lysander's claim that 'reason' and not unregulated will inspires his love for Helena (II. ii. 121–6). Yet, as these examples suggest, imagination is rarely under the control of reason or, to quote Bottom only slightly out of context, 'to say the truth, reason and love keep little company together nowadays' (III. i. 136). The relationship of imagination and reason has strayed far from that recommended by the medieval vision tradition although, for the purposes of irony, that tradition had sometimes shown a soul out of balance. The ironies here, however, cut both ways, for if we laugh at the foolishness of the over-imaginative lovers, we smile as much at Theseus' sense that his 'cool reason' exempts him from their confusion. Shakespeare extends and exceeds the bounds of the genre as he inherited it from the Middle Ages, especially in his commentary on art and imagination; but his play also stands squarely within that tradition, especially of Chaucer's dream visions, poems themselves beset with irony and scepticism at the possibility of imaginative transcendence.

The link between Shakespeare's and Chaucer's visionary practice should come as no surprise to readers of A Midsummer Night's Dream, who have frequently noted that it is Shakespeare's most Chaucerian play. Despite disagreements about degree, there can be little doubt that Shakespeare was drawing on the Knight's Tale for the general romantic predicament of the play.[8] Moving the time-frame of his drama to just before Theseus' and Hippolyta's wedding, rather than positioning the action just after the wedding (as Chaucer had done), Shakespeare squares the romantic triangle of Palamon, Arcite, and Emelye with Demetrius, Lysander, Hermia, and Helena. But, as many have observed, he leaves much of the original situation intact: Theseus remains temperate and controlled; the lovers battle it out for a love that seems arbitrarily provoked; chaos frequently threatens the romantic order of the play; and supernatural interventions are required both to complicate the action and to put things right. The same supernatural interventions, and especially the characters of Oberon and Titania, are also adapted from the Pluto and Proserpina of Chaucer's Merchant's Tale. Yet, while Shakespeare's borrowings from Chaucer's poetry have not been wholly ignored, his debt here has been minimized.

Specifically, Chaucer's early poems, his dream visions, are not generally cited as major sources for the play's overall meaning. To be sure, scattered readers acknowledge local borrowings from the dream visions. Hale, for example, cites Chaucer's Book of the Duchess as a source for two moments in Bottom's attempt to explicate his 'dream': his assertion of its uninterpretability, which echoes lines 276–9 of Chaucer's poem; and his determination to see a 'ballet' written of the vision, taken from Book of the Duchess, lines 1330–3.[9] Similarly, several critics have posited that Theseus' reference to Saint Valentine's Day (IV. i. 136–7) could have come from Chaucer's Parliament of Fowls.[10] In many cases, these local borrowings could be extended even further in

---

[8]   D. Bethurum argues this point forcefully and perceptively in 'Shakespeare's Comment on Mediaeval Romance in Midsummer-Night's Dream', MLN 60 (1945), 85–94, and her argument is confirmed, though rather too cautiously, by N. Coghill, 'Shakespeare's Reading in Chaucer', in H. Davis and H. Gardner (eds.), Elizabethan and Jacobean Studies Presented to F. P. Wilson (Oxford, 1959), 86–99. Thompson's discussion of the play proves the case once and for all in Shakespeare's Chaucer, 88–94; she discusses the critical history of the relationship between the two writers in her introduction, pp. 1–15. See also L. S. Champion, 'A Midsummer Night's Dream: The Problem of Source', PLL 4 (1968), 13–19; Donaldson, Swan at the Well, esp. pp. 1–49.

[9]   D. G. Hale, 'Bottom's Dream and Chaucer', SQ 36 (1985), 219–20. Garber had already suggested the latter reference in Dream in Shakespeare, 11–12.

[10]   e.g. Thompson, Shakespeare's Chaucer, 94.

directions no critic has yet chosen to take. For example, the conclusion of a hunt and the riding homeward of a king ends the dream in the *Book of the Duchess* (called by Thynne 'The Dreame of Chaucer'),[11] just as Theseus 'sets aside' his 'purpos'd hunting' (IV. i. 182) in favour of returning home to feast. Indeed, in both poem and play, the sounds of hunting figure thematically, and there may be an echo of Chaucer's 'This harte roused and stale away' (381) in Egeus' complaint, 'They would have stol'n away' (IV. i. 155), reinforced by the fact that both texts are in a sense about heart-hunting. But these local borrowings need to be considered within Shakespeare's larger debt to the structure of the Chaucerian dream vision.

I can make the latter point most dramatically by looking closely at the relationship between *A Midsummer Night's Dream* and the dream vision to which it most clearly owes significant features of its identity: Chaucer's *Legend of Good Women*. Not only could this poem have served as the source for Theseus' reference to St Valentine's Day (145)[12] and the association of that holiday with the month of May; it is also generally acknowledged to have furnished several details from the story of Pyramus and Thisbe. There can be little doubt that Shakespeare had it in mind, if not before his eyes, while writing the play. I find it quite surprising, therefore, that nobody has noted the importance of the genre and structure of the *Legend*, which in the prologue clearly sets itself out as a dream vision. Here is a poem that provides precedents for the May dream alfresco (108–9); the inclusion of the Ovidian story of Pyramus and Thisbe in a part of the poem structurally set off from the dream; the arbitrary and meddling God of Love whose blindness, we shall see, becomes an object of poetic play; the self-conscious reversal of gender roles; and even for Theseus' misbehaviour, glancingly alluded to in *A Midsummer Night's Dream* (II. i. 77–80). It is even possible, although I would not insist upon it, that the literalistic 'prologue', played by Quince and called for by Bottom, who fears that there are things in their comedy 'that will never please' (III. i. 9), recalls the Prologue to the legendary where such a literal-minded lack of pleasure is also made

[11] All references to Chaucer's poetry will be taken from W. Thynne's 1532 edition, which I have used in W. W. Skeat's facsimile reproduction (London [1905]); line numbers are cited from the *Riverside Chaucer*, ed. Benson, for the convenience of the modern reader.

[12] Thynne's 1532 edition of Chaucer's poetry follows what is currently known as the F-version of the Prologue to the *Legend*. Occasional references to the G-version will be taken from the *Riverside Chaucer*, ed. Benson.

manifest.[13] A more searching analysis of such similarities is clearly called for, one that reads Chaucer's poetry as closely as Shakespeare's.

As Donaldson has observed, much of the modern study of Shakespeare's Chaucerian backgrounds suffers from an oversimplification of Chaucer—an assumption 'that, although the play is a puzzle requiring answers, the Chaucerian works that may provide the answers have settled—one might even say static—meanings that are available to any reader'.[14] Such an assumption diminishes Shakespeare as much as it does Chaucer, for it implies that he would have misunderstood the coy, complicated medieval ironist and mined him for his dross rather than his gold. And this is far from being the case. As Shakespeare reveals in *A Midsummer Night's Dream*, his reading of Chaucer is a reading of a reading of an already sophisticated tradition of readings, in a densely multi-layered intertextuality that underscores and undermines the stable production of meaning, so that even now we can barely excavate the top layers of the relationship between the two poets.

Analysed in its simplest terms, the Prologue to the *Legend of Good Women* tells the story of a poet–dreamer who makes it his practice to rise early during the month of May so that he can worship his mistress. She turns out to be the flower we call the daisy, so named for its precise etymological relationship to the sun: the daisy follows the sun, making them both 'the eye of the day' (184). And so the poet follows the daisy: 'She is the clernesse and the verray lyght | That in this derke worlde me wynt and ledeth' (84–5). She is the hand that makes the poet's harp obey her fingering (90–1). Tired by his day of devotions, the narrator has a bed prepared for himself outside in his garden, benched with turf like a maze. In the dream that follows, he sees the God of Love, accompanied by a beautiful queen who wears a green gown, a golden hairnet, and a crown comprising a single, peerless pearl. The queen, of course, underscores her identity by dressing as a daisy. As the dreamer discovers later, she is Alceste, who died to save her husband Admetus, and in thus making a journey into darkness, from which she returned, as the sun does each day, she is again like the daisy/day's eye. The God of Love is also described, his sun-crowned hair, bright face, angelic wings, darts of love; 'And al be that men sayne that blynde is he | Algate me thought that he myght se' (237–8).

---

[13] J. W. Spisak also notes the possible echo suggested by the 'prologue', in 'Pyramus and Thisbe in Chaucer and Shakespeare', in E. T. Donaldson and J. J. Kollman (eds.), *Chaucerian Shakespeare: Adaptation and Transformation* (Detroit, 1983), 81–95: 90.

[14] Donaldson, *Swan at the Well*, 2.

Following the queen and her lord are a troupe of women led by nine-
teen of the truest ladies who ever lived. The God of Love accosts the
dreamer, kneeling by his flower, with a bill of poetic crimes against love:
poems and translations that cause lovers to mistrust women and
renounce the law of romantic love. (In the G-text, he also includes a list
of stories the poet ought to have translated instead, some of which are,
ironically, far more misogynist than the poems against which he rails.)
Although Alceste then pleads for the dreamer's chance to explain or
excuse himself, suggesting that he may be the victim of false accus-
ations, or of a translator's foolhardiness in failing to understand his
source, or of the irresistible command of a high personage, the poet is
allowed a scant twenty lines to make his case. He does so by arguing vigorously, if briefly, that the underlying intentions of his work were
pure—to chastise the false in love, and praise the true. But the God of
Love, a tyrant of love, cannot be 'countrepleted' with such arguments
(476), Alceste tells the poet impatiently as she cuts him off. She assigns a
penance: to make a legendary of good women and the false men who
betrayed them. The god himself reinforces her instruction with the
explicit direction that, somewhere in his legendary, the poet should tell
the miracle of Alceste herself, though 'At Cleopatras I wol that thou
begynne' (566). Dutifully, and without ever waking from his dream, the
poet takes up the legend of Cleopatra, a queen whose medieval reputation was sullied by charges of incest, luxury, and general debauchery,
and follows it with legends of eight other ladies, several of equally com-
promised virtue. (In the G-version he wakes before undertaking the
legendary.)

On the surface, this little dream vision does not seem much to resemble Shakespeare's dream play, and I do not mean to offer it as a source
for the literal narrative. In addition to all that is missing—the romance
plot ending in marriage, the father's legal opposition, the four lovers
cavorting in the forest under the supervision of mischievous fairies—
there are significant formal differences. Like other medieval dream
visions, Chaucer's Prologue is told from the perspective of the dreamer;
in the broadest terms, it is traditional in recounting the conversion of his
will to the judgement of the god who appears in this vision to guide and
reform him. Although it includes a dialogue, even a trialogue—between
Cupid, the poet, and Alceste—it is not fundamentally dialogic in the
way of a play. As we shall see, his recasting of the conventional dream
narrative permits Shakespeare to manipulate the frame narrative in
order to juxtapose perspectives in a way that is more radical than

anything Chaucer had attempted, although Chaucer's dream visions, with their ambiguous authorities, had already moved the form in this direction.

Moreover, if one such authority, Cupid, is an important influence in both works, in the medieval poem he appears in his own person, and he is sighted, whereas in the Renaissance one he is referred to in the third person and clearly identified as blind: 'Love looks not with the eyes, but with the mind, | And therefore is winged Cupid painted blind' (I. i. 234–5). Yet the explicit reference to Cupid in both texts also points to an underlying similarity; for, if Cupid is sighted in the *Legend*, it is in opposition to his role in the medieval erotic tradition and elsewhere in Chaucer's works.[15] Indeed, this Cupid's literal ability to see signals his inability to perceive deeply or figuratively, as shown by his singularly foolish belief that stories of masculine betrayal will persuade people of the virtues of erotic love, by his misreading of Chaucer's love poems as tracts against love and, in the G-text, by his citation of notoriously misogynist writers like Jerome or Valerian as promoters of women. Cupid's sight thus figures his blindness, calling attention to it more forcefully than if he had been presented with the traditional attribute. Similarly, the lovers in *A Midsummer's Night's Dream* are blind in love, as is indicated by the fungibility of love objects. Sight here, as in Chaucer, is a source of delusion. Indeed, one of the main functions of the supernatural characters in Shakespeare's play is to account for and underscore the quixotic arbitrariness of love. Puck has frequently been named as a Cupid figure; as Holland puts it, he is 'the spirit responsible for creating irrational affection',[16] which he does by applying the venom or juice from Cupid's 'bolt' (II. i. 164) to the 'sleeping eyelids' (II. i. 170) of unsuspecting mortals.

The supernatural similarities, however, go beyond the association of Puck and Cupid. Like Pluto and Proserpina, the quarrelling pagan gods who supervise the action in the Merchant's Tale, Cupid and Alceste in the *Legend* provide another precedent for Oberon and Titania. Indeed, Oberon's assertion of masculine dominance makes *A Midsummer Night's Dream* in some ways closer to Chaucer's *Legend* than to the Merchant's Tale—another text that links gender to the opposition of sight and blindness—where May, and through her Proserpina, really

---

[15]   See S. S. Smith, 'Cupid's Sight in the Prologue to the *Legend of Good Women*', *Centrepoint*, 15 (1981), 95–102.

[16]   Holland, introduction to his edition of *Midsummer Night's Dream*, 41.

have the last word. The queens in Shakespeare's play mediate between the mundane and the divine: Hippolyta in Act V speaks for the lovers' truth, 'strange and admirable' (V. i. 27), and defends the distinctions between good and bad art, or imagination, that Theseus crudely wants to blur. Her holding out for such distinctions is paralleled by the four-day delay before she gives her Amazonian hand and body in marriage, a time she also describes as virtually sanctified by dreaming and moonshine (I. i. 7–11). The delay finds its counterpart within the 'dream' in Titania's withholding of the changeling born from the prattling and pregnant 'vot'ress of [her] order' (II. i. 123). Both women have female worlds worth protecting; and they make possible the space for art, for the play itself—even if, just as the young squire's birth kills his mother, that space is ultimately obliterated and absorbed by the prosaic mortal and masculine world surrounding them. Similarly, Alceste is a mediatrix who finds a compromise between the absolutist demands of Cupid and the claims of the poet's art, likewise a compromise that makes room for his art to continue even if, finally, it too will be destroyed by the masculinist solvent of the God of Love's limited taste and understanding. Titania and Hippolyta, then, play Alceste to Oberon's and Theseus' flat-footed Cupid.

Thus gender dynamics create powerful links between Shakespeare's play and Chaucer's legendary. A chief purpose of Chaucer's poem, if it is read without irony, is the defence of women in love. If women were conventionally regarded as the false and inconstant sex, as Chaucer had recently demonstrated in his narrative about the false Criseyde, the *Legend* ostensibly attempts to overturn that reputation. Similarly, within the patriarchal world of Shakespeare's play, the women remain true to their original loves throughout the confusion of the midsummer madness, while the men, even in their appellations—Demetrius 'the vile name' (II. ii. 113) and Lysander/Lies-Ander—emblematize inconstancy. Demetrius, for example, is associated with the more traditionally female moon, 'spotted and inconstant' (I. i. 110), in his mutable and unpredictable doting. As Helena remarks, such qualities are typical of devotees of the male Cupid: 'As waggish boys in game themselves forswear, | So the boy Love is perjured everywhere' (I. i. 240–1). Although critics frequently find a precedent for Shakespeare's broken sisterhood in the disrupted brotherhood of the Knight's Tale's, Chaucer had already orchestrated his own inversions in the *Legend*, where the tender sisterhood of Procne and Philomela, or of Ariadne and Phedra, had been put asunder by a man's love. Only in Chaucer, in fact, is the story of

Theseus' betrayal of Ariadne told as a parable of sisterly rivalry.[17] And Hermia's famous vow to meet Lysander evokes not only a specific story told in Chaucer's poem but also the tone and structure of the aphoristic endings of several of the legends there:

> And by that fire which burned the Carthage queen
> When the false Trojan under sail was seen;
> By all the vows that ever men have broke—
> In number more than ever women spoke—
> In that same place thou hast appointed me
> Tomorrow truly will I meet with thee.
>
> (I. i. 173–8)

Compare these lines with the dismissals of male virtue at the end of the stories of Cleopatra (702–5), Thisbe (920–3), Lucrece (1879–85), and Philomela (2388–93). As the poet quips flirtatiously at the end of the story of Phyllis: 'trusteth nowe in love no man but me' (2561).

Indeed, several of the individual stories of the legendary are echoed in *A Midsummer Night's Dream*. Although the play takes the character of Theseus primarily from his representation as a seemingly mature and self-reflective ruler in the Knight's Tale, it alludes briefly to a far different and less savoury Theseus—the philandering Theseus, the Theseus of the Legend of Ariadne. Oberon accuses Titania of dalliance with the Athenian king:

> Didst not thou lead him through the glimmering night
> From Perigouna whom he ravishèd,
> And make him with fair Aegles break his faith,
> With Ariadne and Antiopa?
>
> (II. i. 76–80)

Although Perigouna, Aegles, and Antiopa come from North's *Plutarch*, Chaucer also tells the story of Theseus' betrayal of Ariadne in the *Legend of Good Women*, a story Shakespeare knew and used when he transformed Ariadne's headscarf dangling from a pole to Dido's willow wafting her love to Carthage in *Troilus and Cressida* (V. i. 9–12).[18] Shakespeare also refers directly to the tragedy of Dido's love for Aeneas

---

[17] See M. Storm, 'From Knossos to Knight's Tale: The Changing Face of Chaucer's Theseus', in J. Chance (ed.), *The Mythographic Art: Classical Fable and the Rise of the Vernacular in Early France and England* (Gainesville, Fla., 1990), 215–21.

[18] Thompson, *Shakespeare's Chaucer*, 67. Shakespeare refers again to Ariadne's complaint at Theseus' unkindness in *The Two Gentlemen of Verona*, IV. iv. 163–5.

in *A Midsummer Night's Dream* in Hermia's vow cited above, and indirectly there to the story of Philomela, when the chorus of fairies invokes her as muse (II. ii. 13). All three stories were among Chaucer's legends of 'good' women. But the most extensive individual debt the play owes to the legendary comes in the dramatization of the story of Pyramus and Thisbe appended to the marriage plot—itself complete well before Act V,[19] just as the legends of Chaucer's poem are appended to a free-standing dream prologue.

A. B. Taylor has recently mounted a rather elaborate challenge[20] to the growing critical consensus that Chaucer's Legend of Thisbe served as a source for Shakespeare's rendition of the story.[21] He argues that what Shakespeare reputedly got from Chaucer could have been had through the intermediary of other Renaissance writers who themselves knew Chaucer's work. Unless Taylor intends to protect Chaucer from parody or, more likely, Shakespeare from contamination by his medieval predecessor, his argument seems to miss the point. Since Shakespeare knew Chaucer and was clearly referring to the Knight's Tale in this play, what makes it likely that he would overlook Chaucer's telling of the Pyramus and Thisbe story in favour of a more obscure Renaissance version? Source-hunting is not a zero-sum game; the fact that Shakespeare had access to the anonymous 'History of Pyramus and Thisbe' from *A Gorgeous Gallery of Gallant Inventions*, Thomson's ballad from *A Handful of Pleasant Delightes*, or a variety of contemporary Latin–English dictionaries,[22] fails to prove that Chaucer's *Legend* was not an additional source for *A Midsummer Night's Dream*. And finally, in point of fact, Taylor does not provide an adequate explanation for the echoes of Chaucer's 'lyme and eke thy stone' (765) in Shakespeare, noting only that 'Shakespeare would have hardly needed Chaucer to know that a wall between two gardens was built of stones and mortar'.[23]

---

[19] H. F. Brooks, introduction to his edition of *A Midsummer Night's Dream*, The Arden Shakespeare (London, 1979), p. xcix; see also Peter Holland's introduction, pp. 105–6.

[20] A. B. Taylor, 'Chaucer's Non-Involvement in "Pyramus and Thisbe"', *NQ* 234 (NS 36) (1989), 317–20.

[21] Although he diminishes the debt, K. Muir ultimately does affirm it, in *The Sources of Shakespeare's Plays*, rev. edn. (New Haven, 1978), 72–3; see also Thompson, *Shakespeare's Chaucer*, 93; Donaldson, *Swan at the Well*, 18–22; and Holland's introduction, pp. 84, 87–8.

[22] See A. B. Taylor, 'Golding's *Ovid*, Shakespeare's "Small Latin", and the Real Object of Mockery in "Pyramus and Thisbe"', *SS* 42 (1990), 53–64.

[23] Taylor, 'Chaucer's Non-Involvement', 318 n. 8.

In arguing for Shakespeare's use of Chaucer, however, Donaldson had already made this very concession, while noting its irrelevance: 'Shakespeare scarcely needed Chaucer to tell him about the composition of house walls, but he follows his lead in referring to Wall in terms of the synecdoches of its constructional components.'[24] Indeed, Donaldson's and Taylor's arguments are more compatible than Taylor acknowledges, for both critics maintain that Shakespeare is being self-parodic in the Pyramus and Thisbe legend: in Taylor's view, Shakespeare mocks his own 'small Latin' in Quince's malapropisms; in Donaldson's view, Shakespeare makes fun of his previous representation of the Pyramus story in *Romeo and Juliet*. As Donaldson points out, Shakespeare would have found a precedent for self-parody in Chaucer who had, like Shakespeare, already (over)dramatized the Pyramus and Thisbe plot in Book IV of *Troilus and Criseyde*: 'both authors show in these other works their awareness of the perils of using so egregiously melodramatic a situation seriously, and both make some effort to propitiate the gods of absurdity who preside over the theatrics of such suicidal lovers under any name or in any context'.[25] Rather than confirming that Chaucer was not a source here for Shakespeare, Taylor's argument ultimately suggests the reverse: that Shakespeare's comedy is in exactly the same spirit of self-undermining mischief as Chaucer's.

Shakespeare's 'Theseus' suggests a similar relationship between the *Legend of Good Women* and *A Midsummer Night's Dream*, one in which Shakespeare is being sustained by the ironic undercurrents of Chaucer's art. Despite the role the ardent and tolerant Theseus plays here in maintaining the play's festive tone, critics have recently begun to explore his darker side. The reputation Theseus brings with him from classical myth, a reputation surrounded by sexual betrayal and death, disturbs the calm surface of the dream. Holland, for example, has explored the background of the Hippolytus story evoked by Shakespeare's (and I would add Chaucer's) choice to follow the tradition that named Theseus' bride Hippolyta. This background, although it is carefully kept only as background by Shakespeare, powerfully connects Theseus with familial murder.[26] Similarly, Mowat has linked the

[24] Donaldson, *Swan at the Well*, 22.
[25] Ibid. Spisak, 'Pyramus and Thisbe', also stresses the ironic tone of both works, although his interpretation of Chaucer's irony is less broad than either mine or Donaldson's.
[26] P. Holland, 'Theseus' Shadows in *A Midsummer Night's Dream*', SS 47 (1995), 139–51.

ambivalent Theseus of North's *Plutarch* to the poet's interest in ambivalent and self-contradictory literary traditions. According to this account,
Theseus is especially intriguing as a locus of 'self-interrogation'.[27]
In Ovid, he is noted for a particular susceptibility to wondrous tales,
while in Shakespeare he is famed for his scepticism ('I never may
believe | These antique fables, nor these fairy toys', V. i. 2–3). As Mowat
observes, Plutarch had himself seen Theseus as an indicator of the diversity of historical reportage and of the difficulties of resolving conflicts in
our understanding of the distant past.[28]

Chaucer, too, was fascinated by such difficulties. The *House of Fame*,
for example, provided an extended treatment of the conflicting traditions of the Dido and Aeneas story, and of the final impossibility of har-
monizing the Virgilian and Ovidian approaches with it. Less explicitly,
Chaucer's Theseus becomes an emblem of the same problem. In the
House of Fame, directly after accusing Aeneas and just before excusing
him—that is, exactly in the middle of his dilemma over conflicting literary traditions—Chaucer devotes twenty-two lines to Theseus' betrayal
of Ariadne for her sister Phedra (405–26). It is the longest of the enclosed
narratives that he will tell here and one that, like the story of Dido herself, he will repeat at greater length in the *Legend*. Indeed, in the *Legend*,
Theseus is the only villain who reproduces himself in a son who follows
in his nefarious footsteps, the 'false Demophon' (2398): 'wicked frute
cometh of a wicked tre' (2395).

Nor does Chaucer keep the false Theseus completely separate from
his representation of the admirable duke of the Knight's Tale. Just as
Shakespeare obliquely evokes his hero's past as a lover, so also
Chaucer's Theseus in the Knight's Tale good-naturedly recalls his
amorous history: 'A man mote ben a foole, other yong or old | I wote it
by my selfe full yore agone | For in my tyme a servante was I one'
(1812–14). Theseus' jolly reminiscences connect him to these present
lovers; he sees them as younger versions of himself.[29] And yet the love he
sanctions is a 'kind of anarchic egotism', as Aers calls it,[30] which again
links Chaucer's exposition of love to Shakespeare's. Nor does Theseus'
logic or reason go uncriticized by Chaucer, any more than it does by
Shakespeare. Until the women begin to weep at the verdict, Theseus'
first response to the love-quarrel that he interrupts in this scene is a

[27] B. A. Mowat, '"A local habitation and a name": Shakespeare's Text as Construct',
Style, 23 (1989), 335–51: 346.
[28] Ibid. 348.   [29] Patterson, *Chaucer and the Subject of History*, 230.
[30] D. Aers, *Chaucer, Langland and the Creative Imagination* (London, 1980), 181.

peremptory 'Ye shall be deed by myghty Mars the reed' (1747). And on closer examination, the mercy that Theseus appears to show so generously to the two lovers, fighting up to their ankles in blood, is an inappropriate response to 'repentance and . . . drede' (1776). For neither of these knights—and certainly not Palamon, who has been calling not only for his own execution but also for that of his cousin first!—has demonstrated either repentance or dread. His very exhibition of clemency and attention to circumstance, moreover, recall previous occasions when Theseus was less than generous. As Webb wrote almost fifty years ago, these lines 'are an indirect condemnation of several of his past acts'.[31] Chaucer criticism has thus been divided on the subject of Theseus in the Knight's Tale and, although as many Chaucerians as Shakespearians cherish the image of the 'good Theseus', the verdict is by no means unanimous that he is a uniformly laudable, just, or temperate ruler. Indeed, like Shakespeare's duke—and I think it is significant that he borrows that title from Chaucer—the medieval Theseus seems haunted by 'shadows'. Chaucer's complaint, *Anelida and Arcite*, another story of masculine betrayal, likewise begins with the triumph of Theseus, and although the poem remains unfinished, its tone towards Theseus is complicated both by the general subject-matter and by the connection between Theseus and the false Arcite, for each is linked to Mars and the older hero takes the role of the younger in the *Legend*.[32]

Thus, when in the Prologue to the *Legend of Good Women* Alceste offers a version of the Knight's Tale—'And al the love of Palamon and Arcite | Of Thebes though the storie is knowen lyte' (420–1)—as the culminating secular example of Chaucer's fidelity in love, one suspects that the poet is sardonically leading up to the sober translations of Boethius and of Pope Innocent that follow, writings that surely do not prosecute straightforwardly Cupid's agenda of romantic love. As we have seen, if the *Legend of Good Women* is offered explicitly as a palinode to the story of *Troilus and Criseyde*, it also constructs itself in a complex opposition to the narrative of Palamon and Arcite, a version of which Chaucer had to hand. In its recasting of same-sex feuds and compacts, in

---

[31] H. J. Webb, 'A Reinterpretation of Chaucer's Theseus', *RES* 23 (1947), 289–96: 296.

[32] Storm, 'Knossos to Knight's Tale', 222–9, discusses the verbal, heraldic, and iconographic links between the two characters as they emerge consecutively in *Anelida*, the Legend of Ariadne, and the Knight's Tale. His argument is quite different from mine, however, for he sees the composite Theseus/Arcite figure as progressively liberated from enslavement to venereal impulses as he moves through the three works. See also J. Chance, *The Mythographic Chaucer: The Fabulation of Sexual Politics* (Minneapolis, 1995), ch. 6.

its evocation of the traitorous Theseus, it calls forth a vicious underside of love that is powerfully in tension with the poem's ostensible celebration of fidelity to romantic love. Read with any perceptiveness, none of the poems mentioned here, and certainly not the *House of Fame* which heads the list, offers an innocent praise of love. Chaucer seems to be announcing, then, the ambiguity of the story that stars Theseus as its leading man, and to be pointing to the complicated way in which the literary tradition assigns praise and blame. As Patterson puts it, 'The *Legend of Ariadne* is Chaucer's own commentary on the assumptions that make the *Knight's Tale* possible but which it cannot itself make visible.'[33]

Chaucer's deliberate confusions of the time-scheme of Theseus' life also call the reader's attention to the indeterminacy and conflict involved in the telling of the narrative, and especially so in the Legend of Ariadne. Although the version of Theseus' biography that Shakespeare would have known in North's *Plutarch* concentrates doubt in its reworking and synthesizing of differing accounts of the separate events in Theseus' life, by and large it straightens out the sequences. Other classical and medieval commentators, in contrast, were divided about the order of Theseus' adventures. Chaucer's closest source, Boccaccio, for example, protects Theseus' reputation by having him marry Hippolyta before his victory over the Minotaur, while Statius, Ovid, and other writers have him defeat the Minotaur and abandon Ariadne before his Amazonian conquests.[34] Chaucer follows this more widespread order of events at the beginning of the Knight's Tale when Theseus rides into battle against Thebes carrying a golden pennant bearing the image of the Minotaur (980). In the Legend of Ariadne, however, Chaucer invokes the Boccaccian order when he has Ariadne promise her sister Phedra the hand of Hippolytus, son of Theseus and the Amazonian queen, if she assists in the plan of Theseus' release.[35] On top of the

---

[33] Patterson, *Chaucer and the Subject of History*, 240.

[34] Several details in Boccaccio reinforce this order: Aegeus is still living, as is Minos' son Androgeus, vengeance for whose death caused the drawing of lots that brought Theseus to the Minotaur and Ariadne (*Teseide* 6. 46); Boccaccio also makes clear that his noble Theseus' only crime against women up to this point in his life is the atoned-for ravishing of the maiden Helen (*Teseide* 1. 130, 5. 92). See G. Boccaccio, *The Book of Theseus*, trans. B. M. McCoy (New York, 1974). Like Chaucer, Statius in Book 12 of the *Thebaid* represents Theseus as bearing the image of the Minotaur on his arms when he charges into Thebes; see Statius, *Thebaid*, trans. A. D. Melville (Oxford, 1995), 325.

[35] For the identification of the son, see the note to *LGW* 2099, in the *Riverside Chaucer*, p. 1072.

temporal confusion, we are told quite unnecessarily and conspicuously by Chaucer that Theseus is a young man, only 'twenty yere and thre' (2075; ages are not given for the other villains in the *Legend*), too young to have fathered a mate ready to be 'wedded' to his bride's sister directly at their homecoming.[36] Surely, too, the betrothal of Phedra and Hippolytus would have called to any knowledgeable reader's mind the horrible consequences of that love later in Theseus' life, when Phedra's incestuous passion for her stepson leads Theseus to kill his own son, while Demophon's betrayal would also have evoked the pattern of cross-generational treachery. As Ovid's Phaedra exclaims, 'Theseus' son and Theseus have been the undoing of sisters twain—rear ye a double trophy at our house's fall!' ('Thesides Theseusque duas rapuere sorores— | ponite de nostra bina tropaea domo!').[37] The banner of the Minotaur under which Theseus fights would have been itself an ambiguous symbol, signifying the conquest of Unity over Division or of Reason over Disordered Appetite,[38] but also recalling that appetite itself and, in Theseus' particular circumstances, the despicable treason that followed Ariadne's rescue of the Athenian hero. The question remains, though: why is Chaucer invoking all these conflicting traditions?

Rather than being, as Mowat calls them, 'a grid through which the confusing versions of "Theseus" are filtered',[39] Chaucer's stories of the hero, especially taken together, would have suggested the same textual indeterminacy, the same confusions about art and reception, that preoccupied Shakespeare in *A Midsummer Night's Dream*. Just as Plutarch returns again and again to the problems of coming to terms with the competing claims of diverse poets, biographers, and historians, so Chaucer dramatizes those problems in the conspicuously incoherent chronology of Theseus' life. His account of Theseus in the Knight's Tale sends us back to the Minotaur in the Legend of Ariadne, where the reference to Theseus' son in turn reverses the narrative order and moves us back again to the marriage of Theseus and Hippolyta, a union necessary to produce that son. It is an essentially circular, infinitely regressive, and

---

[36] In Chaucer the word generally signifies the act of marriage rather than betrothal, as in WBT 1071–2: 'nedes must he her wedde | And taketh his olde wyfe and gothe to bedde'.

[37] Ovid, *Heroides and Amores*, trans. G. Showerman, rev. G. P. Gould, Loeb Classical Library (Cambridge, Mass., 1977), *Heroides* 4. 65–6 (pp. 48–9).

[38] See R. H. Green, 'Classical Fable and English Poetry in the Fourteenth Century', in D. Bethurum (ed.), *Critical Approaches to Medieval Literature: Selected Papers from the English Institute, 1958–1959* (New York, 1960), 110–33; also Chance, *Mythographic Chaucer*, 79–81, 192–6.

[39] Mowat, '"A local habitation"', 338.

self-consuming set of manoeuvres, calculated to create a kind of narrative vertigo, which Shakespeare would have appreciated. The Theseus of *A Midsummer Night's Dream*, V. i, does not stand, as the Shakespearian critic argues, 'in direct contrast to Chaucer's "gentil duc" ';[40] he is an earlier version of the same challenge to the notion of an accessible unitary tradition, the same enigma of wonder and scepticism.

In Chaucer's dream vision, the *Legend of Good Women*, Shakespeare would have found Theseus' darkest shadow and the strongest indication of the medieval poet's deep preoccupation with problems of language and poetic imagination. Indeed, what links poem and play most profoundly is their interest in the poetic imagination, in its relationship to reason, and in the (im)possibility or (un)likelihood of imagination's accurate representation of a truth that may be reliably perceived or apprehended by its audience. Similarly, both the medieval and Renaissance poets take advantage of the juxtaposition of perspectives offered by the dream form to suggest that relativity of perspective may undermine imaginative poetic truth. As indicated in my summary of the Prologue to the *Legend*, the vision presented there to the poet at first seems to affirm the power of metaphor, and through it of image-making. The poet follows the daisy, whose relationship to the sun, the 'day's eye', is one of transparent reflection. The lady from literature, Alceste, similarly 'kytheth what she ys' (504), that is, shows herself truthfully, in her dress, her literary history, her character, as the straightforward embodiment of daisy and sun. Yet Alceste does not so clearly figure truth when she refuses to consider the poet's intention in the poems that she agrees are crimes against love, while the misreading she encourages in the legendary suggests a much more troubled, unpredictable set of relationships between the artistic blueprint, its realization, and its reception. The same pattern occurs in *A Midsummer Night's Dream*, where the 'pan's eye', flower of the Puck-ish nature god, and source of illusion, will come to obscure the daisy's transparency.[41]

As well as contradicting herself, Alceste lives within a form that can highlight such contradictions. The dream vision offered a framing device that permitted the juxtaposition of competing perspectives. It is partly because the vision of Cupid and Alceste occurs within a dream that we question not only the validity of their perspectives but also the poet's perspective on them. As I have indicated, in the F-version of the

---

[40] Ibid. 342.
[41] I owe this connection of the daisy and pansy to my colleague Yu Jin Ko.

Prologue, the text that Shakespeare would have known, even the individual legends would have been presented as if from inside the poet's dream. Dream visions—and especially Chaucer's—were frequently arranged as a series of enclosed and enclosing boxes, allowing the poet to achieve a sort of double, triple, and even quadruple perspective on the central truth of his poem. For example, in the *Book of the Duchess*, the narrator dreams about a grieving black knight who tells a story of lost love. In the course of his narrative, he ventriloquizes the words of the lady who rejected him—first in love, and later in death. We have her initial 'nay' (1243), framed by his grief, framed by the narrator's incomprehension, all of which weaves a skein of conflicting interpretations to be unravelled by the reader outside the poem. And this is not even to mention the complicated way in which the knight's story relates to the similarly boxed-up set of narratives the narrator finds in the old book he reads to induce sleep, which anticipates and mirrors the plot of his dream, and suggests by analogy that dreams and poetry present their imaginative lessons or losses in similar forms.

Shakespeare seems to be using the layered form of the dream vision in a like way. In *The Taming of the Shrew*, for example, the Induction frames Petruchio's autocratic exercise of control over Kate's perception with Sly's dream of false advancement, thus underscoring the tenuousness of human perception and truth. ('Then, God be blessed, it is the blessed sun, | But sun it is not, when you say it is not. | And the moon changes even as your mind', IV. v. 18–20.)[42] *A Midsummer Night's Dream* makes the point more subtly and embeds it more deeply in the structure of the whole. This is, as many critics have noted, a tightly choreographed play; it has fewer scenes than any other play by Shakespeare. Its shape, like the shape of a medieval dream vision, can be easily diagrammed: Acts I and V, the frame, are set in Athens; Acts II to IV in the surrounding wood. This central section corresponds to the dream. At the same time, the shape articulates a series of competing perspectives on the action. Theseus' (and Hippolyta's) waking perspectives are aligned with the Athenian court, rationalism, and the law, while the point of view of the dream is enclosed in the wood, associated with the imagination, and expressed by the lovers and fairies. Like a dream vision, the play, with its multiplication of voyeuristic readers within the text, points outward to the reader—or the audience—outside the poem so that we watch Theseus and Hippolyta watch the lovers, all watched

---

[42]   W. Shakespeare, *The Taming of the Shrew*, ed. H. J. Oliver (Oxford, 1982).

over by the fairies, who in turn watch each other. The arrangement suggests a complex and disorienting series of dramatic ironies; for if pardon or blessing is required in the final lines of the play (V. i. 415–16), we are also invited, like the mortals within the play, to participate in the illusion: 'If we shadows have offended, | Think but this, and all is mended, | That you have but slumber'd here | While these visions did appear' (V. i. 409–12).

We are seduced into the heart of the liar's paradox, and there is no way out. As Scott puts it,

Try as we may to hold ourselves superior to [the lovers'] examples because they are only fictions . . . their acceptance of mystery after all governs us. There is a dizzying succession of frames: dream is enclosed by fiction which is enclosed by dream. . . . If there is a closure it must be provided by us; but the experience, founded on a liar or dreamer or fabulist or ironist paradox as it is, does not encourage us to close it.[43]

The experience Scott describes is very like the one that Chaucer's *Legend* produces where, as one of the founding premises of the poem, we are torn between the assertions of a narrator who has been tried and found guilty of misogyny, and the indictments of a pair of royals whose misunderstandings subvert as much as ratify his guilt. A similar paradox plagues the morality of the individual legends. In Delany's words: 'If we believe the Narrator's final words about untrustworthy utterances by men [quoted above], then we must hesitate to trust his representation. If we do not believe his concluding essentialist claim, then we have already withdrawn credulity from his utterances and must hesitate again to trust his representation.'[44] The dream vision—in the hands of both Shakespeare and Chaucer—thus becomes a form that embodies the infinite regressiveness of language and its self-undermining deconstructions.

In this way, the form becomes both literally and metaphorically labyrinthine. In fact, several classical and medieval poems within the vision tradition had used the labyrinth as an image of intellectual complexity and confusion that proper guidance could transcend. Philosophia had led Boethius through the labyrinthine paths of dialectic to an understanding of the single meaning of good and evil; Dante's Virgil had rescued the poet–pilgrim from the 'selva oscura' and taken

[43] W. O. Scott, 'Chaucer, Shakespeare, and the Paradoxes of Dream and Fable', *CEACrit* 49 (1986–7), 25–32: 31.

[44] S. Delany, *The Naked Text: Chaucer's Legend of Good Women* (Berkeley and Los Angeles, 1994), 208.

him through the maze-like structures of hell and purgatory. For Chaucer, though, the labyrinth becomes exclusively an image, as Doob writes, 'of confusion and doubt', especially in the *House of Fame* where the 'domus Dedaly' (1920) is explicitly invoked at the poem's end to signify the trap of language and poetic tradition from which the narrator can never emerge.[45] Other Chaucerian dream-vision narrators are similarly 'amazed'; as the dreamer in the *Book of the Duchess* complains, 'I have felynge in nothyng | But as it were a mased thyng, | Alday in poynte to fal adoun' (11–13). And, as we have seen, the dreamer in the *Legend* falls asleep in a garden whose architecture recalls a turf maze (204) and whose dream leads to the retelling of the story of the original labyrinth. Theseus' maze-quest results in the impossibility of recovering Theseus as a stable poetic referent, since the circularity of the hero's history in Chaucer's rendering of it seems itself labyrinthine, leading always to the point at which it began. The hero himself becomes an emblem of abandonment and lack ('Ryght in the dawnyng awaketh she [Ariadne] | And gropeth in the bed and fond right nought', 2185–6).

Shakespeare's play, too, specifically recalls a maze, indeed a turf maze; following Oberon's allusion to her love for Theseus, Titania complains that his jealousies have disrupted the natural order and robbed the world of its cheer: 'The nine men's morris is filled up with mud, | And the quaint mazes in the wanton green | For lack of tread are undistinguishable' (II. i. 98–100). A few lines later, the entire world has become convoluted into a maze by the quarrels of these two gods: 'The spring, the summer, | The chiding autumn, angry winter change | Their wonted liveries, and the mazed world | By their increase now knows not which is which' (II. i. 111–14). The lovers, Hermia 'amazed' at Helena's words (III. ii. 220), or dizzy Lysander who emerges 'amazedly' (IV. i. 145) from the green world, also evoke the labyrinth or maze through which they have trod the night, as well as the confused dreamers of earlier visions. At the centre of this maze we find the play's ultimate visionary, Bottom. His name, which could refer to a spool of thread,[46]

---

[45] In *The Idea of the Labyrinth from Classical Antiquity through the Middle Ages* (Ithaca, NY, 1990), P. R. Doob makes this argument about the relationships between Virgil, Boethius, Dante, and Chaucer; see esp. her chapter on the *House of Fame*, pp. 307–9.

[46] A. Lecercle draws this lexical connection in an essay exploring the play's maze-like structure, 'On Mazes, Merry-Go-Rounds and Immaculate Conceptions: The Dream Logic of *A Midsummer Night's Dream*', in Iselin and Moreau (eds.), *Songe d'une nuit*, 141–53. Another analysis that considers the play as a maze and Bottom as the Minotaur, quite traditionally moralized, is D. Ormerod's '*A Midsummer Night's Dream*: The Monster in the Labyrinth', *SStud* 11 (1978), 39–52.

connects him to Theseus, who found his way out of the Minotaur's den by following a ball of twine; and his occupation as a weaver ties him to the fabric of words he commissions, the *textus* constructed by the carpenter Quince. With his ass's head, Bottom is also the man–beast at the bottom of the labyrinth, the Minotaur himself, although his transformation by an ass's head leaves him a more neutral figure for the transformative powers of the imagination than the man–bull who in traditional iconography heralded lust and enslavement by the sensual world. Bottom, this dreamer at the centre of the play, is also a dreamer like those Chaucer loved to describe—bewildered, astonished, unable to make sense of his experience:

Methought I was—there is no man can tell what. Methought I was, and methought I had—but man is but a patched fool if he will offer to say what methought I had. The eye of man hath not heard, the ear of man hath not seen, man's hand is not able to taste, his tongue to conceive, nor his heart to report what my dream was. (IV. i. 204–10)

The Pauline echoes here, from 1 Corinthians 2 and 2 Corinthians 12, are also quite Chaucerian, reminiscent both of the *Book of the Duchess*, as I noted earlier, and of the *House of Fame*:

> I wote wel I am here
> But whether in body or in goost
> I not ywys but god thou wost
> For more clere entendement
> Nas me never yet ysent.
>
> (980–4)

Neither is 'clere entendement', true understanding, ever made available to Shakespeare's 'dreamers' in *A Midsummer Night's Dream*, who indeed never know for sure if they were dreaming or not. In many ways, Shakespeare's dream vision is a more radically sceptical inversion of form and function than any of Chaucer's. Gone are the putative guides: the eagle of the *House of Fame*, Scipio Africanus of the *Parliament of Fowls*; even the counterparts of Cupid and Alceste, Oberon and Titania, stand back from the action, blessing and tormenting the humans but never instructing them. One might go so far as to say that Boethius' *Philosophia* has become in Shakespeare the prankster Puck. The tracks of the 'quaint mazes in the wanton green' are 'undistinguishable', lacking shape and form, like the 'undistinguishable' memories (IV. i. 186) Demetrius describes upon emerging from the wood, and like the footprints of the dream vision form itself, which are stamped out by the many other sources and traditions competing for ascendancy here. One wonders whether it is even right to call this play a dream vision when it so seriously undermines the visionary and replaces it with the secular and purely festive. But on another level *A Midsummer Night's Dream* offers a comment on the imagination as searching as any Chaucer made, though one that is probably more affirmative.

At first glance, of course, Shakespeare's reading of the imagination seems quite sceptical. Both in medieval faculty psychology, and in Renaissance texts, imagination could be a source of error and illusion,[47] as it certainly is in the play, where a squirt of pansy juice signals 'change partners', and 'Titania waked and straightway loved an ass' (III. ii. 34). Even the immortals lack full control over the vagaries of imagination: Puck mistakes Lysander for 'disdainful' Demetrius (II. i. 261). Rather than moving progressively towards enlightenment, as the high medieval dream vision would have done, this forest world is plunged into confusion at the centre of the play and, finally, the participants in the amorous chase collapse in exhaustion on a stage one imagines as darkened, an action which signifies both literal and metaphorical blindness. With a demon in control of their senses, they can do no more.

But their wild and creative imaginations make them more than passive victims; the dream-world of the play shows imagination's hilarious and terrifying capacity actually to realize its excesses, as we find in Bottom's literal metamorphosis. An ass of sorts in his imagination, he becomes one in fact, although Titania's imagination in turn reinterprets lovingly what she sees. Such metamorphoses were a frequent topic in Renaissance discussions of the power of the imagination. Montaigne, for example, describes a king of Italy 'who because the day before he had with earnest affection, assisted and beene attentive at a bul-baiting, and having all night dreamed of hornes in his head, by the very force of imagination brought them forth the next morning in his forehead'.[48] This passage is interesting partly because of its connection with the dreaming imagination, although it is unlikely that Shakespeare could have seen it

---

[47] W. Rossky, 'Imagination in the English Renaissance', *SR* 5 (1958), 49–73.
[48] Michel de Montaigne, *The Essayes of Michael Lord of Montaigne Translated into English by John Florio*, 3 vols. (London, 1928), bk. I, ch. 20 (vol. i, p. 93). For a discussion of the sceptical affinity between Montaigne and Shakespeare, which entertains the possibility that Shakespeare may have known Florio's translation of the *Essays* in draft before their publication in 1603, see T. Anzai, *Shakespeare and Montaigne Reconsidered*, Renaissance Monographs 12 (Tokyo, 1986).

unless in a very early draft of Florio's 1603 translation. But Montaigne's tongue, of course, is in his cheek—and he no more believed in such transformations than did another source that Shakespeare certainly used, Reginald Scot, who describes several 'fantasticall'[49] illusions that resemble Bottom's transfiguration—for example, anointments that lead to beasts' heads on human bodies, and the case of a man so worked upon that he appears to bystanders to have the head of an ass.[50] In these instances, as Holland observes, 'Scot's emphasis is on a seeming transformation, not an actual one, placing the metamorphosis in the spectator's vision, not in an empirical reality'.[51] Interestingly, only a few pages before describing the bewitched man, Scot has been discussing claims for the incubus, that lecherous body that plagues sleepers, another illusion he ascribes to 'phantasie and vaine imagination'.[52] The conclusion of his book on the incubus consists of sixteen lines from the beginning of Chaucer's Wife of Bath's Tale, where the medieval poet 'smelt out' the popish 'absurdities' of the incubus and 'derided' them.[53] In this context, Chaucer's scepticism is seen as a breath of fresh air.

Indeed, both Shakespeare and Chaucer are sceptics of a similar cast and mind—clear-sighted unmaskers of hypocrisy, disinclined to entertain exaggerated claims of transcendence, alert to the deceptions humans practise upon themselves and others. They know that reason can take a person so far and no further into the labyrinth, but not out of it. His sense of the limitations of reason is what marks Chaucer as a late medieval, Catholic poet, a 'skeptical fideist' as Delany calls him,[54] a nominalist who must turn, finally, to faith and theology for a solution to those problems he cannot untangle himself. Shakespeare, in contrast, moves past the limits of reason; he makes his scepticism finally an opening for the possibility of belief, and belief that finds its ground within, rather than outside, itself. A radical or Pyrrhonist sceptic rather than a dogmatic or Academic one, Shakespeare weighs, as Bradshaw puts it, 'the human need to affirm values against the inherently problematic nature of all acts of valuing'—and human need emerges, if not

---

[49] R. Scot, The Discoverie of Witchcraft (London [1584]), introd. M. Summers ([London], 1930), 5. 3 (p. 55).

[50] Ibid. 13. 19 (pp. 178–9), and 5. 3 (pp. 54–5).

[51] Holland, introduction, p. 74. See also Holland's discussion of Scott and Montaigne in Ch. 5 below.

[52] Scot, Discoverie of Witchcraft, 4. 9 (p. 48).

[53] Ibid. 4. 12 (p. 50).   [54] Delany, Chaucer's House of Fame.

triumphant, at least fighting for the upper hand.[55] Theseus' oft-quoted denunciation of imagination—'The lunatic, the lover, and the poet | Are of imagination all compact' (V. i. 7–8)—is undercut by Hippolyta's even more sceptical critique, by its own sheer lyricism, by the genuinely transformative power of love in this play, and by its source: a cipher, a wizard, a lover himself at his own wedding. We also feel the presence of the poet behind the hero, the one whose imagination has spun this entire play out of 'airy nothing'. Shakespeare propitiates the gods of love and poetry who had punished Chaucer's 'translaciouns', and offers in their place those wonderful vindications of the imagination, the 'translations' of *A Midsummer Night's Dream*, not the least of which is the 'translation' of Chaucer himself. As Quince notes sagely, 'Bless thee, Bottom, bless thee. Thou art translated' (III. i. 112).

[55] G. Bradshaw, *Shakespeare's Scepticism* (1987; repr. Ithaca, NY, 1990), 39. Although his interest is not in scepticism as an intellectual or historical movement, the distinction between radical and dogmatic scepticism, which underlies Bradshaw's study, corresponds roughly to the distinction between Pyrrhonist and Academic scepticism, as explained, for example, in R. H. Popkin, *The History of Scepticism from Erasmus to Descartes*, rev. edn. (Assen, 1964): the radical or Pyrrhonic sceptic doubts even his own scepticism, while the dogmatic or Academic sceptic installs scepticism as a system with its own truth-claims. See also R. B. Pierce's analysis of Shakespeare's Pyrrhonic scepticism in 'Shakespeare and the Ten Modes of Scepticism', *SS* 46 (1994), 145–58.

5. 'The Interpretation of Dreams' in the Renaissance

PETER HOLLAND

In 1929 Maxime Leroy asked Freud to comment on a series of dreams experienced by Descartes on the night of 10–11 November 1619. The three dreams of that night mark a crucial stage in the intellectual life of the young Descartes: their impact on his commitment to research, and on his movement towards formulating the *cogito*, is fully emphasized by Descartes himself. Freud's response to Leroy's invitation was initially hesitant, 'since working on dreams without being able to obtain from the dreamer himself any indications on the relations which might link them to one another or attach them to the external world . . . gives, as a general rule, only a meagre result'.[1] But Freud nonetheless offered a brief response:

Our philosopher's dreams are what are known as 'dreams from above' ('*Träume von oben*'). That is to say, they are formulations of ideas which could have been created just as well in a waking state as during the state of sleep, and which have derived their content only in certain parts from mental states at a comparatively deep level . . .

The analysis of dreams of this kind usually leads us to the following position: we cannot understand the dream, but the dreamer—or the patient—can translate it immediately and without difficulty, given that the content of the dream is very close to his conscious thoughts. (203)

This leaves, for Freud, only a small part of the dream material in need of further analysis. Although he rejects Descartes's own explanation of the most enigmatic moment in the account of the dreams, the strange present made to the dreamer in the first dream of 'a melon which someone had brought him from some foreign country',[2] Freud is frustrated in his

---

[1] S. Freud, 'Some Dreams of Descartes', in Freud, *The Standard Edition of the Complete Psychological Works*, ed. J. Strachey, vol. xxi (London, 1961), 203; page references in the text are to this edition.

[2] Descartes recorded the dreams and his analysis of them in an important manuscript known as the 'Olympica', now lost. The material is known through a paraphrase in

analysis both by his own rules for dream interpretation and by the limitations of historical analysis: 'The philosopher interprets them for himself and, in accordance with all the rules for the interpretation of dreams, we must accept his explanation, but it should be added that we have no path open to us which will take us any further' (204). Freud's definition of Descartes's dreams as 'dreams from above' is precisely the conditioning factor for leaving most of the analysis to the dreamer and Freud strongly emphasizes that the term 'must be understood in a psychological, not in a mystical, sense' (203). Descartes himself is not in any way reluctant to analyse the dream, yet he understands it as being 'from above' in exactly the contrary sense to Freud's. The account of the dreams in Baillet is introduced as 'three consecutive dreams in a single night which he thought to himself could only have come from above [*d'enhaut*]' (181).

Clearly sensing his life was at a crossroads, exhausted and excited by his research, Descartes was both ready for a revelation and expecting one: '[his research] tired him out to such a degree that his brain was fired up and he fell into a kind of enthusiasm which put his already battered spirit into the right frame so that he was in a state to receive the impressions of dreams and visions' (181). But the distinction between dreams and visions, fundamental to Macrobian dream theory, is already present within the dream account itself. Descartes analyses while asleep: during the third dream, according to Baillet, 'what is singular to note is that, wondering whether what he had seen was dream or vision, not only did he decide, while sleeping, that it was a dream [*songe*], but he made this interpretation even before sleep left him' (184). This definition of the experience as 'songe' makes it into a Macrobian *somnium*, a prophetic dream. Browne, in a fine account of the dreams, suggests, fairly cynically, that

In a state of uncertainty he went to bed expecting a dream-revelation strongly enough for Macrobian technical terms to find their way into his dream; he needed a dream which could be interpreted to show that he was on the right path in life, something as all-embracing as a prophet's call, and given this situation almost any dream would have served his purpose.[3]

French by the Abbé Baillet used for his *La Vie de Monsieur Des-Cartes* (1691). The relevant sections are reprinted in Descartes, *Oeuvres*, ed. C. Adam and P. Tannery, vol. x (Paris, 1966), 180–8 (here 181): page references in the text are to this edition. The translations are my own.

[3] A. Browne, 'Descartes's Dreams', *JWCI* 40 (1977), 256–73: 270–1. For very different analyses see G. Sebba, *The Dream of Descartes*, ed. R. A. Watson (Carbondale, Ill., 1987);

Baillet is careful to show that, even though the dreams were on the evening of the feast of St Martin, when 'it is the custom to go on a spree in the place where he was . . . he assures us that he had passed the evening and all the day before in great sobriety and that he had not drunk wine for the whole of the previous three months' (186). Convinced of its divine source, Descartes placed great weight on his state of enthusiasm, 'l'enthousiasme', a condition of spiritual excitement: 'he adds that the Spirit [*le Génie*] which excited in him the enthusiasm with which for some days he had felt his brain heated had predicted these dreams to him before he went to bed and that the human soul [*l'esprit humain*] had no part in it' (186). Given this state of expectation, it is hardly surprising that the dreams should so explicitly focus on choice, and that he should find himself in one of them looking at an idyll by Ausonius beginning 'Which journey of life shall I follow?' (183: 'Quod vitae sectabor iter?').

Descartes's response to his own sense of the revelatory nature of the dreams of this night was profoundly affected by his firm belief in their non-human agency. The elimination of the possibility of the effects of alcohol or a heavy meal—recurrent sources, according to most medieval and Renaissance dream theory, of powerful dreams as the fumes from the stomach head up towards the brain—left only divine revelation. Descartes turned immediately to God 'to pray him to make known his will' and to the Virgin Mary 'to dedicate to her this event which he judged to be the most important of his whole life' and 'in order to try to interest [her] in the matter with some urgency, he took the opportunity of a trip he was thinking of making to Italy in a few days' time to make a vow of a pilgrimage to Our Lady at Loretto' (187).

My interest in Descartes's dreams has nothing to do with the specific details of their content, with the strengths and weaknesses of Descartes's own analysis of their meaning and implications, or with the analyses of subsequent commentators. I am concerned instead with the framework within which Descartes's analysis took place. For there seems something pleasingly paradoxical in the way that these dreams, enabling causes for the development of an ontological epistemology based on rationality, on the process of thought itself, are defined by the dreamer through their non-human agency. The act of thinking about these dreams does not lead Descartes to a reliance on his own subjectivity as the source of thinking, but instead to a belief in the dreams'

F. Hallyn, 'Les Songes du jeune Descartes', in F. Charpentier (ed.), *Le Songe à la Renaissance* (Saint-Etienne, 1987), 41–51.

externality, their dissociation from his thought. The context for the experience of the dreams—Descartes's indecision about his career—is defined by Descartes most explicitly as a form of heightened spiritual readiness, the sensitivity of enthusiasm, within which the receptivity of the brain to divine revelation is most discriminatingly attuned.

Descartes's dreams, a vital step in his own life and hence in the history of Western philosophy, are caught up in the tension between human and non-human agency central to dream analysis in classical and post-classical writing on the subject. The study of dreams had one other crucial function: they were held to be a major aid to diagnosis for doctors. Most dreams are classified as natural dreams, a product of the individual's balance or complexion of humours. As Camden summarizes the traditional view,

The choleric man dreams of wars, fire, or debates; the phlegmatic man dreams of waters, drownings, and storms; the sanguine man dreams of love and happy things; the melancholic man dreams of death, dangers, and fears. It is very necessary for the physician to be familiar with these facts so that he may be able to know the complexion and constitution of his sick patient, for no man can minister to physical ills unless he knows the dominant humor of his patient.[4]

As Thomas Wright argued, 'we proove in dreames, and Phisitians prognosticate by them, what humour aboundeth'.[5] The view was still standard at the end of the seventeenth century: Thomas Tryon, a 'student in Physick', had no doubt that one of the major uses for dreams was that 'the secret Diseases of persons are as soon, or better found out by their *Dreams*, than by any outward signs'.[6]

Yet the medical diagnostic function, while widely explored in the full range of medical writing in the Renaissance, was less problematic than the sustained negotiation for each dreamer and each dream theorist with the complex of thinking surrounding the possible prophetic purpose and non-human agency of dreams. It is with the range of formulations of that problem—with the variety of intellectual and religious traditions as they interacted with the dreams and dream analysis of people placed in different contexts in the period—that I shall be concerned.

In a rhetorical flourish at the end of a chapter examining dream theory across what he dubs 'the superstitious centuries', MacKenzie argued that 'Almost 1500 years separate Goethe from St. Augustine—a

⁴ C. Camden, 'Shakespeare on Sleep and Dreams', *RIP* 23 (1936), 123–4.
⁵ T. Wright, *The Passions of the Minde in Generall* (London, 1621), 65.
⁶ T. Tryon, *A Treatise of Dreams & Visions*, 2nd edn. (London [1700]), 6.

millennium and a half in which no really important new ideas about the dream entered European thought; a period in which, according to experience, education, and religion, men largely repeated the insights or prejudices of much earlier writers.[7] He is largely right. Although I shall be suggesting some moments at which new ideas entered the stream of dream theory, there is nothing radical in the reappraisals accomplished. Different parts of the tradition are re-examined, re-emphasized and, gently, revised. But the sort of shock to the system administered by Freud in *The Interpretation of Dreams* (1900) has no precedent in the Renaissance.

None the less, the relationship of Freud to his tradition is precisely analogous to the relationships which Renaissance interpretations of dreams sought to make and, indeed, were required to make with the traditions as perceived and understood. The title of Freud's work already establishes its connection with the past, with the long perspective of the tradition: *Die Traumdeutung*, as Pontalis remarks, 'already links, indeed irrevocably unites, the dream and its interpretation'.[8] But *Die Traumdeutung*, *The Interpretation of Dreams*, is also the appropriate and accurate translation for the title of the *Oneirocritica* of Artemidorus of Daldis.[9] The first published translation of Artemidorus into English, almost certainly by Robin Wood, moves a little further away from its original in calling itself *The Judgement or Exposition of Dreames* (1606)—though the relationship between 'interpretation' and 'judgement' or 'exposition' is an intriguing one—but Thomas Hill's book, the crucial English Renaissance text on the topic, elaborates the core terms only slightly in being named *The moste pleasaunte Arte of the Interpretacion of Dreames*.[10]

For Pontalis, Freud's work is itself a rearticulation of a crucial balance

---

[7] N. MacKenzie, *Dreams and Dreaming* (London, 1965), 83.

[8] J.-B. Pontalis, 'Dream as an Object', in S. Flanders (ed.), *The Dream Discourse Today*, New Library of Psychoanalysis 17 (London, 1993), 108.

[9] See e.g. the translation of Artemidorus by R. J. White as *The Interpretation of Dreams: Oneirocritica* (Pack Ridge, NJ, 1975).

[10] The date of first publication of Hill's book is problematic and worth setting out here. The earliest complete copies are dated 1576 (*STC* 13498) but it may well have existed earlier. A title-page for a 1571 edition is in the Huntington Library (*STC* 13497.5), but it would be rash to assume from it that the rest of the volume was printed. Reginald Scot refers to Hill's book as having been published in 1568 (*The Discovery of Witchcraft* [1584], 180). Thomas Marsh, the printer of the 1571 and 1576 editions, entered in the Stationers' Register in 1558–9 a book of 'sertayne Dreames made by Artemedorus' (see E. Arber, *A Transcript of the Registers of the Company of Stationers of London 1554–1640 A.D.*, vol. i (London, 1875), 33) which may have been an earlier version of Hill's work. William Copland entered in the Register 'a breaf and pleasaunte trestese of the Interpretation of Dreames' (Arber, *Transcript*, 154) which probably corresponds to

in dream analysis between meaning and experience: 'Freud, at the same time as he totally revises it, places himself in the tradition of the various seers, secular and religious, where the dream is consecrated to its meaning, thus to some extent neglecting the dream as *experience*.'[11] But that balance is sustainedly and intensely investigated in most traditional thinking. The validity and value of the meaning of a dream, its status as *somnium* or *insomnium*, as divine or natural, are precisely dependent on the nature of the dream as experience as well as on whether there is any eventuating proof. The traditional forms of dream classification are always circumscribed by their mode of connection to the particularity of a dreamer's experience, and only from that combination can the interpretation be matched to the listings available in Artemidorus, the *Somniale Danielis*, or the other manuals of interpretation.[12]

The circumstances of Descartes's dreams, his own sense of the context within which the dream vision occurred, led him to an unequivocal assessment of the dreams as a divinely visited religious experience. Although nothing in the content of the dreams necessarily signalled their divine origin—there were, as it were, no angels present—his response in committing himself to the pilgrimage to Loretto amply attests to his understanding of the night's dreams, placing them firmly within the conventional band of divine dreams.

But Descartes's experience was, as he himself certainly realized and accepted, quite exceptional. Others took a much more limited view of the source of dreams. A quatrain by Abraham Fleming was included by Reginald Scot in his blast against dream-divining in *The Discoverie of Witchcraft* (1584):

> Regard no dreames, for why the mind
> Of that in sleepe a view dooth take,
> Which it dooth wish and hope to find,
> At such time as it is awake.[13]

another work usually ascribed to Hill (*STC* 13498.5), the only surviving copy of which, printed by Copland, has a title-page supplied describing it as 'A little treatise of the interpretation of dreams' (1566–7).

[11] Pontalis, 'Dream as an Object', 108.

[12] For an interesting comparison of three dream-classification systems (in ancient Mesopotamia, Artemidorus, and modern Morocco) see B. Kilborne, 'On Classifying Dreams', in Tedlock (ed.), *Dreaming*, 171–93; see also B. Mannheim's study of the consistencies and shifts in the cultural understanding of the meaning of dreams in the Quechua communities of the southern Andes from 1631 to the 1970s, 'A Semiotic of Andean Dreams', in Tedlock (ed.), *Dreaming*, 132–53.

[13] Professor John Burrow has kindly pointed out to me that Fleming's quatrain 'is a translation of the 31st distich in the second book of the *Disticha Catonis*, the widely-used

Scot himself, while accepting that in the past God used to make revelations to his prophets in dreams, is now unwilling to believe that there is any such form of divine revelation in dream visions: dreams 'are the inward actions of the mind in the spirits of the braine, whilest the bodie is occupied with sleepe',[14] and the very idea that dreams could still be revelatory is for Scot almost blasphemous, for 'if we expect revelations in our dreames, now, when Christ is come, we shall deceive our selves: for in him are fulfilled all dreames and prophesies'.[15] Scot's greatest venom, even beyond the stupidity of those who trust their dreams, is reserved for those who set themselves up as analysts:

And as for dreames, whatsoever credit is attributed unto them, proceedeth of follie: and they are fooles that trust in them, for whie they have deceived many . . . and therefore those witches, that make men beleeve they can prophesie upon dreames, as knowing the interpretation of them, and either for monie or glorie abuse men & women therby, are meere couseners, and worthie of great punishment.[16]

Scot is perfectly well versed in the traditional classical texts on dream analysis—Plato and Macrobius, Avicenna and Aristotle, Averroes and Cicero—but the last authority, in particular, 'confuteth the vanitie and follie of them that give credit to dreames'.[17] What is more, the dream interpreters are practitioners of a distinctly inexact science: 'as they knowe not before the dreame, nor yet after, any certeintie; yet when any thing afterwards happeneth, then they applie the dreame to that which hath chanced'.[18]

Descartes's response to his dream is essentially self-reliant. He turns to God and the Virgin Mary for reassurance about the implications of the dream, and makes no attempt to consult a dream diviner. While so much Renaissance thinking and so many of the period's habits of mind are deeply distrustful of dreams, they are even more strenuously dubious about the likelihood of a dream analyst being able to assist. Dreams may be troubling, but for the most part it was thought better to wrestle with their meaning oneself.

Yet the temptation to record and analyse or at least be aware of one's dreams is extremely strong. Archbishop Laud, for instance, who in Scot's terms might reasonably have been expected to have known

medieval schoolbook. The edition by Otto Arntzenius, *Dionysii Catonis Disticha* (Amsterdam, 1754), has rich annotation on pp. 200–3, quoting the distich.' See Scot, *Discoverie of Witchcraft*, 10. 2 (p. 102).

[14] Ibid., p. 101.   [15] Ibid. 10. 10 (p. 107).   [16] Ibid. 10. 1 (p. 101).
[17] Ibid. 10. 4 (p. 102).   [18] Ibid.

better, recorded a considerable number of dreams in his diary, with the account of the dream often being the only entry for particular days. The act of recording the dream seems in itself to be sufficient, whether the dream is troubling (like the dream of 14 December 1623 'that the Lord Keeper was dead . . . This dream did trouble me')[19] or a solace ('Sunday night, my dream of my Bl. Lord and Saviour Jesus Christ. One of the most comfortable passages that ever I had in my life').[20] Even when a dream prediction comes true it is not something that fills Laud with anything more than suspicion: 'Wednesday night, Towards the morning, I dreamed, that L. M. St. came to me the next day, and showed me all the kindness I could ask. And that Thursday he did come, and was very kind towards me. *Somniis tamen haud multum fido.*'[21]

Laud, more distrustful of dreams than Descartes, still dutifully records them. But Montaigne, whose alignment with Descartes must be a central part of any project of redefining the originality of Renaissance thought, claimed to have had few dreams to record. Montaigne is, characteristically, both forthright in his statements and a dancer as he allows them to perform, complicating the notion of dream until it comes to occupy a central space of delicious imprecision: 'Our waking sleeps more than our sleeping; our wisdom is less wise than our folly; our dreams are worth more than our discourse; and to remain inside ourselves is to adopt the worst place of all.'[22] This suggests a delight in the world of dreams or, at least, the necessity of sustained consideration of this area, ambiguously within and without the self, a part of experience to which he appears here to be according high value.

Montaigne is predictably mocking about the usefulness of dreams for predictions: 'I would rather order my affairs by casting dice, by lots than by [dreams].'[23] But it is much more surprising that, though he often writes of the significance of dreams, he seems to identify them as the kind of event that mostly happens to others, as if they are alien to Montaigne's project of writing his self: 'I do not dream much: when I do

[19] W. Laud, *The Works*, ed. W. Scott and J. Bliss, 7 vols. (Oxford, 1847–60), iii. 144.

[20] Ibid. 157, 30 Jan. 1625.

[21] 'However I don't put much trust in dreams': ibid. 227, 4 Aug. 1636.

[22] Michel de Montaigne, 'An Apology for Raymond Sebond', in *The Essays*, trans. and ed. M. A. Screech (London, 1991), 640. On Montaigne and dreams, see also G. Mathieu-Castellani, 'Veiller en dormant, dormir en veillant: Le Songe dans les Essais', in Charpentier (ed.), *Le Songe à la Renaissance*, 231–8.

[23] 'Dreams' is my own translation. Screech translates 'que par les songes' unnecessarily freely as 'than by such fanciful nonsense' ('On Prognostications', in *Essays*, 44); Florio offers 'than by such frivolous dreames' (*Essayes*, i. 55).

it is of grotesque things and of chimeras usually produced by pleasant thoughts, more laughable than sad.'[24] Dream becomes for Montaigne more conceptual than experiential, available primarily as a metaphor for a form of definition of existence rather than constituting an area of experience that needs documenting and analysing. Throughout the *Essays*, in the course of the immense act of recording and interpreting his thoughts and his sense of his own existence, he displays no strong interest in recording and interpreting his dreams.

Unlike so much else about himself, dreams seem to Montaigne to be unsurprising and therefore effectively uninteresting. The labour of dream interpretation might seem to be necessary since 'I maintain that dreams are loyal interpreters of our inclinations', especially, given Montaigne's reluctance to take easy options in such analysis, since 'there is skill in classifying them and understanding them'.[25] But the quotation that follows this statement, beautifully caught in Florio's translation, suggests that the act of interpreting dreams could be seen as unnecessary, a deviation and useless appendix to the crucial exercise of analysing the waking self:

> It is no wonder if the things, which we
> Care-for, use, thinke, doe-oft, or waking see,
> Unto us sleeping represented be.[26]

Precisely because dreams are, for Montaigne, unquestionably human, because they are nothing more than a transfer and reformulation of the day-residue, they do not warrant further investigation. The act of analysing the waking self is sufficient to account for the material of dreams, indeed more than sufficient, since the analysis of the waking self is the aim of the project and dream analysis would not necessarily be a helpful guide to the larger goal.

Montaigne is content to note that Plato, Socrates, Xenophon, and Aristotle are prepared to argue that it is 'the office of wisedome to draw divining instructions from them [dreams], against future times', but he seems far more intrigued by the connection between dreams and diet, moving elegantly from the historical record to applying the advice of Pythagoras to his own situation:

The history books tell us that the Atlantes never dream; they add that they never eat anything which has been slaughtered, a fact which I mention because

---

[24] Montaigne, 'On Experience', *Essays*, trans. Screech, 1247.
[25] Ibid.   [26] Montaigne, *Essayes*, trans. Florio, iii. 364.

it may explain why they do not dream, since Pythagoras prescribed a certain preparatory diet designed to encourage dreams. My dreams are weak things: they occasion no twitching of the body, no talking in my sleep.[27]

He immediately follows this not with a sustained discussion of his dreams but by a disquisition on what he eats and why. The particularity of dreams and of his dreaming is a fact only worth passing notice before he moves on to the intricacies of his menus. Dreams do not delay or interest Montaigne precisely because their causation is known or at least knowable and because that suggests that their content can be recuperated through the sustained analysis of the waking self, the self in the fullest state of dreaming that waking life constitutes.

Dreams could, of course, be used as a literary format, a structure for argument and a framework for the presentation of complex ideas. The astronomer Johannes Kepler, for example, embodied his most searching thoughts on the moon in a dream form. Kepler's *Dream or Lunar Astronomy*, written in 1609 but not printed until 1634, exemplifies this transposition of the tradition of dream writing into the most advanced areas of Renaissance scientific exploration. The examination of the moon's geography, a combination of observation and hypothetical extrapolation, could not easily have been presented in the conventional forms of Renaissance prose. Instead, as the most recent editor of Kepler's *Dream* suggests, Kepler 'devised this *Dream* framework in order to introduce a supernatural agency for the purpose of transporting a professional astronomical observer to the moon'.[28]

But the intellectual study of dreams themselves, as opposed to the utilization of dream as a structure for the communication of other research, was likely to run into problems because of constrictions in the structures of Renaissance academic enquiry. In March 1520 Juan Luis Vives was at Louvain and wanted to lecture on Cicero's *Somnium Scipionis*, offering a new, post-Macrobian, commentary on it. But Vives' request for official permission for the lecture met a difficulty. As he wrote jokingly to a friend,

As soon as the rector and certain other deputies heard 'dream,' they burst into laughter. I think this was because when they heard a reference to dreaming, that beloved pastime in which they take such delight, a rush of hilarity overcame them. They then directed me to take the matter before the faculty that had the proper charge over the volume to be lectured upon. Yesterday, when the high

[27]   Montaigne, 'On Experience', trans. and ed. Screech, 1247.
[28]   Kepler, '*Somnium*', ed. E. Rosen (Madison, Wis., 1967), p. xix.

and mighty Senate was in session, it referred to the Fathers the new issue concerning the faculty of Dreams. That day was dragged out in opinions and quarrels, and many more will be eaten up over the question what faculty is it to which dreams belong.[29]

Vives' attempt to produce a revisionary account of dreams through constructing a new commentary on Cicero, his *Somnium et vigilia in Somnium Scipionis*, was written in a combination of two conventional forms: it constitutes a commentary in the tradition of Macrobius' highly significant and influential study, but is written in the style of a Lucianic satire, 'a wild, dreamlike vision of the underworld of Dream'.[30] The satiric framework was the enabling mechanism for Vives' revision of Macrobius, a rejection of the priority which had been given to the reading of prophetic dream in the work of Artemidorus and Macrobius and their progeny in favour of a radical reappraisal of Aristotle's writings in the *Parva naturalia*. This reinvestigation of Aristotle shows Vives, as Palley comments, to be 'true to his humanist mission of returning to the sources, the Greek and Latin classics, rather than their medieval interpretations and misinterpretations'.[31] Where most dream analysis was emphatically concerned with the unusual and exceptional prophetic dream, Macrobius' *somnium*, Vives allowed unusual weight to the advantages of ordinary dreams as wish-fulfilment, those dreams 'whose function consists specifically in introducing in the spirit of man false joys, false sadness, those same things which one desires or fears during wakefulness, imagining that they are fulfilled at the time of sleep'.[32]

Though he does not explore it in his commentary on the *Somnium Scipionis*, Vives even, remarkably, identifies and is intrigued by the phenomenon of the 'lucid dream', the dream in which the dreamer is aware of dreaming and, while asleep, analyses the dream experience. Some Renaissance dreamers record this type of dream event. Descartes's third dream is clearly of this kind, an analysis of a dream in the course of sleep. Laud, too, had a dream on 8 March 1626, in which 'I was reconciled to the Church of Rome. This troubled me much; and I wondered

---

[29] J. L. Vives, *Somnium et vigilia in Somnium Scipionis*, ed. E. V. George (Greenwood, SC, 1989), p. xxxviii.

[30] J. Palley, *The Ambiguous Mirror: Dreams in Spanish Literature* (Valencia, 1983), 68. On Vives' *Somnium et vigilia* see also D. Baker-Smith, 'Juan Vives and the *Somnium Scipionis*', in R. R. Bolgar (ed.), *Classical Influences on European Culture A.D. 1500–1700* (Cambridge, 1976), 239–44; J.-C. Margolin, 'Vives, lecteur et critique de Platon et d'Aristote', ibid. 245–58.

[31] Palley, *Ambiguous Mirror*, 68.   [32] Ibid.

exceedingly, how it should happen . . . And while I wearied myself with these troublesome thoughts, I awoke. Herein I felt such strong impressions, that I could scarce believe it to be a dream.'[33] Vives, almost alone, adds this kind of dream to his theorizing of dream analysis in his account of dreams in *De anima* (1538): 'at times the dream turns back on itself . . . and we believe that we are dreaming or that we are not dreaming; this phenomenon is produced in agreeable dreams, in which we fear the image may result in a vain phantom, or in very sad ones, in which we desire that all may be false'.[34]

Vives' frame in his commentary on the *Somnium Scipionis* is satiric, in part as a self-defensive measure. The first half of the title of his work, *Somnium et vigilia*, is an attempt to balance the contradictory responses the study itself was likely to produce:

I have not searched out titles for their sublimity or their extravagant promises. 'Dream': what label could be found more insignificant, more lowly? One might have said 'Trivia'. Nor do I wish what I say in the piece to be valued at any more than that, in case anyone is likely to get offended. 'Vigil' . . . Vigils were indeed needed in the explication of the Ciceronian Dream, which owing to its rich and varied wisdom demands a vigilant, truly sober interpreter and diviner.[35]

Vives' witty 'Dream', a dream on a dream, needs protecting if its essential seriousness is to stand any chance of being perceived. Hamstrung by the impossibility of accommodating dreams into Renaissance systems of thought, Vives chooses the mocking meta-dream metaphor as a means of letting the ideas flourish imaginatively, circumventing the parameters of traditional thought by the literary and creative style of his exposition.

Vives' dream fantasia is, at the same time, a demand for a revaluation of Aristotelian scepticism about dreams, of the suspicious unwillingness of Aristotle to accept divine causation for any dreams. Aristotle's three essays on dreams in the *Parva naturalia*, 'On Sleep and Waking', 'On Dreams', and 'On Prophecy in Sleep', consistently hesitate over finding in the connection between dreams and subsequent events anything more than coincidence. As he argues in the last of the three, 'it is absurd to hold that it is God who sends out such dreams, yet that He sends them not to the best and wisest, but to any chance persons. But if we dismiss the theory of causation by God, none of the other causes seems

---

[33] Laud, *Works*, ed. Scott and Bliss, iii. 201–2.
[34] Quoted in Palley, *Ambiguous* Mirror, 70.
[35] Vives, 'Prefatory Epistle' to *Somnium et vigilia*, ed. George, 5.

probable.'[36] But the traditions of oneiromancy, the fulfilment of the understandable human need to find value in dreams and to have dreams interpreted as divine, had led to an undervaluing of Aristotle's argument. Vives attempts to redress the balance. In the debate on dreams in the senate of the realm of sleep, Vives ably marshals the arguments for the validity of dreams before rapidly demolishing these claims through the final and triumphant interventions of Aristotle and Carneades.[37]

Vives' structure imposes on him an acceptance of resolution as the contradictory voices of the dream debate are effectively silenced by the sceptical arguments of the last speakers. In a different rhetorical structure the multivocality of thinking about dreams can more comfortably coexist. Jean Bodin's *Colloquium of the Seven about Secrets of the Sublime*, completed in 1586, allows a number of the speakers to offer their consideration of dreams. Senamus, the voice of scepticism, warns against overvaluing dreams: 'If true dreams of present and future occurrences are called prophecies, there will be innumerable prophets. Has not everyone learned something true in a dream or nocturnal vision which he could not have known otherwise?' His doubts about the inflationary increase in prophets through the validation of dream experiences is echoed by the Lutheran speaker, Fridertius: 'If we reduce the apex of our religion and salvation to idle dreams, religions are done for.'[38]

But the most unusual of Bodin's other voices is Salomon, who represents Judaism, a religious and ethical position hardly ever included in contemporary discussion, least of all with the sympathy and understanding that Bodin displays. Salomon consistently argues for the significance of dreams and is prepared to annex for the realm of dreams a number of visions that are conventionally excluded from it. Believing that 'God surely spoke to no one when he was awake except Moses', Salomon claims that 'we should understand that the voice of the angel who spoke to Balaam or the voice of the ass came to him in a dream, as we should interpret all the foreknowledge given to Abraham and the prophets'.[39]

Bodin's Salomon is not prepared to find all dreams necessarily significant, any more than was customary in classical or Christian dream

[36] Aristotle, *Parva naturalia*, ed. and trans. W. S. Hett, 375.
[37] Vives, *Somnium et vigilia*, ed. George, 29–31.
[38] J. Bodin, *Colloquium of the Seven about Secrets of the Sublime*, ed. M. Leathers and D. Kuntz (Princeton, 1975), 181–2.
[39] Ibid. 99.

interpretation. But after enumerating the conventional criteria for exclusion he still finds a residual possibility of prophetic and divine dreams:

Certain dreams are true, yet many are false such as those which result from a soul upset with cares. Dreams follow worry, according to a wise teacher, and when there are many dreams, there are many deceptions. Dreams often come after a heavy meal. Yet when a sober man whose soul is free from baseness, lust, idle cares, and greed sleeps soberly he often has true dreams and excellent visions . . . [40]

Bodin's Salomon is not simply a rhetorical construct, a device for creating an alternative voice in the *Colloquium*. The autobiographical writings of Leon Modena, a rabbi in Venice in the seventeenth century, show that dream interpretation and dream divination were regular parts of his activities. Dream divination appears not to have been in any way incompatible with his work as a rabbi; indeed, his work as a preacher and teacher was intimately bound up with his dream analyses or his selling of amulets to protect households against the outbreaks of plague in 1630 and 1631, amulets containing a prayer 'based on a divine name, which he said he had learned in a dream in which he had seen prophets' and which were claimed to be entirely efficacious.[41]

Rabbi Modena saw dream divination as part of his religious activity, using, as preparation for the activity, a prayer he had written especially for such occasions.[42] He also used it for his own needs. At the point at which he records that his mother is trying to persuade him to marry his cousin Esther, Rabbi Modena notes that he had, some time earlier, 'engaged in dream divination, using prayer without conjuration, in order to see the woman intended as my mate'. In the dream an old man showed him a portrait covered by a veil, and 'when he drew aside the veil I saw a portrait of my cousin Esther, as well as the color of her garment'. Though he reported this dream to his parents, 'they did not believe it'. But when the marriage agreement with Esther was completed, Rabbi Modena notes that 'I pointed out to my mother that she [Esther] was wearing clothes of the same color and ornamentation that I had described more than a year previously when I had seen her in my dream.'[43]

---

[40] Bodin, *Colloquium*, ed. Leathers and Kuntz, 181–2.
[41] H. E. Adelman, 'Leon Modena: The Autobiography and the Man', in Leon Modena, *The Autobiography of a Seventeenth-Century Venetian Rabbi: Leon Modena's 'Life of Judah'*, ed. M. R. Cohen (Princeton, 1988), 40.
[42] Ibid. 199.   [43] Ibid. 90–1.

Modena's autobiography illustrates the placing of dreams and their interpretation within a specific culture, here the community of Venetian Jews. Each culture necessarily provides an equally specific context for the cultural existence of dreams. Hence, for example, most of the essays in Charpentier's collection explore dreams in the intellectual, medical, and social culture of Renaissance France. The reconstruction of that culture and its dream theories would be possible by sustained exploration of the manuscript and printed works on dream generated in France, a bibliography the first stages of which have been excitingly established by Cooper.[44]

Work with a broader perspective on the Spanish culture within which Vives' writings take their place—as much as they do within the pan-European humanist culture of which Vives was so influential a part—is also possible through the extraordinary corpus recording over 400 of the dreams of a young Spanish woman, Lucrecia de León, between 1587 and 1590, mostly transcribed at the time by Fray Lucas de Allende and Dr Alonso de Mendoza. This important dream corpus has recently been intriguingly explored by Kagan.[45]

Lucrecia's reputation as a dreamer seems to have begun early in childhood, and she rapidly became known to her family and to the community as someone whose dreams had a prophetic tendency. The dream corpus she dictated and which eventually brought her into trouble with the Spanish Inquisition in Madrid are, for the most part, strikingly short on material derived from day-residue or autobiographical sources. They are not 'of a type that would necessarily interest a Freudian analyst . . . and do not lend themselves to psychobiographic analysis' (1–2). Instead, Lucrecia generated 'a series of dreams alleged to contain a variety of blasphemous and heretical propositions as well as seditious statements injurious to the honor and reputation of the Spanish monarch, Philip II' (1). While some of the dreams may well have been real, it seems probable that many were invented to please Mendoza, as Lucrecia responded to his questions and, presumably, was flattered by the attention her dreams were provoking.

While the substance of Lucrecia's dreams was obviously such that they were likely to create interest and bound eventually to lead to charges

---

[44] R. Cooper, 'Bibliographie sommaire d'ouvrages sur le songe publiés en France et en Italie jusqu'en 1600', in Charpentier (ed.), Songe à la Renaissance, 255–71.

[45] See R. L. Kagan, Lucrecia's Dream (Berkeley and Los Angeles, 1990). My comments on Lucrecia are entirely dependent on Kagan's fine study and all quotations are taken from it.

before the Inquisition for their explicitly political content, the context within which dreams could be explored in Catholic Spain was as a significant part of religious life. Dreams played an even more significant role than they did in the professional work of Rabbi Modena: Spanish Catholic priests were specifically 'instructed to become knowledgeable about dreams, to inquire about them in the confessional, and to be alert for dreams that might have a divine or diabolical source' (37). Priests, in fulfilling their religious obligations as codified by the Church, acted as dream interpreters in direct competition with what Kagan dubs the 'free-market dream analysts', like the community's wise women. What is extraordinary is the sheer number of people, mostly women, working as oneiromancers: according to one estimate 'Spain alone contained over ten thousand such individuals' (37). Such practices, defined as magic, were attacked by the Church and investigated by the Inquisition. Dream analysis is, then, trapped between the strong popular fascination with dreams, ably supported by the economics of the profession of oneiromancy, and the equally strong religious culture which wished their study to be placed within the bounds of the Church and hence the state. Dreams become an important locus for the battle between the community and the systems of authority to an extent unknown in, say, England in the period.

In the Inquisition's judgements in the cases of Lucrecia, Allende, Mendoza, and the others who were arrested and tried, there is an awkward balance between the competing claims of involvement in and exclusion from dream analysis. Hence, for instance, the ruling on Allende included 'a warning to avoid future encounters with dreams, prophecies, and related phenomena' (156). But Mendoza claimed obstinately that he had a 'right as a theologian to transcribe Lucrecia's dreams' (157). Pedro de Sotocameño, the Inquisition's prosecuting counsel in the case,

evidently considered Mendoza the author of Lucrecia's dreams. In his view the canon was guilty not only of various errors of faith in matters of prophecy but also of believing in dreams that were patently 'scandalous, seditious, and prejudicial to the Catholic Church and which gave rise to great dissensions and riots' and to 'libels against the ministers of the king'. (157)

If the form of Sotocameño's complaints is to be taken at face value, it is the content of Lucrecia's dreams that should have stopped Mendoza from investigating them, whereas, of course, it was precisely the content that so fascinated him. But on matters to do with errors of faith one might reasonably expect the rule of the Inquisition to be beyond question.

In less authoritarian contexts, more subtle redefinitions of the classical traditions of dream theory were possible. Girolamo Cardano (Jerome Cardan) was endlessly fascinated by his own dreams and they fill the pages of his autobiography.[46] One dream so impressed Cardano with its encouraging intimations of his own fame, a matter of considerable importance to him, that he had a medal cast bearing an image from the dream. The plan for his major study of natural philosophy, *De subtilitate rerum*, was set out for him in a recurrent dream which he understood to be a compulsion for him to complete the work.

Cardano's own study of dreams was constructed as a commentary on Synesius of Cyrene's 'On Dreams'. Though the two recent studies of Cardano's *Somniorum Synesiorum libri IIII* (Basle, 1562) finely praise it for its subtle rethinking of the Aristotelian position,[47] it seems to me most remarkable for its inclusion of a chapter devoted to a group of Cardano's own dreams. This collocation of dream theory with a dream corpus or dream diary, following the recommendation of Synesius, is extremely rare, an acceptance by the dream theorist that his/her own dreams are a part of the study, a connection between the theory and the theorist, between the analysis and the analyst as subject of analysis as a dreaming self, that is almost unprecedented. Artemidorus and his successors do not choose to write about their own dreams. The pages of the *Somniale Danielis* encode the materials of dream for interpretation but do not mention an individual dreamer. Thomas Hill, the inheritor of this tradition, lists the details of dream events so that the readers can analyse their dreams, but nothing suggests that Hill himself has ever had a dream. Yet for Cardano his awareness of himself as dreamer is integral to the possibility of the analysis of dreams.

Cardano's major theoretical contribution is in his redefinition of the source of events in dreams: the materials of 'all dreams without exception are composed of memory-images, and prophetic dreams are not direct, if distorted, reflections of future events and their causes, as they are for Aristotle and Synesius, but are composed by astral influence out of imagery already in the dreamer's mind'.[48] Cardano's elegant

---

[46] J. Cardan, *The Book of My Life*, trans. J. Stoner (New York, 1930), e.g. pp. 156–61.

[47] See A. Browne, 'Girolamo Cardano's *Somniorum Synesiorum Libri IIII*', *BHR* 41 (1979), 123–35; C. S. Rupprecht, 'Divinity, Insanity, Creativity: A Renaissance Contribution to the History and Theory of Dream/Text(s)', in id. (ed.), *The Dream and the Text* (Albany, NY, 1993), 112–32. My understanding of Cardano's work is substantially dependent on these two accounts.

[48] Browne, 'Girolamo Cardano', 127.

explanation places all dreams within the category of natural occurrences, the product of the dreamer's experience, rather than separating out the classification of dreams according to their truth or falsity or their human or non-human agency. Cardano's listing of the objects and events which are to be found in dreams, what Rupprecht calls 'a veritable encyclopedia of phenomena which appear in dreams,'[49] is more completely conditioned and circumscribed by their placing in relation to a particular dreamer than in any other major account of dream theory in the Renaissance.

By comparison, the English Renaissance attempts to provide a theory of dream seem extremely thin. Reginald Scot mocked all dream analysis but singled out Thomas Hill for particular scorn: 'And therefore in mine opinion, it is time vainelie emploied, to studie about the interpretation of dreames. He that list to see the follie and vanitie thereof, maie read a vaine treatise, set out by Thomas Hill, Londoner, 1568.'[50] Scot is unkind: Hill's *The moste pleasaunte Arte of the Interpretacion of Dreames* is the most substantial attempt in English Renaissance writing to produce an account of dream theory.

Hill read widely and used most of the standard classical authorities. What is most remarkable is his heavy reliance on Aristotle and on Averroes. Averroes' important commentary on Aristotle's *Parva naturalia* includes his reformulation of the Aristotelian theory of dream[51] but this section of Averroes' writings had rarely been used. Hill turns again and again to Averroes to define the nature of dreams, following Averroes, for instance, in his location of dreams firmly in the imagination.

Unsurprisingly, Hill finds Averroes' abstract thought extremely difficult, and at times he seems to be doing little more than regurgitating chunks of the commentary, often garbling it completely in the process. His account is unsystematic, leaping from topic to topic arbitrarily; Hill fails to find a way of setting out dream theory any more completely as a rational, organized science than his predecessors had done.

But at the heart of the book is Hill's belief in the high value that should be placed on dream interpretation as an art, a technical skill and mystery that is underrated: 'But great pitty it were that so noble a knowledge, so necessarye to all men bee troden underfote, and so lightly

---

[49] Rupprecht, 'Divinity, Insanity, Creativity', 116.

[50] Scot, *Discoverie of Witchcraft*, 180.

[51] For a modern English translation based on the Arabic original as well as the Hebrew and Latin versions see Averroes, *Epitome of 'Parva Naturalia'*, ed. H. Blumberg, Corpus Commentariorum Averrois in Aristotelem, Versio Anglica 7 (Cambridge, Mass., 1961).

estemed' (sig. A. iv^b).[52] While there may be bad dream analysts, for Hill it is they who should be attacked, and not the 'Art' itself, for 'this art of the interpretation of Dreames, doth especially consiste of wysedome, and by conjecture in that he which coniectureth cunninglye, is counted a natural Prophet' (sig. A. iii^b).

When it comes to the detail of dream phenomena, Hill's book degenerates into a series of lists culled from anything to hand. One section, for instance, is of 'Certain briefe Dreames gathered out of the Pamphlettes of the wyse Salomon holye Joseph, and Daniell the Prophet, with others newly added' (sig. N. vi^b), taken from the conventional collections of the *Somniale Danielis* or the *Sompnile Joseph*. The dreams are often introduced by phrases like 'a certayn man dreamed' or 'he that thinketh in his dreame', and the book eventually grinds to an arbitrary halt in mid-list when Hill—or the printer—appears to feel it is long enough. The whole series of lists is aggregated in such a way that it is not a usable manual for dream interpretation. As with other listings, the reader in search of illumination about a particular dream would have to read the whole work in search of anything that might help.

But Hill's understanding of the circumstances that need to be considered for interpreting dreams is broadly based. The analyst needs 'to inquire orderlye, whether the dreame appeared pleasaunt or otherwyse unpleasaunte . . . what the persone tradeth or occupyeth, & of what birth hee is & what possessions he hath & what state he is in for the healthe of bodye & of what age he is also which seeth ye dream' (sig. B. vi^a). Hill is careful to give the standard warnings about the falsity of dreams when the dreamer is affected by 'the burthen of meate or drinckes, or superfluous humors' or 'geven to any other bodelie pleasures' (sig. A. ii^b), even though he asserts, relying on Hippocrates and Galen, the usefulness of dreams to medical diagnosis so that 'the Phisitionnes by the Dreames of the sicke maye the redyar and aptlyar appoynt a perfite diet and due medecines' (sig. A. iii^a). Other determinants include the season of the year, since 'men have truer dreames in the Sommer and Wynter then in the Springe, and the Harveste' (sig. D. vii^b), or even particular days, since 'dreames happeninge on Christmas day, and on the day of the salutation of the virgin Marye, shewe marvelous matters to follow' (sig. E. ii^a).

Hill defines two pairs of causes for dreams: whether they are 'bodilye' or not and whether they are 'newe' or 'before wrought' (sig. D. vi^b). This

---

[52] References to Hill are to the 1576 edition.

gives him four kinds of dream: new and bodily (which are caused by meat and drink), precedent and bodily (caused by the imbalance of the humours), precedent and not bodily (caused by cares and worries), and, the last and crucial group, new and not bodily 'which frame the superior cause come unto the soule' (sig. D. vii^a).

For all its faults of methodology and misunderstanding, Hill's little book is a considerable achievement, an attempt to bring together the full range of dream theory. It was less influential, however, than Wood's translation of Artemidorus (from a French version of a Latin translation of the Greek) in 1606, a work frequently reprinted and reworked. By the late seventeenth century dream analysis had fragmented into a variety of separate fields that had no means of speaking to each other. Three books amply represent the field. The theological area is exemplified by Moses Amyraldus (Moise Amyraut), *A Discourse concerning the Divine Dreams mention'd in Scripture* (1676), with its strong warning that 'if the frequency of certain dreams, and their evil quality, do inform us that we are inclin'd to some vicious passions . . . we then endeavour to correct them by Christian Morality' (129–30). The second edition of Thomas Tryon's *A Treatise of Dreams and Visions* (1695), after devoting considerable space to outlining dream theory, ends with a recommendation of a vegetarian diet as the best way to have 'sublime converse' (243), a view which had been considered by Sir Thomas Browne:

There is an Art to make dreames as well as their interpretations, and physitians will tell us that some food makes turbulent, some gives quiet dreames. Cato who doated upon cabbadge might find the crude effects thereof in his sleepe . . . Pythagoras might have more calmer sleepes if hee totally abstained from beanes. Even Daniel, that great interpreter of dreames, in his leguminous dyet seems to have chosen no advantageous food for quiet sleepes according to Græcian physick.[53]

The lunatic fringe of pseudo-science with occultist overtones and bizarrely encoded diagrams can be found in Richard Saunders's *Saunders Physiognomie, and Chiromancie, Metoposcopie, with the Subject of Dreams made plain* (1671) which, in its third book, 'the physiognomie of Dreams explained' (223), defines seventy-two types of dream, of which the fifteen 'more diviner than the rest' (233) are linked to the rungs of Jacob's ladder.

---

[53] Browne, 'On Dreames', in *Works*, ed. Keynes, iii. 232.

Hill's book represents a serious attempt to return to classical authorities, to place the study of dreams on a scientific and humanist basis within the terms of English Renaissance practice. But it is Thomas Nashe's pamphlet *The Terrors of the Night* (1594) that most fully embodies the energies of English Renaissance writing, inserting dream study into the continuum of witty pamphleteering. Posing as a means of whiling away some time ('A little to beguile time idly discontented, and satisfy some of my solitary friends here in the country'),[54] Nashe's brilliant squib hides its considerable learning behind the sheer verve of its style. No account of dream as the product of day-residue has a fraction of the delight of Nashe's 'A dream is nothing else but a bubbling scum or froth of the fancy, which the day hath left undigested; or an after-feast made of the fragments of idle imagination' (153). No contempt for dream interpreters can match Nashe's for 'aged mumping beldams as they sat warming their knees over a coal' (163). No analysis of the potentially therapeutic effects of dreams and nightmares reaches for analogies like Nashe: 'There were gates in Rome out of which nothing was carried but dust, and dung, and men to execution: so, many of the gates of our senses serve for nothing but to convey out excremental vapours and affrighting deadly dreams that are worse than executioners unto us' (155). No description of the effect of the humours on the brain as a cause of dream can compete with Nashe's version:

Discontent also in dreams hath no little predominance; for even as, from water that is troubled, the mud dispersingly ascendeth from the bottom to the top, so, when our blood is chased, disquieted, and troubled, all the light, imperfect humours of our body ascend like mud up aloft into the head. The clearest spring a little touched is creased with a thousand circles: as those momentary circles, for all the world such are our dreams. (154)

If *The Terrors of the Night* represents no substantial attempt to discriminate among the competing theories, if it lacks the re-evaluation of the tradition of some of the works I have been examining, it none the less embodies the popular pleasure in talking and more particularly in writing about dreams. The enjoyment of its own act is shared with its pleasure in the bizarre realms of dream analysis; its self-mockery imitates and parallels its mockery of the quirks of those who take dreams too solemnly. Nashe's wit embraces his essential seriousness, for dreams clearly matter to him, but dreams are also a source of energy and

[54] T. Nashe, *The Terrors of the Night*, in *Selected Works*, ed. S. Wells, The Stratford-upon-Avon Library 1 (London, 1954), 146; references in the text are to this edition.

excitement, part of the fun of existence. Nashe's musings on dreams have none of the important consequences of Descartes's dream experiences. But, far more than Descartes, *The Terrors of the Night* is the quintessence of the pleasures Renaissance writers found in the interpretation of dreams, with the solemn face of the professional engaged in the quasi-scientific analysis of dream theory masked by the laughing grin of the professional writer.

6. The 'Candy-Colored Clown': Reading Early Modern Dreams

Kathleen McLuskie

I

As every devotee of Sixties retro knows, the 'candy-colored clown' is the sandman who, in Roy Orbison's song 'In Dreams', 'comes to my window every night'. He brings the dreams which compensate for romantic loss but which are sadly insubstantial:

> In dreams you're mine, all of the time,
> But it's only in dreams,
> And just about the dawn
> I awake, and find you're gone;
> I can't help it, I can't help it if I cry—
> I remember when you said goodbye.

The song gets its sentimental effect partly from the throb of the music and the powerful range of Orbison's wailing voice; it also plays on a familiar opposition between the worlds of dreams and reality which is a standard metaphor for emotional loss, the leitmotif of the genre.

Some twenty years after the success of the Roy Orbison ballad, released in 1963, it was given a new twist in David Lynch's film, *Blue Velvet* (1986). The song is sung, karaoke-style, by the drug dealer who supplies the psychotic anti-hero and whose code-name is Candy-Colored Clown. Roy Orbison's sentimental dream of love is transmuted into the dream of drug-induced hallucination as the schmaltz of the music is placed in an ironic relationship to the film's enactment of the irresistible trauma of the Oedipal triangle. The hero views a primal scene in which the drugged rapist attempts to get back inside the woman he calls 'Mommy'; the innocent young man fulfils the Oedipal fantasy by making love to the woman who takes the position of mother;[1] and the

---

[1] She is called 'mother' by her rapist; she is the actual mother of the child whose abduction, before the action begins, triggers the action; and when she appears, naked, on the

ensuing conflict with the rapist/father-figure is enacted in a scene of violence where 'In Dreams' throbs across the soundtrack. When the drug supplier sings 'In Dreams', his position in the film's Oedipal economy becomes clear: he is figured as the good mother who whispers 'go to sleep, everything is all right'.

Lynch's use of this, and other, classic rock'n'roll ballads in the film reanimates the dead metaphors of dreaming by literalizing them into psychoanalytic meaning. He is able to extend the dream metaphor even further by his parodic use of film convention. After the sequence in which the hero witnesses the primal scene and narrowly escapes with his life, the film cuts to a scene of his waking up in his own bed. Within the diegesis, the action has not been a dream, but the familiar connection between dreams and the unconscious, dreams and the denied world of sexuality and vice, is made and mocked in the same moment.

Reading the Oedipal analogues in this film is one of its most seductive pleasures. The ease with which every episode offers itself up for a vulgar Freudian reading teases its audience in characteristic Lynch fashion. The imagery of dreams is part of this tease. The flatness of the colour in the opening images of flowers against a white picket fence, the mechanical wave of the jolly neighbourhood fireman, and the jaunty skip of the schoolchildren being helped across the road parody the American dream of the hero's daytime world. But that self-conscious invocation of an already much-mocked image itself mocks the smart 'reading' spectator. It is a mockery which continues right through to the final sequence when the hero wakes from a doze on the same suburban lawn on which the action began. Surely it cannot be that all the violence and horror of the action are merely a dream?

In the post-modern moment of Lynch's film-making, images and cultural echoes are in constant play, always accompanied by their ironized counterpart, always looking over their shoulder and being looked at, always second-guessing the reader who wants, as it were, to catch them and tie them down. Lynch's film reminds us that the commonplace images of a culture, including the ways in which it reads dreams, are only its raw material. These images in the hands of the film-maker or dramatist can be turned to effects and meanings which are very different from their original ones. Lynch's film comments neither on the effectiveness with which the Oedipal model explains the organization of male

hero's lawn at the end of the film, the ruffian football player who is beating up the hero asks in astonishment or sarcasm: 'Is that your mother?'

desire, nor on the simpler version of human relationships offered by rock ballads or the American dream. Any reading which turned those motifs into paradigms of contemporary culture would seem tiresomely reductive compared with the wit and sparkle of Lynch's film.

II

In its complex intertextuality and its play with vulgar Freudianism, *Blue Velvet* seems very much of its time. Yet the range of cultural reference which every spectator must bring to this film offers a model of the complexities required to provide an adequate account of dreams in earlier cultures. Lynch is able to play with images of dreaming since he is making films in a long tradition which associates films with dreaming, and which uses dreams and dream sequences as part of the language of the cinematic 'dream factory'. Reading dreams in early modern culture requires a similar attention to the connections between dreams and theatre, to the available models for the interpretation of dreams, and to the ways in which this cultural raw material contributes to the development of a dramatic and theatrical language of representation.

References to dreams in early modern drama vary from the fully dramatized dream vision (Queen Catherine in *Henry VIII*, Queen Elizabeth in Heywood's *If You Know Not Me*, Part 1), to the description of dreams, to reflections on the state and nature of dreaming. One of the clearest features of all these references is that dreams are thought of as alternative realities which parallel the reality of waking existence, particularly when that waking existence seems hard to understand. When Antipholus of Syracuse in *The Comedy of Errors* finds himself addressed as husband by Adriana, he asks: 'What, was I married to her in my dream? | Or sleep I now, and think I hear all this?' (II. ii. 185–6);[2] and later in the same play, when the identical twins are revealed to one another, he says to Luciana, to whom he has made love:

> What I told you then
> I hope I shall have leisure to make good,
> If this be not a dream I see and hear.
>
> (V. ii. 377–9)

[2] All Shakespeare quotations in this chapter are from *The Complete Works*, ed. S. Wells and G. Taylor (Oxford, 1986).

It is difficult to distinguish between dreams and waking reality because the sensual reality which authenticates waking can be equally present in dreams, an idea which is wittily played on in the Induction to *The Taming of the Shrew*. When the practical-joking Lord plans to make 'the beggar then forget himself', he suggests that this unexpected change of status will be 'Even as a flatt'ring dream or worthless fancy' (Induction 1. 42). However, the dream-like illusion can be given a greater reality by sensual experience:

> Carry him gently to my fairest chamber,
> And hang it round with all my wanton pictures.
> Balm his foul head in warm distillèd waters,
> And burn sweet wood to make the lodging sweet.
>
> (Induction 1. 44–7)

Sly's insistence on the reality of his former existence is also presented in terms of his material circumstances which define his identity:

Ne'er ask me what raiment I'll wear, for I have no more doublets than backs, no more stockings than legs, nor no more shoes than feet . . . Am not I Christopher Sly, old Sly's son of Burton-heath, by birth a pedlar, by education a cardmaker, by transmutation a bearherd, and now by present profession, a tinker? (Induction 2. 6–9, 17–20)

However, faced with a new material reality, he is equally prepared to believe that his former life, in all its materiality, was a dream:

> Or do I dream? Or have I dreamed till now?
> I do not sleep. I see, I hear, I speak.
> I smell sweet savours, and I feel soft things.
> Upon my life, I am a lord indeed.
>
> (Induction 2. 68–71)

Behind Antipholus' and Sly's confusion about whether and when they were dreaming lies the commonplace connection between dreaming and the illusory and transitory nature of honour and love. In *Dekker his Dreame*, an old-fashioned dream vision of the horrors of hell, worldly honour is dismissed as 'a fruitlesse golden Dreame',[3] and in *The Duchess of Malfi* Bosola, finding that his evil deeds on behalf of his patron will not be rewarded, chides himself as 'one | That long hath ta'en a sweet and golden dream— | I am angry with myself, now that I wake'

---

[3] *Dekker his Dreame: in which . . . the great volumes of Heaven and Hell to Him were opened . . .* (London, 1620), 8.

(IV. ii. 324–5).[4] The association of dreams with both pleasure and loss ('In dreams I walk with you') allows them to serve as powerful images for the experience of love. In *Romeo and Juliet*, just before the false news arrives that Juliet is dead, Romeo soliloquizes:

> I dreamt my lady came and found me dead—
> Strange dream that gives a dead man leave to think!—
> And breath'd such life with kisses in my lips
> That I reviv'd and was an emperor.
>
> (V. i. 5–9)

This dream creates local dramatic ironies. Romeo welcomes it as 'dreams presage some joyful news at hand', and the audience knows that Juliet both is and is not dead. Moreover, it foreshadows the tragic finale of the play in which Romeo will die on a kiss and Juliet, kissing his dead body, will kill herself rather than revive him. But its combination of the images of sensual love and highest honour encapsulates the central fantasy of the play: that the lovers' passion will provide them with a dream world which will transcend the pressing demands of their real social situation.

Their passionate commitment to dragging the dream world of love into the reality of marriage and banishment is contrasted with Mercutio's eloquent fantasy in his set piece about Queen Mab. In that speech, dreams are reduced to the outcome of purely physical impulses interacting with the characteristic aspirations of different categories of people, as the Queen of Fairies

> gallops night by night
> Through lovers' brains, and then they dream of love;
> O'er courtiers' knees, that dream on courtesies straight;
> O'er lawyers fingers, who straight dream on fees;
> O'er ladies lips, who straight on kisses dream ...
>
> (I. iv. 70–4)

These examples of a dream world which echoes the sensual reality of the waking world, in which aspirations for love and honour could be realized, had obvious analogies with the world of theatre. In a mock legal action, the organizers of the *Gesta Grayorum* at Gray's Inn in 1594 were accused 'that those things which they all saw and perceived sensibly to be in very deed done, and actually performed were nothing

[4] J. Webster, *The Duchess of Malfi*, ed. J. R. Brown, The Revels Plays (London, 1964).

else but vain Illusions, Fancies, Dreams and Enchantments'.[5] The sense that theatre was a dream could be turned into an expression of the transitoriness of all human experience—as in Prospero's elegy, which connects the vision of his masque with 'the stuff that dreams are made on'. It could equally be turned to comic effect in the parodic metatheatricality of Shakespeare's *A Midsummer Night's Dream*. After his experiences with the Fairy Queen, Bottom assumes that he has been dreaming. He is quite unable to provide a coherent account of the events of his 'dream', but sees the potential for a transformation into art: 'I will get Peter Quince to write a ballad of this dream: it shall be called "Bottom's Dream", because it hath no bottom; and I will sing it at the latter end of the play, before the Duke' (IV. i. 212–16).

III

The poetic connections and contrasts between dreaming and waking reality suggest a range of ways in which dreams could be seen and used as poetic and theatrical effects, structuring the emotional movement of the plays and constructing character. Mercutio's scepticism is evident in his belief that dreams are no more than reactions to physical sensation which induce conventional reactions from different social types; Romeo's imaginative power is dramatized in his invocation of a dream world which will fulfil his hopes of consummated love; and Bottom's opportunist creativity recognizes that dreams could be turned into art that might ensure aristocratic patronage. However, these dreams themselves are such close analogues of waking existence, representing the characters' aspirations so clearly in their manifest content, that they offer frustratingly limited material for a wider reading of early modern culture. They invoke neither the large social concerns nor the telling insight into individual psychology which might interest the cultural historian.

When Louis Montrose offered a new historicist reading of *A Midsummer Night's Dream*, he found it necessary to posit a very different model of the relationship between dreams and the waking reality of culture. He read the play in the light of Simon Forman's dream in which Forman saves Queen Elizabeth from low-life ruffians and then makes a pass at her which she eagerly reciprocates: 'And so we talked merrily;

---

[5] *Gesta Grayorum*, Malone Society Reprints (Oxford, 1914), 24.

then she began to lean upon me, when we were past the dirt and to be very familiar with me, and methought she began to love me. When we were alone, out of sight, methought she would have kissed me.'[6] For-man's dream, like 'Bottom's dream', could be read as a dream of love and honour, but Montrose prefers a psychoanalytic model in which love and honour have an anterior abstracted connection to Oedipal fantasy in the desire for the powerful mother. A reading of Shakespeare's play which concentrates on the absent mothers in the play and its fantasies of patriarchal power makes a telling connection between Forman's dream and Bottom's experience. Both dreams, according to Montrose, repre-sent a fantasy of 'fleeting intimacy with a powerful female who is at once lover, mother, and queen'.[7] However, the details of the play leave open some questions about such a satisfyingly totalizing interpretation. Can we really read Bottom's desire for physical comfort as necessarily infant-ile—as against low culture—and can we be satisfied with a reading which makes no concession to genre or literary tradition in its elegant slide from 'the dream life of Dr Forman' to 'the dream play' by Master Shakespeare?

The theory and method of Montrose's reading are informed by Fred-erick Jameson's *The Political Unconscious*, which sees

the literary text in such a way that the latter may itself be seen as a rewriting or restructuration of a prior historical or ideological subtext, it being understood that the 'sub-text' is not immediately present as such, not some commonsense external reality . . . but rather must itself always be (re)constructed after the fact.[8]

In other words, the 'dream work of Master Shakespeare' is not a prod-uct of his individual psychology. It is, rather, the manifestation of a cul-tural unconscious, unavailable to him or his contemporaries, now revealed by the theoretical tools of a later age. By dealing with the elem-ents excluded by the play (the mothers) these tools can investigate and find a coherence which seems more satisfying, because more complete, than the simple connections made by the characters in the play between dreams and waking aspirations.

The drive towards coherent explanations for dreams is equally evident in early modern accounts of dreams and dreaming. In the

---

[6] *The Casebooks of Simon Forman*, ed. A. L. Rowse (London, 1974), 31.

[7] Montrose, '"Shaping Fantasies"', 65.

[8] F. Jameson, *The Political Unconscious*, quoted in Montrose, '"Shaping Fanta-sies"', 87.

dedicatory epistle to his *Pleasaunte Arte of the Interpretacion of Dreames* (1576), a book also discussed by Peter Holland in Chapter 5, Thomas Hill carefully refines his theoretical tools by insisting on the distinction between those which are 'properly dreames' and 'vain dreams, no true signifiers of matters to come but rather shewers of the present affections and desiers of the body' (sig. A. ii^b). In his 'Preface to the reader' he warns against dismissing dream material as 'thinges casual, natural, or impossible' (sig. A. vii^a) because like all dream theorists he wishes to organize the extraordinarily disparate material of dreams into a theory which can take into account existing assumptions about representation and signification. In doing so he deals with the somatic causes of dreams in terms of the theory of excesses of bodily vapours and humours, but is continually holding back from the completely materialist position which, as he writes in his treatise, would 'reduce mens dreames, unto the inward or bodily cause' (sig. D. iii^b). However, he does recognize the interaction of the past and the future in which, although dreams take account of the physical and mental situation of the dreamer, the evidence of his dreams are always in excess of the physical evidence so that they can be considered to 'signifye many matters upon the issue of the busines of the hap to come' (sig. D. iv^a).

Because Hill is not dealing with a therapeutic context which will provide him with dream material, his categorization is entirely schematic. Like Mercutio, who deals with the lovers, courtiers, lawyers, and ladies, Hill divides his subjects according to the familiar social categories of women and men, poor and rich, and so on. He is torn between providing a dream dictionary, a ready reckoner of interpretative significance, and a sense of the idiosyncracy of the dreamer's experience. Hill has access to a firm schema of allegorical and symbolic interpretation which is culturally specific not only in the particular examples but also in the closed character of the cultural field in which he exercises his interpretation. For example, 'To dreame that he meeteth women in black garmentes, with their heade couered declareth priuy deceytes intended against him' (sig. E. [viii]^b), or 'To dreame that hee seeyth a harlotte, or commoneth wyth her, signifieth deception or variances' (sig. E. [viii]^b). The habit of allegorical and symbolic correspondences which permeates the literary discourses of his time is echoed in the expectation that connections of this kind will seem self-evident. However, on some occasions the correspondences seem so unexpected as to suggest special pleading amounting to denial: 'If he, whiche is in loue with a woman, dreameth to have founde a birdes neaste, and that he reaching or puttyng his hand into the neast, feeleth it could, it is a token of hasty or sodayne sadnes, and sorrowe' (sig. F. i^b). The imagery seems unusual because it is not part of a traditional scheme of allegorical signification, but its significance depends upon connecting it none the less to an interpretation which makes sense through correspondences. Coming to the image from a modern, post-Freudian, perspective we make the connection between love, woman, and nest as a physical, sexual correspondence. For Hill, however, the correspondences are more innocent: 'For that neast signified and is the place of byrth, and coldnes expresseth death' (sig. F. i^b).

The vividness of many of Hill's more extended examples begs the modern reader to apply a different explanatory model to the extended dream sequences which he offers as examples of the prophetic power of dreams:

And one thought in his sleepe that hee kepte his mothers funeral and that be bewayled, and sighed bitterly for her, insomuch that he waked out of sleepe for feare of the same. And the next morrow, when he had told his dreame unto his frend he noted that day, and within a few dayes after he received letters that the day before the same day he had his dreame at night the mother whom hee supposed to be alyue dyed. (sig. H. ii^b)

This dream and the surrounding circumstances offer evidence of the prophetic power of dreams, but its powerful effect of authenticity—the attention to the day and time—suggests, from a Freudian perspective, a compensatory anxiety which needs to be read psychoanalytically. For the significant innovation of Freud's work was his insistence on the presence of wish-fulfilment even in the most anxious dreams, and on the importance of the initiating impulses in infantile memories which, translated into the daytime residue, provide the manifest content of the dream narrative. We do not have enough evidence from Hill's dream to trace it back to its impulses, but he does tell us that 'hee kepte his mothers funeral'. The activity in his dream seems startlingly like Freud's examples of 'compensatory activity which temporarily prevents the anxiety of the dream from breaking through sleep'.[9]

Hill's dream is very similar to Ben Jonson's dream recounted to Drummond of Hawthornden. Having abandoned his family in London during the plague in order to join his patron, Robert Cotton, in the country, Jonson

---

[9] See Freud's statement that dreams are 'the guardians of sleep': S. Freud, *The Interpretation of Dreams*, ed. A. Richards, The Pelican Freud Library 4 (Harmondsworth, 1971), 330–1.

saw in a vision his eldest sone (then a child in London) appear unto him with the Marke of a bloodie crose on his forehead as if it had been cutted with a suord, at which amazed he prayed unto God . . . in the meane tyme comes thr letters from his wife of the death of that Boy in the plague. He appeared to him he said of a Manlie shape & of that Grouth that he thinks he shall be at the resurrection.[10]

Ben Jonson told the story as proof of the prophetic qualities of dreams but, as David Riggs has shown, it could be interpreted very differently. In his biography of Ben Jonson he reads Jonson's dream as 'an embodiment of the dreamer's wish to abandon his family . . . and his guilt over the gratification of that wish into a single harrowing image'.[11] Riggs describes the conflict throughout Jonson's life as being between his need for a natural family (as a compensation for his own utterly inadequate childhood) and the alternative satisfactions of a family politic in the stable hierarchies of aristocratic patronage. His interest is in Jonson's psyche but he is also aware that that psyche functioned in a specific historical context. However, he cannot extend his acknowledgement of a historical context into accepting Jonson's model for interpreting dreams since it is a model so at odds with his own as to be, for him, completely unpersuasive.

IV

The fact that the same dreams can be interpreted so differently using modern and early modern models is not surprising. However, it throws into relief the methodological problems involved in reading the dreams of early modern culture. In his important article on the possibilities of a social history of dreaming, Burke works with the sceptical rigour of his discipline. He warns the historian to 'remember that he does not have access to the dream itself, but to its written account, modified by the subconscious or conscious thought in the course of its recall and transcription'.[12] His warning seems otiose in view of the fact that no one, not even the dreamer, has access to 'the dream itself' after it is ended. Most remembered dreams are a muddle of somatic impulses, memories, and daytime residue; as Freud found:

---

[10] 'Ben Jonson's Conversations with Drummond of Hawthornden', in *Ben Jonson*, ed. C. H. Herford and P. and E. Simpson, 11 vols. (Oxford, 1925–52), i. 139–40.

[11] D. Riggs, *Ben Jonson: A Life* (Cambridge, Mass., 1989), 95.

[12] P. Burke, 'L'Histoire sociale des rêves', *Annales*, 28 (1973), 329–42: 333; my translation.

Even the most truth loving of men is scarcely able to relate a note-worthy dream without some addition or embellishments. The tendency of the human mind to see everything connectedly is so strong that in memory it unwittingly fills in any lack of coherence that there may be in an incoherent dream.[13]

What is at issue is not the truth or otherwise of the dream, or even the a priori validity of a particular model of interpretation, but the processes by which one dream seems more significant than another because it offers more scope for interpretation within the readily available models. These processes can be illustrated by returning to *Blue Velvet*.

The only actual dream in the film is recounted by Sandy, the hero's girlfriend. She dreams of a world of darkness which is gradually transformed into a scene filled with light brought by, of all things, a flock of robins. Her account of the dream marks her increasing intimacy with the hero, but its simple contrast between darkness and light, and its use of a banal Christmassy image, seem sentimental and stupidly inconsequential (why robins?). The dream is given a significance in the film by the connecting images of light and darkness, and by Sandy's reported feelings of great happiness, which slot the dream into a recognizable cultural pattern: it moves from being a private, physical experience to being an image for hopes and wishes and aspirations. And at the end of the film the appearance of a robin in the garden, albeit swallowing a bug, offers an ironized, happy conclusion to the action. Conversely, the scene where the hero watches the rape of the character called 'Mommy' is not a dream. It is connected to symbolically significant dreams both by the Roy Orbison song and by the cultural familiarity of the interpretative model offered by the Oedipus complex. The hero's experience of the primal scene, and his subsequent conflict with the father-figure, provide an interpretation of the film which contrasts the violence of the Oedipal dream with the desirable fantasies of both the American dream and the dream of innocent love.

However much Freud and other commentators on dreams insist on the inadequacy of a 'dream dictionary' for individual analysis, dreams can only function socially, in the culture as a whole, through these correspondences. Keith Thomas describes how Francis Tilney, the Suffolk minister, may have 'felt a little sheepish about the "night visions" which came to him during the opening years of the civil war, but he nevertheless thought it worth sending an account of them to his MP, Sir Harbottle Grimstone, on the grounds that they were almost certainly

[13] Freud, *Interpretation of Dreams*, ed. Richards, 110.

premonitory'.[14] He presumably had numerous other dreams which seemed too inconsequential to remember, far less record or communicate to others.

Dreams will seem significant or banal according to the complexity of the interpretative work required to explain them, and the extent to which they fit with the prevailing interests of the interpreter.[15] Burke, for example, is dismissive of one of Cellini's dreams which took place when he was seriously ill. He dreamt that 'a terrifying old man appeared at my bed head and tried to carry me away by the force of his enormous boat'. Burke applies his knowledge of Renaissance iconography to assume that the old man must be Charon and concludes 'we have no need to apply a theory of archetypes to explain the appearance of Charon to an Italian Renaissance artist'.[16] Conversely, Forman's dream of seducing Queen Elizabeth seems more receptive to interpretation in terms of the political unconscious than many of his other recorded dreams. His dreams are often preoccupied with sexuality, but they also deal with law suits, or with the sense of paranoia produced by his constant battle with the College of Physicians or, as in Ben Jonson's case, by his unhappy family life.

It is possible to contrast the rather random character of Forman's dreams, as recorded in the casebooks, with his subsequent attempts to organize dream material in the interests of particular thematic or theoretical preoccupations. There is clearly a theoretical impulse in the very way in which Forman opens his autobiography with an account of his childhood dreaming:

So soon as he was laid down to sleep he should see in visions many mountains and hills come rolling against him. Although they would overrun him and fall on his head and bruise him, yet he got up always to the top of them and with much ado went over them. Then he should see many great waters like to drown him, boiling and raging against him as though they would swallow him up, yet he thought he did overpass them.

For Forman, the meaning of the dreams was self-evident:

These visions God did show him in his youth to signify his troubles in his riper years. For the mighty mountains might signify the great and mighty potentates

---

[14] K. Thomas, *Religion and the Decline of Magic: Studies in Popular Beliefs in Sixteenth- and Seventeenth-Century England* (Harmondsworth, 1973), 152.

[15] Cf. Freud, *Interpretation of Dreams*, ed. Richards, 457, on the conditions of representability for dreams.

[16] Burke, 'Histoire sociale des rêves', 334; my translation.

that he had controversy with afterwards. The waters might signify the great counsels that were holden against him to overthrow him. Yet God, the only defender of all that be his, would never let him to be overthrown, but continually gave him always in the end the victory of all his enemies.[17]

Forman's flattering and self-justifying interpretation of his dreams for the purposes of constructing an autobiographical self can be contrasted with the more random character of the dreams in his casebooks. But the fact that we believe the random dreams, and are suspicious of the coherent ones, reflects a modern distinction between autobiographical discourse and the satisfying opportunities for interpretation which incoherence seems to provide.

V

The relationship between coherence, interpretability, and meaning is focused in a particularly apt way in the case of Archbishop Laud's dreams, to which Peter Holland alludes in Chapter 5. Laud recorded his dreams in a diary which, after his imprisonment, was seized by his old enemy, William Prynne. Prynne published selections from the diary with his own editorial introduction and brief commentary, in which he paid considerable attention to the dreams. At his trial Laud noted 'every Lord present with a new thin book in folio, in a blue coat', a copy of Prynne's *Breviate of the Life of William Laud*.

The manifest content of Laud's recorded dreams have the ring of authenticity because most of them are easily connected to the events of his life. For example, he records several dreams in which his enemy, the Lord Keeper, is discomfited; and he dreams that 'the King was offended and would cast me off and tell me no cause why' (14 October 1636).[18] He also has the familiar anxiety dreams that his teeth fall out (9 February 1626, 7 July 1627), that he cannot find his clothes (31 January 1628), or that he cannot perform an important but familiar task, finding the Order of Marriage in his service book (12 February 1638). Some of his dreams, such as the one in which he finds himself publicly in bed with Buckingham (21 August 1625), or when he dreams of the mysterious K.B. or E.B., offer tantalizing conundrums for the biographer,[19] because

---

[17] Forman, *Casebooks*, ed. Rowse, 273.
[18] Laud, *Works*, ed. Scott and Bliss, vol. iii.
[19] e.g. C. Carleton, *Archbishop William Laud* (London, 1987) who uses the dreams extensively to flesh out his account of Laud's inner life and personality.

they confirm a modern sense of an identity which locates sexual, religious, and political conflict in an interior unconscious revealed by dreams that corroborate and explain the actions of a waking life.

Laud rarely interprets his dreams and, when he does, he assumes a position of dry intellectual scepticism. His troubled relations with K.B. were frequently mentioned in the diary entries for the early months of 1633. On 6 June Laud

dreamed that K.B. sent to me in Westminster church, that he was now as desirous to see me as I him, and that he was then entering into the church. I went with joy, but met another in the middle of the church, who seemed to know the business, and laughed; but K.B. was not there.

On 8 June Laud notes that he has received letters from K.B. and adds drily that if he returns from Scotland 'I shall see how true or false my dream is'. Late in his life, Laud dreamed of his father 'Who died 46 years since': 'And after some speech, I asked him how long he would stay with me? He answered he would stay until he had me away with him.' Faced with this dream, which offered up an obvious premonitory meaning, Laud merely observes: 'I am not moved with dreams; yet I thought fit to remember this' (24 January 1639). For Laud, the over-interpretation of dreams seems to have been associated with the vulgar enthusiasms of his political opponents. On 11 August 1634,

One Rob. Seal, of St Alban's, came to me to Croydon; told me somewhat wildly about a vision he had at Shrovetide last, about not preaching the word sincerely to the people. And a hand appeared unto him, and death; and a voice bid him go tell the Metropolitan of Lambeth, and made him swear he would do so; and I believe the poor man was overgrown with fancy. So I troubled not myself further, with him, or it.

Prynne's interpretations of Laud's dreams were another matter. Laud's anxieties about them were recorded in his annotations on a copy of Prynne's *Breviate* which reveal Laud's view of dreams as well as his wish to exonerate himself from Prynne's charges.[20] What was at issue in the publication of the diary was not only Laud's actions but also his intentions and the question of how far the dreams could reveal them. Laud's comments both refute Prynne's allegations, and show him suggesting a quite different connection between dreamer and dreaming than that urged by Prynne. Prynne had predictably noted

---

[20]   See Laud, *Works*, ed. Scott and Bliss, iii. 261–72; page references to Laud's annotations are given in the text.

Laud's dream 'that I had been reconciled to the Church of Rome'. Laud refers the reader back to the diary with 'I hope ye reader will note my trouble at ye dream, as well as ye dream' (264). Where Prynne paid attention to a dream in which Sir George Wright 'whispering in my ear, told me I was the cause why the Bishop of Lincoln was not again admitted to favour', Laud's note protests 'yt this allso was a wild fancy in a dream' (264); and where Prynne found events ominous, Laud noted 'So then Mr Pryn's superstition can take some things as ominous' (271). Nevertheless, there was no hard and fast distinction between the superstitious Prynne and the rational archbishop. On 27 October 1640, Laud's diary records that he went into his study and found his portrait 'fallen down upon the face and lying on the floor'. He noted 'I am almost every day threatened with my ruin in Parliament. God grant this be no omen.'

Laud's greatest anxiety in his notes on Prynne seems to have centred on an alleged 'fatall dream at Oxford'. Laud refutes the charge that he had this dream, 'Upon ye faith of a Christian'. He enquires: 'I wonder how it came to pass that I should set down so many dreams in my Diary and omitt this more memorable then any of ye rest' (271). However, the ellipses and omissions in the records of many of his dreams suggest that Laud was all too aware of why he might not have recorded this dream and a good deal seems to have hung on its meaning. The dream appears to have dogged him throughout his career:

When I was first Archbishop, one Mr Badger, an atturney at law, my kinsman by marriage, but a separatist, came to me to Lambeth, and told me he heard yt when I was young I had had this dream, but could not or would not tell of whom he heard it. I verily think ye credulous and bold man was purposely sent to abuse me to my face. I told him he was set on to abuse me and protested to him yt I never had any such dream. Yet not long after he told it to Mr Pryn. (271–2)

The dream itself, as recorded by Prynne, seems both too coherent to be genuine and too obvious to bear this weight of anxious interpretation:

That when he was a young Scholler in Oxford, he dreamed one night, that he came to farre greater preferment in the Church, and power in the State, then ever any man of his birth and Calling before him; in which greatenesse and worldly happines he continued many yeares; but after all this happiness, before he awaked, he dreamed he was hanged.[21]

---

[21] W. Prynne, *A Breviate of the Life of William Laud, Arch-bishop of Canterbury: extracted (for the most part) verbatim out of his owne Diary* (London, 1644).

Prynne's interpretation, however, is both a triumphant vindication of the power of dreams as prophecy and a direct exhortation to his readers in parliament:

The first part of this Dreame hath been long since verified, and the conclusion of it, is in all probability like to be speedily accomplished upon the close of his Tryall: The exact Complete Relation whereof, may (God assisting and the Parliament commanding) hereafter follow in its order, wherein the criminal part of his life will appear most foule, and detestable, in all Particulars of his impeachment.

Prynne records the dream in a list of things to observe appended to the main text of the *Breviate*, which includes 'That he tooke speciall notice of Sundry Dreames presages and Omens of his owne downfall, to which, for a Close to this Breviate of his life, some other memorable ominous passages yet unmentioned shall be added.' However, concern for omens had been the organizing principle of Prynne's document, and in the context he needs to make no pretence of objective judgement, since he was reading the diary quite explicitly as evidence of Laud's ambition, closet Catholicism, and desire above all to further his own political ends. Laud's own anxiety at the allegation is more interesting. He recognizes the direct threat in Prynne's hope for the speedy fulfilment of the prophecy, but he also seems anxious to deny that he dreamt of the power and status he achieved before they came about. The politician's 'sweet and golden dream' of success could not be acknowledged.[22] The fact that its acknowledgement was at issue suggests a conflict of interpretation between dream as prophecy and dream as aspiration. In his protest against Prynne's interpretation of his dreams, Laud was coming close to a notion of dream as expression of the unconscious.

VI

The suspicious coherence of Laud's alleged dream, and the conflict between his and Prynne's models of interpretation, highlight the extent to which reading dreams is always a process of translation. The dreamer translates incoherence into memory; the dream theorist translates dream into theory—in Hill's case dream into prophecy; Montrose

---

[22] Laud's notes also protest that Prynne had exaggerated the poverty of his family and the humbleness of his origins. See Laud, *Works*, ed. Scott and Bliss, iii. 262.

translates dramatic text into psychoanalytic text; and Jameson concludes that there is no alternative to 'rewriting or restructuration of a
prior historical or ideological subtext' which 'must itself always be
(re)constructed after the fact'. Yet the process of translation is culturally
determined not by a single model of interpretation, but by conflicts in
the range of interpretation offered by a variety of texts.

The tension between Prynne's allegorical reading of Laud's dreams,
and Laud's insistence that his dreams came to him unbidden, is similar
to formal shifts in the varied models of dreams available in the drama. In
the collaborative play *Sir Thomas More*, for example, there is a play
within a play which includes an account of a dream:

> In an arbour green, asleep whereas I lay,
> The birds sang sweetly in the midst of the day.
> I dreamed fast of mirth and play—
> In youth is pleasure, in youth is pleasure.
> Methought I walked still to and fro,
> And from her company I could not go,
> But when I waked it was not so.
> In youth is pleasure, in youth is pleasure.
> Therefore my heart is surely plight
> Of her alone to have a sight,
> Which is my joy and heart's delight.
> In youth is pleasure, in youth is pleasure.
>
> (III. ii. 181–92)[23]

This dream takes the old-fashioned form of a medieval dream vision,
and its position in the play within the play makes it quite distinct from
the dreams of the principal actors. However, their dreams too involve
models of literary symbolism which make them interpretable. Lady
More, for example, dreams that

> the king and queen went on the Thames
> In barges to hear music. My lord and I
> Were in a boat, methought—Lord, Lord,
> What strange things live in slumbers!—and being near,
> Ye grappled to the barge that bare the king.
> But after many pleasing voices spent
> In that still moving music house, methought
> The violence of the stream did sever us

---

[23] A. Munday *et al.*, *The Book of Sir Thomas More*, ed. V. Gabrieli and G. Melchiori
(Manchester, 1990).

> Quite from the golden fleet and hurried us
> Unto the bridge which with unused horror
> We entered at full tide; thence some flight shoot
> Being carried by the waves, our boat stood still
> Just opposite the Tower, and there it turned
> And turned about, as when a whirlpool sucks
> The circled waters. Methought that we both cried
> Till that we sunk, where arm in arm we died.
>
> (IV. ii. 11–26)

Roper, Lady More's son-in-law, tries to comfort her by dismissing dreams as 'slight illusions of the blood'. However, he confesses to his wife that he is anxious about More's fate and she then recounts her dream, in which she sees her father 'standing upon the rood loft' in Chelsea church:

> And whilst he kneeled and prayed before the image,
> It fell with him into the upper choir,
> Where my poor father lay all stained in blood.
>
> (IV. ii. 38–41)

Both dreams can be read symbolically in terms of the action of the play, but they use different degrees of symbolism. Lady More's is a realistic image taken from the life of the court, but its symbolism also draws in the conventional tropes of the ship of the individual life on the river of time. Margaret Roper's also takes a real image from Harpsfield's *Life of More*, but More's fall is metaphorical and is connected through the image of 'the rood loft now defaced' with the fall of the old religion.

The contrast between the 'literary' dream of the play within the play and the striking, though still conventionally symbolic, material of the women's dreams indicates in a single text the ways in which dreams in dramatic material can be read. There is a recognition of the literary dream, and an ability to use it for a dramatic function; of contemporary ideas about dreams as prophecy, disputed by the rationalist Roper, but nevertheless realized through the play's vivid imagery as a focus for its emotional content and narrative coherence. The *Life of More* suggests a complex relationship between dream as literature, dream as a set of symbolic images, and dream as a route into the feelings, if not of the unconscious, of its characters.

A similar process is evident in the use of dreams in plays more widely separated in time, for example in the contrasting uses of dreams in Shakespeare's *Richard III* and Webster's *The White Devil*. In Act I, scene iv of *Richard III*, Clarence reports a dream in which he escapes from the Tower, is 'embarked to cross to Burgundy', and is thrown into the water while trying to save his brother Gloucester from falling overboard. He then dreams that he is drowned and after death encounters his enemies, Warwick and Rutland, from the Wars of the Roses, who hand him over to fiends and the torments of hell. The dream serves a number of dramatic functions. It reminds the audience of Clarence's past, ironically foreshadows his imminent murder, and indicates the political role his murder will fulfil in advancing Gloucester's progress to the usurped throne. The power of its poetry generates a local sympathy for Clarence which is vital to the effect of the scene of murder, but at the same time indicates that he too has a guilty part in the current political situation of which he is about to become a victim.

But the dream is also a poetic set piece, a theatrical aria with its accumulated imagery of the horrors of the deep and its acknowledged classical sources in the description of crossing the Styx: 'With that sour ferryman which poets write of, | Unto the kingdom of perpetual night' (I. iv. 46–7). Its narrative coherence and poetic eloquence have none of the compressed inconsequentiality of real dreams. Nevertheless, there is some attempt to link it to character as an expression of Clarence's guilt. The striking image of Rutland—'a shadow like an angel, with bright hair | Dabbled in blood'—suggests the dream-work which has partly transformed Clarence's victim into a consoling vision of his apotheosis after death. The dream's effect is to link the play's past and its future in a single poetically powerful moment which also reveals the internal conflict in the character's mind.

The connection between dreams and subjectivity is more fully achieved in Vittoria's dream in *The White Devil*. Both the occasion and the subject-matter of the dream integrate dramatic and narrative function with the representation of character. In the opening scene of the play Vittoria is introduced to Brachiano, and the seduction is initiated in the bawdy exchange about jewels. In order both to hold off and extend the moment of consummation, Vittoria tells Brachiano of her 'foolish idle dream' in which she encounters her husband and Brachiano's Duchess, who accuse her of an intention to root up 'That well grown yew, and plant i'th' stead of it | A withered blackthorn' and vow to bury her alive. She is rescued by a whirlwind

> which let fall a massy arm
> From that strong plant
> And both were struck dead by that sacred yew
> In that base shallow grave that was their due.

(I. ii. 252–5)[24]

Both Brachiano and Flamineo are sceptical that the dream is anything more than a veiled instruction to Brachiano to act as a 'yew' that will 'make away his duchess and her husband'. However, the dream's meaning is not made clear by a set of simple allegorical or prophetic correspondences. The yew is Brachiano, the wished murderer of the spouses who stand in the way of the lovers' consummation, but it could also be Vittoria herself who is to be removed and replaced by 'A withered blackthorn'. Flamineo's interpretation is both excessive and inadequate, for the dream's form expresses both the prophetic nature of dreams and the idiosyncracy of the dream experience. It makes a significant contribution to the sense of Vittoria as a character autonomous from the action, one who can both manipulate symbolic imagery to her own advantage and who has a mysterious emotional life just out of reach of the action of the play. The emotional action is now located inside the characters and is psychologically accounted for in such speeches as Flamineo's bitter memories of being 'fain to heel his tutor's stockings' (I. ii. 322), or Vittoria's disingenuous self-characterization as one whose only faults are 'beauty and gay clothes, a merry heart, | And a good stomach to a feast' (III. ii. 208–9).

Such shifts in the representations of dreams show the dramatists using the rich and varied traditions of dream representation to create particular dramatic effects. The dramatists were aware of and could exploit the interpretation of dreams as a constant interplay between convention and the particularity of individual experience. In formal terms, the representation of dreams acts as a transitional form between fully realized external, allegorical action and the compressed metaphors and symbolism of a character's speech suggestive of the psychological density of that character's experience. Where the interpreters of real dreams attempt to realize the latent action which results in the manifest content of the dream narrative, the movement of the drama goes in the opposite direction, from the moral and allegorical schemata of

---

[24] J. Webster, *The White Devil*, ed. J. R. Brown (London, 1960).

providential or prophetic action to the complex interconnections of imagery which characterize the individual mind.

Dreams in drama are quite explicitly represented through this interplay between latent and manifest content. The forms of prophetic dreams are integrated into the explanatory schemata of action—either as ironically prophetic or as a correlative for motivation. The location of the dream impulse similarly presents an interaction between the notion of dreams as internal and external—a tension which is equally evident in the shifting contemporary theory of dreams. But perhaps most important of all, dreams in the drama enact and demonstrate the processes by which some texts authenticate themselves by appearing to move beyond the rigid schemata of static correspondence to something which appears to represent the idiosyncracy of individual identity.

The use of dreams as textual strategies and means of characterization, or a shorthand of imagery, may seem to the historicizing critic a limited formalist undertaking. However, the form which dreams take determines not only the ways in which they can be interpreted but their very capacity for interpretation. Dreams, like Cellini's, or Laud's, or Clarence's, or even Vittoria's, which seem too closely linked to outmoded or instrumental modes of interpretation, call into question their own authenticity and thus their own validity as historical evidence. Nevertheless, the range of forms in which dreams are represented does provide an insight into models of perception which are a vital part of the mental life of a past culture.

David Lynch's mocking play with vulgar Freudianism in *Blue Velvet* reveals the balance between filmic convention and interpretative knowledge which constitutes the mental life of his audience. A rather different balance informs the representation of dreams in early modern culture, but we need not assume that it is any less delicately poised.

Bibliography

ADELMAN, H. E., 'Leon Modena: The Autobiography and the Man', in L. Modena, *The Autobiography of a Seventeenth-Century Venetian Rabbi: Leon Modena's 'Life of Judah'*, ed. M. R. Cohen (Princeton, 1988).

AERS, D., 'Altars of Power: Reflections on Eamon Duffy's *Stripping of the Altars*', *LitHist*, 3rd ser. 3 (1994), 90–105.

—— *Chaucer, Langland and the Creative Imagination* (London, 1980).

—— 'Chaucer's *Book of the Duchess*: An Art to Consume Art', *DUJ*, NS 38 (1977), 201–5.

—— *Community, Gender, and Individual Identity: English Writing 1360–1430* (London, 1988).

—— *Piers Plowman and Christian Allegory* (London, 1975).

—— 'A Whisper in the Ear of Early Modernists; or, Reflections on Literary Critics Writing the "History of the Subject"', in id. (ed.), *Culture and History: Essays on English Communities, Identities and Writing 1350–1600* (Hemel Hempstead, 1992), 177–202.

—— and HODGE, R., '"Rational burning": Milton on Sex and Marriage', *MiltonS* 12 (1979), 3–33.

AIKEN, P., 'Vincent of Beauvais and Dame Pertelote's Knowledge of Medicine', *Speculum*, 10 (1935), 281–7.

ALAIN DE LILLE, *The Plaint of Nature* [*De planctu naturae*], trans. J. J. Sheridan (Toronto, 1980).

ALBERTUS MAGNUS, *Opera omnia*, ed. A. Borgnet, 38 vols. (Paris, 1890–9).

ALGAZALI, *Algazel's Metaphysics: A Mediaeval Translation*, ed. J. T. Muckle (Toronto, 1933).

ALIGHIERI, D., *The Divine Comedy*, i: *Inferno*, ed. and trans. J. D. Sinclair, rev. edn. (London, 1948).

ANDERSON, J. H., *The Growth of a Personal Voice*: Piers Plowman *and* The Faerie Queene (New Haven, 1976).

ANDERSON, J. J., 'The Narrators in the *Book of the Duchess* and the *Parlement of Foules*', *ChauR* 26 (1991–2), 219–34.

ANDREAS, J. R., 'Festive Liminality in Chaucerian Comedy', *ChauN* 1/1 (1979), 3–6.

ANZAI, T., *Shakespeare and Montaigne Reconsidered*, Renaissance Monographs 12 (Tokyo, 1986).

APPIGNANESI, L., and FORRESTER, J., *Freud's Women* (London, 1992).

ARBER, E., *A Transcript of the Registers of the Company of Stationers of London 1554–1640 A.D.*, vol. i (London, 1875).

ARISTOTLE, *Aristotle's Psychology: A Treatise on the Principle of Life* (De anima *and* Parva naturalia), trans. W. A. Hammond (London, 1902).

—— *De insomniis et De divinatione per somnum: A New Edition of the Greek Text with the Latin Translations*, ed. H. J. Drossaart Lulofs, 2 vols. (Leiden, 1947).

—— *De somno et vigilia liber, adiectis veteribus translationibus et Theodori Metochitae commentario*, ed. H. J. D. Lulofs (Leiden, 1943).

—— *Parva naturalia*, ed. and trans. W. S. Hett, rev. edn., Loeb Classical Library (London, 1964).

ARTEMIDORUS, *The Interpretation of Dreams: Oneirocritica*, trans. R. J. White (Pack Ridge, NJ, 1975).

ASTELL, M., *Reflections upon Marriage* (London, 1706).

AUGUSTINE, *De cura pro mortuis gerenda, PL* 40, cols. 591–610.

—— *De Genesi ad litteram libri duodecim*, ed. J. Zycha, Corpus Scriptorum Ecclesiasticorum Latinorum 28, 3. 1 (Prague, 1894); trans. J. H. Taylor as *The Literal Meaning of Genesis*, Ancient Christian Writers: The Works of the Fathers in Translation 42, 2 vols. (New York, 1982).

—— *On Care to Be Had for the Dead*, trans. H. Browne, A Select Library of the Nicene and Post-Nicene Fathers of the Christian Church 3 (Buffalo, 1887), 537–51.

AVERROES, *Epitome of 'Parva Naturalia'*, ed. H. Blumberg, Corpus Commentariorum Averrois in Aristotelem, Versio Anglica 7 (Cambridge, Mass., 1961).

AVICENNA, *Liber canonis* (Venice, 1507; repr. Hildesheim, 1964).

—— *The Poem on Medicine*, trans. H. C. Krueger (Springfield, Ill., 1963).

BAKER, D. C., 'Imagery and Structure in Chaucer's *Book of the Duchess*', *SN* 30 (1958), 17–26.

BAKER-SMITH, D., 'Juan Vives and the *Somnium Scipionis*', in R. R. Bolgar (ed.), *Classical Influences on European Culture A.D. 1500–1700* (Cambridge, 1976), 239–44.

BARKER, F., *The Tremulous Private Body: Essays on Subjection* (London, 1984).

BARNEY, S. A., 'Allegorical Visions', in J. A. Alford (ed.), *A Companion to* Piers Plowman (Berkeley and Los Angeles, 1988), 117–33.

BAUMGARTNER, E., 'The Play of Temporalities; or, The Reported Dream of Guillaume de Lorris', in K. Brownlee and S. Huot (eds.), *Rethinking the Romance of the Rose: Text, Image, Reception*, Middle Ages ser. (Philadelphia, 1992), 21–38.

BENNETT, J. A. W., *Chaucer's* Book of Fame: *An Exposition of 'The House of Fame'* (Oxford, 1968).

BERNHEIMER, C., and KAHANE, C. (eds.), *In Dora's Case: Freud, Hysteria, Feminism* (London, 1985).

BETHURUM, D., 'Chaucer's Point of View as Narrator in the Love Poems', *PMLA* 74 (1959), 511–20.

—— 'Shakespeare's Comment on Mediaeval Romance in *Midsummer-Night's Dream*', *MLN* 60 (1945), 85–94.

Biblia sacra iuxta vulgatam Clementinam, ed. A. Colunga and L. Turnado, 4th edn., Biblioteca de Autores Cristianos 14. 1 (Madrid, 1965); English translations are from *The Holy Bible: Douay Version Translated from the Latin Vulgate (Douay A.D. 1609: Rheims, A.D. 1582)* (London, 1956).

BOARDMAN, P. C., 'Courtly Language and the Strategy of Consolation in the *Book of the Duchess*', *ELH* 44 (1977), 567–79.

BOCCACCIO, G., *The Book of Theseus*, trans. B. M. McCoy (New York, 1974).

BODENHAM, C. H. L., 'The Nature of the Dream in Late Mediaeval French Literature', *MÆ* 54 (1985), 74–86.

BODIN, J., *Colloquium of the Seven about Secrets of the Sublime*, ed. M. Leathers and D. Kuntz (Princeton, 1975).

BOETHIUS OF DACIA, *De somniis*, in *Opera*, vol. vi, pt. 2, ed. N. G. Green-Pederson, Corpus Philosophorum Danicorum Medii Aevi (Copenhagen, 1976).

—— *On the Supreme Good, On the Eternity of the World, On Dreams*, trans. J. F. Wippel (Toronto, 1987).

BOSWELL, J., *Christianity, Social Tolerance, and Homosexuality: Gay People in Western Europe from the Beginning of the Christian Era to the Fourteenth Century* (Chicago, 1980).

BRADSHAW, G., *Shakespeare's Scepticism* (1987; repr. Ithaca, NY, 1990).

BREWER, D., 'Escape from the Mimetic Fallacy', in id. (ed.), *Studies in Medieval English Romances: Some New Approaches* (Cambridge, 1988), 1–10. [Excerpted from his 'The Interpretation of Dream, Folktale and Romance with Special Reference to *Sir Gawain and the Green Knight*', *NM* 77 (1976), 569–81.]

BRODY, S. N., *The Disease of the Soul: Leprosy in Medieval Literature* (Ithaca, NY, 1974).

BRONSON, B. H., 'The *Book of the Duchess* Re-opened', *PMLA* 67 (1952), 863–81.

BROWN, J. N., 'Narrative Focus and Function in *The Book of the Duchess*', *MSE* 2 (1969–70), 71–9.

BROWN, P., and BUTCHER, A., *The Age of Saturn: Literature and History in the Canterbury Tales* (Oxford, 1991).

BROWNE, A., 'Descartes's Dreams', *JWCI* 40 (1977), 256–73.

—— 'Girolamo Cardano's *Somniorum Synesiorum Libri IIII*', *BHR* 41 (1979), 123–35.

BROWNE, SIR T., 'On Dreams', in *The Works of Sir Thomas Browne*, ed. G. Keynes, new edn., vol. iii (London, 1964).

BROWNLEE, K., *Poetic Identity in Guillaume de Machaut* (Madison, 1984).

BUCKLER, P. P., 'Love and Death in Chaucer's *The Book of the Duchess*', in J. S. Mink and J. D. Ward (eds.), *Joinings and Disjoinings: The Significance of Marital Status in Literature* (Bowling Green, Oh., 1991), 6–18.

BUNDY, M. W., *The Theory of Imagination in Classical and Mediaeval Thought*, University of Illinois Studies in Language and Literature 12/2–3 (Urbana, Ill., 1927).

BURKE, P., 'L'Histoire sociale des rêves', *Annales*, 28 (1973), 329–42.

BURLIN, R. B., *Chaucerian Fiction* (Princeton, 1977).

BURNLEY, D., 'Some Terminology of Perception in the *Book of the Duchess*', *ELN* 23 (1986), 15–22.

BURTON, R., *The Anatomy of Melancholy*, ed. H. Jackson (New York, 1977).

BUTTERFIELD, A., 'Lyric and Elegy in *The Book of the Duchess*', *MÆ* 60 (1991), 33–60.

—— 'Pastoral and the Politics of Plague', *SAC* 16 (1994), 3–27.

BYNUM, C. W., *Fragmentation and Redemption: Essays on Gender and the Human Body in Medieval Religion* (New York, 1991).

CALIN, W., *The French Tradition and the Literature of Medieval England* (Toronto, 1994).

—— *A Poet at the Fountain: Essays on the Narrative Verse of Guillaume de Machaut* (Lexington, Ky., 1974).

CAMDEN, C., 'Shakespeare on Sleep and Dreams', *RIP* 23 (1936), 123–4.

CARDAN, J., *The Book of My Life*, trans. J. Stoner (New York, 1930).

CARLETON, C., *Archbishop William Laud* (London, 1987).

CARSON, M. A., 'Easing of the "Hert" in the *Book of the Duchess*', *ChauR* 1 (1966–7), 157–60.

CHAMPION, L. S., '*A Midsummer Night's Dream*: The Problem of Source', *PLL* 4 (1968), 13–19.

CHANCE, J., The *Mythographic Chaucer: The Fabulation of Sexual Politics* (Minneapolis, 1995).

CHAUCER, G., *The Riverside Chaucer*, ed. L. D. Benson (Boston, Mass., 1987).

—— *The Works of Geoffrey Chaucer and Others*, ed. W. Thynne (1532); facsimile reproduction, ed. W. W. Skeat (London [1905]).

CHERNISS, M. D., *Boethian Apocalypse: Studies in Middle English Vision Poetry* (Norman, Okla., 1987).

CIXOUS, H., *Portrait de Dora* (Paris, 1976).

CLANVOWE, SIR J., *The Works of Sir John Clanvowe*, ed. V. J. Scattergood (Cambridge, 1965).

CLEMEN, W. H., *Chaucer's Early Poetry*, trans. C. A. M. Sym (London, 1963). [First published as *Der junge Chaucer* (1938).]

COGHILL, N., 'Shakespeare's Reading in Chaucer', in H. Davis and H. Gardner (eds.), *Elizabethan and Jacobean Studies Presented to F. P. Wilson* (Oxford, 1959), 86–99.

COLERIDGE, S. T., *Aids to Reflection*, ed. J. Beer, in *The Collected Works*, vol. ix (Princeton, 1993).

COLLIN-ROSET, S., 'Le *Liber thesauri occulti* de Pascalis Romanus (un traité d'interprétation des songes du XIIᵉ siècle)', *AHDLMA* 30 (1963), 111–98.

COOPER, R., 'Bibliographie sommaire d'ouvrages sur le songe publiés en France et en Italie jusqu'en 1600', in F. Charpentier (ed.), *Le Songe à la Renaissance* (Cannes, 1987), 255–71.

CRAMPTON, G. R., 'Transitions and Meaning in *The Book of the Duchess*', *JEGP* 62 (1963), 486–500.

CUNNINGHAM, J. V., 'The Literary Form of the Prologue to the *Canterbury Tales*', *MP* 49 (1952), 172–81.

CURRY, W. C., *Chaucer and the Mediaeval Sciences*, rev. edn. (New York, 1960).

D'ALVERNY, M.-T., 'Translations and Translators', in R. L. Benson and G. Constable (eds.), *Renaissance and Renewal in the Twelfth Century* (Cambridge, Mass., 1982).

DAMIAN, P., *Liber Gomorrhianus*, *PL* 145, cols. 159–90.

DAVIDOFF, J. M., *Beginning Well: Framing Fictions in Late Middle English Poetry* (London, 1988).

DE BECKER, R., *The Understanding of Dreams, or the Machinations of the Night*, trans. M. Heron (London, 1968). [Originally published as *Les Machinations de la nuit* (Paris, 1965).]

DE CONDÉ, J., '*La Messe des oiseaux' et 'Le Dit des Jacobins et des Fremeneurs'*, ed. J. Ribard, Textes Littéraires Français (Geneva, 1970).

DE DEGUILEVILLE, G., *The Pilgrimage of the Lyfe of the Manhode: Translated Anonymously into Prose from the First Recension of Guillaume de Deguileville's Poem* Le Pèlerinage de la vie humaine, ed. A. Henry, vol. i, EETS os 288 (Oxford, 1985).

—— *The Pilgrimage of the Soul: A Critical Edition of the Middle English Dream Vision*, ed. R. P. McGerr, vol. i, Garland Medieval Texts 16 (New York, 1990).

DE GRANDSON, O., *Le Songe Saint Valentin*, ed. A. Piaget, in his *Oton de Grandson: Sa vie et ses poésies*, Mémoires et Documents Publiés par la Société d'Histoire da la Suisse Romande, ser. 3, vol. i (Lausanne, 1941).

Dekker his Dreame: in which, being rapt with a Poeticall Enthusiasme, the great volumes of Heaven and Hell to Him were opened, in which he read many Wonderfull Things (London, 1620).

DELANY, S., *Chaucer's House of Fame: The Poetics of Skeptical Fideism* (Chicago, 1972).

—— *The Naked Text: Chaucer's Legend of Good Women* (Berkeley and Los Angeles, 1994).

DELASANTA, R., 'Christian Affirmation in *The Book of the Duchess*', *PMLA* 84 (1969), 245–51.

DE MACHAUT, G., *Le Dit dou lyon*, ed. E. Hoepffner, in his *Œuvres de Guillaume de Machaut*, vol. ii, SATF (Paris, 1911).

—— *The Fountain of Love (La Fonteinne amoureuse) and Two Other Love Vision Poems*, ed. and trans. R. B. Palmer, Garland Library of Medieval Literature 54, ser. A (New York, 1993).

—— *The Judgment of the King of Navarre*, ed. and trans. R. B. Palmer, Garland Library of Medieval Literature 45, ser. A (New York, 1988).

DE MARGIVAL, N., *Le Dit de la panthère d'Amours*, ed. H. A. Todd, SATF (Paris, 1883).

DESCARTES, R., *Oeuvres*, ed. C. Adam and P. Tannery, vol. x (Paris, 1966).

DESCHAMPS, E., *Le Lay de franchise*, ed. le marquis de Queux de Saint-Hilaire, in *Œuvres complètes de Eustache Deschamps*, ed. Saint-Hilaire and G. Raynaud, vol. ii, SATF (Paris, 1880).

De spiritu et anima, PL 40, cols. 779–832; trans. E. Leiva and B. Ward in *Three Treatises on Man: A Cistercian Anthropology*, ed. B. McGinn (Kalamazoo, Mich., 1977), 179–288.

DILORENZO, R. D., 'Wonder and Words: Paganism, Christianity, and Consolation in Chaucer's *Book of the Duchess*', UTQ 52 (1982), 20–39.

Dionysii Catonis disticha, ed. O. Arntzenius (Amsterdam, 1754).

Dives and Pauper, ed. P. H. Barnum, vol. i, pt. 1, EETS os 275 (Oxford, 1976).

DOD, B. G., 'Aristoteles latinus', in N. Kretzmann, A. Kenny, J. Pinborg, and E. Stump (eds.), *The Cambridge History of Later Medieval Philosophy: From the Rediscovery of Aristotle to the Disintegration of Scholasticism, 1100–1600* (Cambridge, 1982), 45–79.

DONALDSON, E. T., *The Swan at the Well: Shakespeare Reading Chaucer* (New Haven, 1985).

DONNELLY, C., 'Challenging the Conventions of Dream Vision in *The Book of the Duchess*', PQ 66 (1987), 421–35.

DOOB, P. R., *The Idea of the Labyrinth from Classical Antiquity through the Middle Ages* (Ithaca, NY, 1990).

DUTTON, P. E., *The Politics of Dreaming in the Carolingian Empire*, Regents Studies in Medieval Culture (Lincoln, Nebr., 1994).

EADE, J., and SALLNOW, M. J. (eds.), *Contesting the Sacred: The Anthropology of Christian Pilgrimage* (London, 1991).

EDWARDS, R. R., 'The *Book of the Duchess* and the Beginnings of Chaucer's Narrative', NLH 13 (1982), 189–204. [Presented in revised form in Edwards, *Dream of Chaucer*, 65–91.]

—— *The Dream of Chaucer: Representation and Reflection in the Early Narratives* (Durham, NC, 1989).

ELDREDGE, L., 'The Structure of the *Book of the Duchess*', RUO 39 (1969), 132–51.

ELLMANN, M., 'Blanche', in J. Hawthorn (ed.), *Criticism and Critical Theory* (London, 1984), 99–110.

ERICKSON, C., *The Medieval Vision: Essays in History and Perception* (New York, 1976).

EVANS, C., *Landscapes of the Night: How and Why We Dream* (London, 1983).

Li Fablel dou Dieu d'amors, in *Les Débats du clerc et du chevalier dans la littéraire poétique du moyen-âge*, ed. C. Oulmont (Paris, 1911), 197–216.

FATTORI, M., 'Sogni e temperamenti', in T. Gregory (ed.), *I sogni nel medioevo*, Seminario Internazionale, Rome, 2–4 Oct. 1983 (Rome, 1985), 87–109.

FERRIS, S., 'John Stow and the Tomb of Blanche the Duchess', *ChauR* 18 (1983–4), 92–3.

FERSTER, J., *Chaucer on Interpretation* (Cambridge, 1985).

FIORAVANTI, G., 'La "scientia somnialis" di Boezio di Dacia', *Atti della Accademia delle Scienze di Torino*, ii: *Classe di scienze morali, storiche e filologiche*, 101 (1966–7), 329–69.

FISCHER, S. R., *The Complete Medieval Dreambook: A Multilingual, Alphabetical* Somnia Danielis *Collation* (Berne, 1982).

FORMAN, S., *The Casebooks of Simon Forman*, ed. A. L. Rowse (London, 1974).

FOUCAULT, M., *The History of Sexuality*, i: *An Introduction*, trans. R. Hurley (Harmondsworth, 1981), 62–7. [First published as *La Volonté de savoir* (Paris, 1976).]

FRADENBURG, L. O., ' "Voice Memorial": Loss and Reparation in Chaucer's Poetry', *Exemplaria*, 2 (1990), 169–202.

FREUD, S., *Case Histories I: 'Dora' and 'Little Hans'*, trans. A. and J. Strachey, ed. A. Richards, The Pelican Freud Library 8 (Harmondsworth, 1977). ['Dora' first published as *Bruchstück einer Hysterie-Analyse* (1905).]

—— *The Interpretation of Dreams*, ed. A. Richards, The Pelican Freud Library 4 (Harmondsworth, 1971).

—— 'Some Dreams of Descartes', in Freud, *The Standard Edition of the Complete Psychological Works*, ed. J. Strachey, vol. xxi (London, 1961).

FROISSART, J., *Oeuvres de Froissart: Poésies*, vol. i, ed. M. A. Scheler (Brussels, 1870).

—— *Le Paradis d'Amour; L'Orloge amoureus*, ed. P. Dembowski, Textes Littéraires Français (Geneva, 1986).

FRYE, N., *The Secular Scripture: A Study of the Structure of Romance* (Cambridge, Mass., 1976).

FYLER, J. M., 'Irony and the Age of Gold in the *Book of the Duchess*', *Speculum*, 52 (1977), 314–28. [Re-presented in Fyler, *Chaucer and Ovid* (New Haven, 1979), 65–81.]

GALWAY, M., 'Chaucer's Hopeless Love', *MLN* 60 (1945), 431–9.

GARBER, M. B., *Dream in Shakespeare: From Metaphor to Metamorphosis* (New Haven, 1974).

GARDINER, F. C., *The Pilgrimage of Desire: A Study of Theme and Genre in Medieval Literature* (Leiden, 1971).

GELLRICH, J. M., *The Idea of the Book in the Middle Ages: Language Theory, Mythology, and Fiction* (Ithaca, NY, 1985).

GEREMEK, B., 'The Marginal Man', in J. le Goff (ed.), *Medieval Callings*, trans. L. G. Cochrane (Chicago, 1987), 347–73. [Book originally published as *L'uomo medievale* (Rome, 1987).]

Gesta Grayorum, Malone Society Reprints (Oxford, 1914).

GOWER, J., *Confessio Amantis*, ed. J. A. W. Bennett, in his *Selections from John Gower* (Oxford, 1968).

—— *The Major Latin Works of John Gower:* The Voice of One Crying *and* The Tripartite Chronicles, trans. E. W. Stockton (Seattle, 1962).

—— *Vox Clamantis*, ed. G. C. Macaulay, in *The Complete Works of John Gower*, iv: *The Latin Works* (Oxford, 1902).

GREEN, R. H., 'Classical Fable and English Poetry in the Fourteenth Century', in D. Bethurum (ed.), *Critical Approaches to Medieval Literature: Selected Papers from the English Institute, 1958–1959* (New York, 1960), 110–33.

GREGORY THE GREAT, *Dialogues*, ed. A. de Vogüé, Sources Chrétiennes 251, 260, 265 (Paris, 1978–80); trans. O. J. Zimmerman, The Fathers of the Church: A New Translation 39 (New York, 1959).

—— *Moralia in Iob*, ed. M. Adriaen, Corpus Christianorum, Series Latina 143, 143A, 143B (Turnholt, 1979–85); trans. as *Morals on the Book of Job*, 3 vols., A Library of Fathers of the Holy Catholic Church, translated by members of the English church (Oxford, 1844–50).

GREGORY, T., 'I sogni e gli astri', in id. (ed.), *I sogni nel medioevo*, Seminario Internazionale, Rome, 2–4 Oct. 1983 (Rome, 1985), 111–48.

GRENNEN, J. E., '*Hert-Huntyng* in the *Book of the Duchess*', *MLQ* 25 (1964), 131–9.

GRUNER, O. C., *A Treatise on the Canon of Medicine of Avicenna, Incorporating a Translation of the First Book* (London, 1930; repr. New York, 1973).

HAGEN, S. K., *Allegorical Remembrance: A Study of* The Pilgrimage of the Life of Man *as a Medieval Treatise on Seeing and Remembering* (Athens, Ga., 1990).

HALE, D. G., 'Bottom's Dream and Chaucer', *SQ* 36 (1985), 219–20.

—— 'Dreams, Stress, and Interpretation in Chaucer and his Contemporaries', *JRMMRA* 9 (1988), 47–61.

HALLYN, F., 'Les Songes du jeune Descartes', in F. Charpentier (ed.), *Le Songe à la Renaissance*, Colloque International de Cannes, 29–31 mai 1987 (Saint-Etienne, 1987), 41–51.

HANNING, R. W., 'Chaucer's First Ovid: Metamorphosis and Poetic Tradition in *The Book of the Duchess* and *The House of Fame*', in L. A. Arrathoon (ed.), *Chaucer and the Craft of Fiction* (Rochester, Mich., 1986), 121–63.

HANSEN, E. T., *Chaucer and the Fictions of Gender* (Berkeley and Los Angeles, 1992).

HARVEY, E. R., *The Inward Wits* (London, 1975).

HASKINS, C. H., *Studies in Mediaeval Culture* (Oxford, 1929).

HEFFERNAN, C. F., 'That Dog Again: *Melancholia Canina* and Chaucer's *Book of the Duchess*', *MP* 84 (1986), 185–90.

HENRYSON, R., *The Poems of Robert Henryson*, ed. D. Fox (Oxford, 1981).

HERZOG, M. B., 'The *Book of the Duchess*: The Vision of the Artist as a Young Dreamer', *ChauR* 22 (1987–8), 269–81.

HIEATT, C. B., '*Un Autre Forme*: Guillaume de Machaut and the Dream Vision Form', *ChauR* 14 (1979–80), 97–115.

—— *The Realism of Dream Visions: The Poetic Exploitation of the Dream-Experience in Chaucer and his Contemporaries*, De Proprietatibus Litterarum, series practica 2 (The Hague, 1967).

HILL, C., *Milton and the English Revolution* (London, 1977).

HILL, J. M., '*The Book of the Duchess*, Melancholy, and that Eight-Year Sickness', *ChauR* 9 (1974–5), 35–50.

HILL, T., *The most pleasaunte Arte of the Interpretacion of Dreames . . .* (London, 1576).

HOBSON, J. A., *The Dreaming Brain* (New York, 1988).

HOCCLEVE, T., *Selections from Hoccleve*, ed. M. C. Seymour (Oxford, 1981).

HOFFMEISTER, G., 'Rasis' Traumlehre: Traumbücher des Spätmittelalters', *AK* 51 (1969), 137–59.

HOLKOT, R., *In librum sapientiae regis Salomonis praelectiones CCXIII* (Basle, 1586).

HOLLAND, P., 'Dreaming the *Dream*', in J. Iselin and J.-P. Moreau (eds.), '*Songe d'une nuit d'été*' et '*La Duchesse de Malfi*', Trames: Actes des Journées Shakespeare–Webster (Limoges, 1989), 9–27.

—— 'Theseus' Shadows in *A Midsummer Night's Dream*', *SS* 47 (1995), 139–51.

HULT, D. F., *Self-Fulfilling Prophecies: Readership and Authority in the First Roman de la rose* (Cambridge, 1986).

HUPPÉ, B. F., and ROBERTSON, D. W., Jr., *Fruyt and Chaf: Studies in Chaucer's Allegories* (Princeton, 1963).

JACQUART, D., and THOMASSET, C., *Sexuality and Medicine in the Middle Ages*, trans. M. Adamson (1985; Princeton, 1988).

JAMES, M., *English Politics and the Concept of Honour* (Oxford, 1978).

JONASSEN, F. B., 'The Inn, the Cathedral, and the Pilgrimage of *The Canterbury Tales*', in S. G. Fein, D. Raybin, and P. C. Braeger (eds.), *Rebels and Rivals: The Contestive Spirit in* The Canterbury Tales, Studies in Medieval Culture 29 (Kalamazoo, Mich., 1991), 1–35.

JONSON, B., 'Conversations with Drummond of Hawthornden', in *Ben Jonson*, ed. C. H. Herford and P. and E. Simpson, 11 vols. (Oxford, 1925–52), i. 139–40.

KAGAN, R. L., *Lucrecia's Dream* (Berkeley and Los Angeles, 1990).

KELLOGG, A. L., *Chaucer, Langland, Arthur: Essays in Middle English Literature* (New Brunswick, NJ, 1972).

KEPLER, J., 'Somnium', ed. E. Rosen (Madison, Wis., 1967).

KERMODE, F., 'The Mature Comedies', in J. R. Brown and B. Harris (eds.), Early Shakespeare, Stratford-upon-Avon Studies 3 (London, 1961), 211–27.

KILBORNE, B., 'On Classifying Dreams', in B. Tedlock (ed.), Dreaming: Anthropological and Psychological Interpretations, School of American Research Advanced Seminar ser. (Cambridge, 1987), 171–93.

KISER, L. J., 'Sleep, Dreams, and Poetry in Chaucer's Book of the Duchess', PLL 19 (1983), 3–12.

KITTREDGE, G. L., 'Chaucer and Froissart (with a discussion of the date of the Méliador)', EStn 26 (1899), 321–36.

—— Chaucer and his Poetry (1915; Cambridge, Mass., 1967).

KLIBANSKY, R., PANOFSKY, E., and SAXL, F., Saturn and Melancholy: Studies in the History of Natural Philosophy, Religion, and Art (London, 1964).

KOLVE, V. A., Chaucer and the Imagery of Narrative: The First Five Canterbury Tales (Stanford, 1984).

KREUZER, J. R., 'The Dreamer in the Book of the Duchess', PMLA 66 (1951), 543–7.

KRUGER, S. F., Dreaming in the Middle Ages, Cambridge Studies in Medieval Literature 14 (Cambridge, 1992).

—— 'Imagination and the Complex Movement of Chaucer's House of Fame', ChauR 28 (1993–4), 117–34.

—— 'Mirrors and the Trajectory of Vision in Piers Plowman', Speculum, 66 (1991), 74–95.

KURATH, H., KUHN, S. M., REIDY, J., and LEWIS, R. E. (eds.), Middle English Dictionary (Ann Arbor, Mich., 1952–   ).

LACAN, J., 'Intervention on Transference', in C. Bernheimer and C. Kahane (eds.), In Dora's Case: Freud, Hysteria, Feminism (London, 1985), 92–104.

LADNER, G. B., 'Homo Viator: Mediaeval Ideas on Alienation and Order', Speculum, 42 (1967), 233–59.

LANGLAND, W., Piers Plowman: An Edition of the C-Text, ed. D. Pearsall, York Medieval Texts, 2nd ser. (London, 1978).

—— The Vision of Piers Plowman: A Critical Edition of the B-Text, ed. A. V. C. Schmidt (London, 1978).

LAUD, W., The Works, ed. W. Scott and J. Bliss, 7 vols. (Oxford, 1847–60).

LAWLOR, J., 'The Pattern of Consolation in The Book of the Duchess', Speculum, 31 (1956), 626–48.

LEACH, E., Culture and Communication. The Logic by which Symbols are Connected: An Introduction to the Use of Structuralist Analysis in Social Anthropology, Themes in the Social Sciences (Cambridge, 1976).

LECERCLE, A., 'On Mazes, Merry-Go-Rounds and Immaculate Conceptions: The Dream Logic of A Midsummer Night's Dream', in P. Iselin and J.-P. Moreau (eds.), 'Le Songe d'une nuit d'été' et 'La Duchesse de Malfi', Trames: Actes des Journées Shakespeare–Webster (Limoges, 1989), 141–53.

LE GOFF, J., 'Dreams in the Culture and Collective Psychology of the Medieval West', in his *Time, Work, and Culture in the Middle Ages*, trans. A. Goldhammer (Chicago, 1980), 201–4. [Essay first published as 'Les Rêves dans la culture et la psychologie collective de l'Occident médiéval', *Scolies*, 1 (1971), 123–30; book first published as *Pour un autre Moyen Age: temps, travail et culture en Occident* (Paris, 1977).]

LEYERLE, J., 'The Heart and the Chain', in L. D. Benson (ed.), *The Learned and the Lewed: Studies in Chaucer and Medieval Literature*, Harvard English Studies 5 (Cambridge, Mass., 1974), 113–45.

LINCOLN, J. S., *The Dream in Primitive Cultures* (London, 1935).

LOFTIN, A. C., 'Visions', in J. R. Strayer (ed.), *Dictionary of the Middle Ages*, vol. xii (New York, 1989), 475–8.

LOOMIS, R. S., 'Chaucer's Eight Years' Sickness', *MLN* 59 (1944), 178–80.

LOWES, J. L., *Geoffrey Chaucer and the Development of his Genius* (Boston, Mass., 1934).

—— 'The Loveres Maladye of Hereos', *MP* 11 (1914), 491–546.

LUISI, D., 'The Hunt Motif in *The Book of the Duchess*', *ES* 52 (1971), 309–11.

LUMIANSKY, R. M., 'The Bereaved Narrator in Chaucer's *Book of the Duchess*', *TSE* 9 (1959), 5–17.

LYNCH, K. L., 'The *Book of the Duchess* as a Philosophical Vision', *Genre*, 21 (1988), 279–305.

—— *The High Medieval Dream Vision: Poetry, Philosophy and Literary Form* (Stanford, 1988).

—— 'The Logic of the Dream Vision in Chaucer's *House of Fame*', in R. J. Utz (ed.), *Literary Nominalism and the Theory of Rereading Late Medieval Texts: A New Research Paradigm* (Lewiston, NY, 1995), 179–204.

—— '*The Parliament of Fowls* and Late Medieval Voluntarism (Parts 1 and 2)', *ChauR* 25 (1990–1), 1–16 and 85–95.

MACKENZIE, N., *Dreams and Dreaming* (London, 1965).

MACROBIUS, *Ambrosii Theodosii Macrobii Commentarii in Somnium Scipionis*, ed. J. Willis, Bibliotheca Scriptorum Graecorum et Romanorum Teubneriana (Leipzig, 1963).

—— *Commentary on the Dream of Scipio*, trans. W. H. Stahl, Records of Civilization: Sources and Studies 48 (New York, 1952).

MAHONY, P. J., *Freud's Dora: A Psychoanalytical, Historical, and Textual Study* (New Haven, 1996).

MALONE, K., *Chapters on Chaucer* (Baltimore, 1951).

MANNHEIM, B., 'A Semiotic of Andean dreams', in B. Tedlock (ed.), *Dreaming: Anthropological and Psychological Interpretations*, School of American Research Advanced Seminar ser. (Cambridge, 1987), 132–53.

MARCUS, S., 'Freud and Dora: Story, History, Case History', in C. Bernheimer and C. Kahane (eds.), *In Dora's Case* (London, 1985), 56–91.

MARGHERITA, G., *The Romance of Origins: Language and Sexual Difference in Middle English Literature* (Philadelphia, 1994).

MARGOLIN, J.-C., 'Vives, lecteur et critique de Platon et d'Aristote', in R. R. Bolgar (ed.), *Classical Influences on European Culture A.D. 1500–1700* (Cambridge, 1976), 245–58.

MARTIN, C. A. N., 'Mercurial Translation in the *Book of the Duchess*', *ChauR* 28 (1993–4), 95–116.

MATHIEU-CASTELLANI, G., 'Veiller en dormant, dormir en veillant: Le Songe dans les Essais', in F. Charpentier (ed.), *Le Songe à la Renaissance*, Colloque International de Cannes, 29–31 mai 1987 (Saint-Etienne, 1987), 231–8.

MIGNE, J.-P. (ed.), *Patrologia cursus completus . . . series (Latina) prima [Patrologia Latina]*, 221 vols. (Paris, 1844–64).

MILTON, J., *The Poems of John Milton*, ed. J. Carey and A. Fowler (London, 1968).

MODENA, L., *The Autobiography of a Seventeenth-Century Venetian Rabbi: Leon Modena's 'Life of Judah'*, ed. M. R. Cohen (Princeton, 1988).

MOI, T., 'Representations of Patriarchy: Sexuality and Epistemology in Freud's Dora', in C. Bernheimer and C. Kahane (eds.), *In Dora's Case* (London, 1985), 181–99.

MONTAIGNE, M. DE, *The Essayes of Michael Lord of Montaigne Translated into English by John Florio*, 3 vols. (London, 1928).

—— *The Essays*, trans. and ed. M. A. Screech (London, 1991).

MONTROSE, L. A., ' "Shaping Fantasies": Figurations of Gender and Power in Elizabethan Culture', *Representations*, 2 (1983), 61–94; repr. in S. Greenblatt (ed.), *Representing the English Renaissance* (Berkeley, 1988), 31–64.

MOWAT, B. A., ' "A local habitation and a name": Shakespeare's Text as Construct', *Style*, 23 (1989), 335–51.

MUIR, K., *The Sources of Shakespeare's Plays*, rev. edn. (New Haven, 1978).

MUIR, L. R., *Literature and Society in Medieval France: The Mirror and its Image 1100–1500*, New Studies in Medieval History (Basingstoke, 1985).

Mum and the Sothsegger, ed. M. Day and R. Steele, EETS OS 199 (Oxford, 1936).

MUNDAY, A., *et al.*, *The Book of Sir Thomas More*, ed. V. Gabrieli and G. Melchiori (Manchester, 1990).

MUSCATINE, C., *Poetry and Crisis in the Age of Chaucer*, University of Notre Dame Ward-Phillips Lectures in English Language and Literature 4 (Notre Dame, Ind., 1972).

NAGERA, H., *et al.*, *Basic Psychoanalytic Concepts on the Theory of Dreams*, Hampstead Clinic Psychoanalytic Library 2 (London, 1969).

NASHE, T., *The Terrors of the Night*, in *Selected Works*, ed. S. Wells, The Stratford-upon-Avon Library 1 (London, 1954).

NEAMAN, J. S., 'Brain Physiology and Poetics in *The Book of the Duchess*', *RPL* 3 (1980), 101–13.

NOLAN, B., 'The Art of Expropriation: Chaucer's Narrator in *The Book of the*

Duchess', in D. M. Rose (ed.), *New Perspectives in Chaucer Criticism* (Norman, Okla., 1981), 203–22.

—— *Chaucer and the Tradition of the Roman Antique*, Cambridge Studies in Medieval Literature 15 (Cambridge, 1992).

—— *The Gothic Visionary Perspective* (Princeton, 1977).

NYQUIST, M., 'The Genesis of Gendered Subjectivity in the Divorce Tracts and in *Paradise Lost*', in M. Nyquist and M. W. Ferguson (eds.), *Re-membering Milton: Essays on the Texts and Traditions* (New York, 1987), 99–127.

OLSON, G., *Literature as Recreation in the Later Middle Ages* (Ithaca, NY, 1982).

ORMEROD, D., '*A Midsummer Night's Dream*: The Monster in the Labyrinth', *SStud* 11 (1978), 39–52.

OVID, *Heroides and Amores*, trans. G. Showerman, rev. G. P. Gould, Loeb Classical Library (Cambridge, Mass., 1977).

PACK, R. A., 'De pronosticatione sompniorum libellus Guillelmo de Aragonia adscriptus', *AHDLMA* 33 (1966), 237–92.

PALLEY, J., *The Ambiguous Mirror: Dreams in Spanish Literature* (Valencia, 1983).

PALMER, J. J. N., 'The Historical Context of the *Book of the Duchess*: A Revision', *ChauR* 8 (1973–4), 253–61.

The Parlement of the Thre Ages, ed. M. Y. Offord, EETS os 246 (Oxford, 1959).

PARR, J., 'Cresseid's Leprosy Again', *MLN* 60 (1945), 487–91.

PATTERSON, L., *Chaucer and the Subject of History* (Madison, Wis., 1991).

—— 'On the Margins of the Post-modern', *Speculum*, 65 (1990), 87–108.

Pearl-poet, *The Poems of the Pearl Manuscript: Pearl, Cleanness, Patience, Sir Gawain and the Green Knight*, ed. M. Andrew and R. Waldron, York Medieval Texts, 2nd ser. (London, 1978).

PEARSALL, D., *Old English and Middle English Poetry*, Routledge History of English Poetry 1 (London, 1977).

PECK, R. A., 'Theme and Number in Chaucer's *Book of the Duchess*', in A. Fowler (ed.), *Silent Poetry: Essays in Numerological Analysis* (London, 1970), 73–115.

PEDEN, A. M., 'Macrobius and Mediaeval Dream Literature', *MÆ* 54 (1985), 59–73.

PELEN, M. M., 'Machaut's Court of Love Narratives and Chaucer's *Book of the Duchess*', *ChauR* 11 (1976–7), 128–55.

PHILLIPS, H., 'Structure and Consolation in the *Book of the Duchess*', *ChauR* 16 (1981–2), 107–18.

PIEHLER, P., *The Visionary Landscape: A Study in Medieval Allegory* (London, 1971).

PIERCE, R. B., 'Shakespeare and the Ten Modes of Scepticism', *SS* 46 (1994), 145–58.

PISON, T., 'Liminality in *The Canterbury Tales*', *Genre*, 10 (1977), 157–71.

POLLARD, A. W., and REDGRAVE, G. R., *A Short-Title Catalogue of Books Printed in England, Scotland, and Ireland, and of English Books Printed Abroad 1475–1640*, 2nd edn., rev. W. A. Jackson, F. S. Ferguson, and K. F. Pantzer, 3 vols. (London, 1976–91).

PONTALIS, J.-B., 'Dream as an Object', in S. Flanders (ed.), *The Dream Discourse Today*, New Library of Psychoanalysis 17 (London, 1993).

POPKIN, R. H., *The History of Scepticism from Erasmus to Descartes*, rev. edn. (Assen, 1964).

PRATT, R. A., 'Some Latin Sources of the Nonnes Preest on Dreams', *Speculum*, 52 (1977), 538–70.

PRIOR, S. P., '*Routhe and Hert-Huntyng* in the *Book of the Duchess*', *JEGP* 85 (1986), 3–19.

PRYNNE, W., *A Breviate of the Life of William Laud, Arch-bishop of Canterbury: extracted (for the most part) verbatim out of his owne Diary* (London, 1644).

RAMBUSS, R., ' "Processe of Tyme": History, Consolation, and Apocalypse in the *Book of the Duchess*', *Exemplaria*, 2 (1990), 659–83.

RÉGNIER-BOHLER, D., 'Imagining the Self', in P. Ariès and G. Duby (eds.), *A History of Private Life*, ii: *Revelations of the Medieval World*, trans. A. Goldhammer (Cambridge, Mass., 1988), 311–94. [Book originally published as *Histoire de la vie privée*, ii: *De l'Europe féodale à la Renaissance* (Paris, 1985).]

RIGGS, D., *Ben Jonson: A Life* (Cambridge, Mass., 1989).

ROBERTSON, D. W., Jr., 'The Historical Setting of Chaucer's *Book of the Duchess*', in J. Mahoney and J. E. Keller (eds.), *Mediaeval Studies in Honor of Urban Tigner Holmes, Jr.*, University of North Carolina Studies in the Romance Languages and Literatures 56 (Chapel Hill, NC, 1965), 169–95.

—— *A Preface to Chaucer: Studies in Medieval Perspectives* (Princeton, 1962).

ROSSKY, W., 'Imagination in the English Renaissance', *SR* 5 (1958), 49–73.

RUBIN, M., *Corpus Christi: The Eucharist in Late Medieval Culture* (Cambridge, 1991).

RUPPRECHT, C. S., 'Divinity, Insanity, Creativity: A Renaissance Contribution to the History and Theory of Dream/Text(s)', in id. (ed.), *The Dream and the Text* (Albany, NY, 1993), 112–32.

RUSSELL, J. S., *The English Dream Vision: Anatomy of a Form* (Columbus, Oh., 1988).

SADLER, L. V., 'Chaucer's *The Book of the Duchess* and the "Law of Kinde"', *AM* 11 (1970), 51–74.

SARTRE, J.-P., *Nausea*, trans. R. Baldick (Harmondsworth, 1965).

—— *The Psychology of Imagination*, trans. B. Frechtman (New York, 1966).

SAVONOROLA, M., *Libreto de tutte le cosse che se magnano: Un opera di dietetica del sec. XV*, ed. J. Nystedt (Stockholm, 1988).

SCHMIDT, A. V. C., 'The Inner Dreams in *Piers Plowman*', *MÆ* 55 (1986), 24–40.

SCOT, R., *The Discovery of Witchcraft* (London [1584]); introd. M. Summers ([London], 1930).

SCOTT, W. O., 'Chaucer, Shakespeare, and the Paradoxes of Dream and Fable', *CEACrit* 49 (1986–7), 25–32.

SCOTT-MACNAB, D., 'A Re-examination of Octovyen's Hunt in *The Book of the Duchess*', *MÆ* 56 (1987), 183–99.

SEBBA, G., *The Dream of Descartes*, ed. R. A. Watson (Carbondale, Ill., 1987).

SEDGWICK, E. K., *Between Men: English Literature and Male Homosocial Desire* (New York, 1985).

SEVERS, J. B., 'Chaucer's Self-Portrait in the *Book of the Duchess*', *PQ* 43 (1964), 27–39.

—— 'The Sources of "The Book of the Duchess"', *MS* 25 (1963), 355–62.

SHAKESPEARE, W., *The Complete Works*, ed. S. Wells and G. Taylor (Oxford, 1986).

—— *A Midsummer Night's Dream*, ed. H. F. Brooks, The Arden Shakespeare (London, 1979).

—— *A Midsummer Night's Dream*, ed. P. Holland, The Oxford Shakespeare (Oxford, 1994).

—— *The Taming of the Shrew*, ed. H. J. Oliver (Oxford: 1982).

SHOAF, R. A., 'Stalking the Sorrowful H(e)art: Penitential Lore and the Hunt Scene in Chaucer's *The Book of the Duchess*', *JEGP* 78 (1979), 313–24.

SIRAISI, N. G., *Medieval and Early Renaissance Medicine: An Introduction to Knowledge and Practice* (Chicago, 1990).

Sir Orfeo, ed. A. J. Bliss, 2nd edn. (Oxford, 1966).

SMITH, N., *Perfection Proclaimed: Language and Literature in English Radical Religion 1640–1660* (Oxford, 1989).

SMITH, S. S. [now Stanbury, S.], 'Cupid's Sight in the Prologue to the *Legend of Good Women*', *Centrepoint*, 15 (1981), 95–102.

SPEARING, A. C., 'Literal and Figurative in *The Book of the Duchess*', *SAC: Proceedings*, 1 (1984), 165–71.

—— *Medieval Dream-Poetry* (Cambridge, 1976).

SPERONI, C., 'Dante's Prophetic Morning-Dreams', *SP* 45 (1948), 50–9.

SPISAK, J. W., 'Pyramus and Thisbe in Chaucer and Shakespeare', in E. T. Donaldson and J. J. Kollman (eds.), *Chaucerian Shakespeare: Adaptation and Transformation* (Detroit, 1983), 81–95.

SPURGEON, C. F. E., *Five Hundred Years of Chaucer Criticism and Allusion, 1357–1900*, 3 vols. (New York, 1960). [First published by the Chaucer Society, ser. 48–50, 52–6 (London, 1908–17); 3-vol. edn., Cambridge, 1925.]

STAKEL, S., 'Structural Convergence of Pilgrimage and Dream-Vision in Christine de Pizan', in B. N. Sargent-Baur (ed.), *Journeys Toward God: Pilgrimage and Crusade*, Studies in Medieval Culture 30; also as Occasional Studies ser., Medieval and Renaissance Studies Program, University of Pittsburgh 5 (Kalamazoo, Mich., 1992), 195–203.

STANBURY, S., *Seeing the* Gawain-*Poet: Description and the Act of Perception*, Middle Ages ser. (Philadelphia, 1991).

STATIUS, *Thebaid*, trans. A. D. Melville (Oxford, 1995).

STEARNS, M. W., 'A Note on Chaucer's Attitude Toward Love', *Speculum*, 17 (1942), 570–4.

—— 'Robert Henryson and the Leper Cresseid', *MLN* 59 (1944), 265–9.

STEVENS, M., 'Narrative Focus in *The Book of the Duchess*: A Critical Revaluation', *AM* 7 (1966), 16–32.

STORM, M., 'From Knossos to Knight's Tale: The Changing Face of Chaucer's Theseus', in J. Chance (ed.), *The Mythographic Art: Classical Fable and the Rise of the Vernacular in Early France and England* (Gainesville, Fla., 1990), 215–21.

SUMPTION, J., *Pilgrimage: An Image of Mediaeval Religion* (London, 1975).

SYPHERD, W. O., 'Chaucer's Eight Years' Sickness', *MLN* 20 (1905), 240–3.

TAYLOR, A., 'Epic Motifs in Chaucer's "Tale of Ceyx and Alcyone"', *Helios*, 14 (1987), 39–45.

TAYLOR, A. B., 'Chaucer's Non-Involvement in "Pyramus and Thisbe"', *NQ* 234 (NS 36) (1989), 317–20.

—— 'Golding's *Ovid*, Shakespeare's "Small Latin", and the Real Object of Mockery in "Pyramus and Thisbe"', *SS* 42 (1990), 53–64.

TEDLOCK, B., 'Zuni and Quiché Dream Sharing and Interpreting', in id. (ed.), *Dreaming: Anthropological and Psychological Interpretations*, School of American Research Advanced Seminar ser. (Cambridge, 1987), 105–31.

THIÉBAUX, M., *The Stag of Love: The Chase in Medieval Literature* (Ithaca, NY, 1974).

THOMAS, K., *Religion and the Decline of Magic: Studies in Popular Beliefs in Sixteenth- and Seventeenth-Century England* (Harmondsworth, 1973).

THOMPSON, A., *Shakespeare's Chaucer: A Study in Literary Origins* (Liverpool, 1978).

THORNDIKE, LYNN, *A History of Magic and Experimental Science*, ii: *During the First Thirteen Centuries of Our Era* (New York, 1923).

TISDALE, C. P. R., 'Boethian "Hert-Huntyng": The Elegiac Pattern of *The Book of the Duchess*', *ABR* 24 (1973), 365–80.

TRINKAUS, C., and OBERMAN, H. A. (eds.), *The Pursuit of Holiness in Late Medieval and Renaissance Religion* (Leiden, 1974).

TRYON, T., *A Treatise of Dreams & Visions*, 2nd edn. (London [1700]).

TUPPER, F., 'Chaucer and Lancaster', *MLN* 32 (1917), 54.

—— 'Chaucer and Richmond', *MLN* 31 (1916), 250–2.

TURNER, E., 'The Literary Roots of Victor Turner's Anthropology', in K. M. Ashley (ed.), *Victor Turner and the Construction of Cultural Criticism: Between Literature and Anthropology* (Bloomington, Ind., 1990), 163–9.

TURNER, V., *Dramas, Fields, and Metaphors: Symbolic Action in Human Society*, Symbol, Myth, and Ritual ser. (Ithaca, NY, 1974).

—— The Forest of Symbols: Aspects of Ndembu Ritual (Ithaca, NY, 1967).

—— 'Liminal to Liminoid, in Play, Flow, and Ritual: An Essay in Comparative Symbology', in his From Ritual to Theatre: The Human Seriousness of Play (New York, 1982), 20–60.

—— 'Pilgrimage and Communitas', SMiss 23 (1974), 305–27.

—— The Ritual Process: Structure and Anti-Structure, The Lewis Henry Morgan Lectures, 1966 (Chicago, 1969).

—— and TURNER, E., Image and Pilgrimage in Christian Culture: Anthropological Perspectives, Lectures on the History of Religions Sponsored by the American Council of Learned Societies, NS 11 (New York, 1978).

TUVE, R., Seasons and Months: Studies in a Tradition of Middle English Poetry (Paris, 1933; repr. Cambridge, 1974).

USK, T., The Testament of Love, ed. W. W. Skeat, in his The Complete Works of Geoffrey Chaucer, vii: Chaucerian and Other Pieces (London, 1897).

VAN GENNEP, A., The Rites of Passage [1908], trans. M. B. Vizedom and G. L. Caffee (Chicago, 1960).

VINCENT OF BEAUVAIS, Speculum naturale (Douai, 1624; repr. Graz, 1964).

VIVES, J. L., Somnium et vigilia in Somnium Scipionis, ed. E. V. George (Greenwood, SC, 1989).

VOLOSINOV, V. N. [M. Bakhtin], Marxism and the Philosophy of Language (Cambridge, Mass., 1986). [First published as Marksizm i filosofiia iazyka, osnovnye problemy sotsiologicheskogo metoda v nauke o iazyke (Leningrad, 1929).]

WACK, M. F., Lovesickness in the Middle Ages: The Viaticum and its Commentaries (Philadelphia, 1990).

WALKER, D., 'Narrative Inconclusiveness and Consolatory Dialectic in the Book of the Duchess', ChauR 18 (1983–4), 1–17.

WARD, B., Miracles and the Medieval Mind: Theory, Record and Event 1000–1215 (London, 1982).

WEBB, H. J., 'A Reinterpretation of Chaucer's Theseus', RES 23 (1947), 289–96.

WEBSTER, J., The Duchess of Malfi, ed. J. R. Brown, The Revels Plays (London, 1964).

—— The White Devil, ed. J. R. Brown (London, 1960).

WEIDHORN, M., Dreams in Seventeenth-Century English Literature (The Hague, 1970).

WILSON, E., 'The "Gostly Drem" in Pearl', NM 69 (1968), 90–101.

WIMSATT, J. I., 'The Book of the Duchess: Secular Elegy or Religious Vision?', in J. P. Hermann and J. J. Burke, Jr. (eds.), Signs and Symbols in Chaucer's Poetry (University, Ala., 1981), 113–29.

—— Chaucer and the French Love Poets: The Literary Background of the Book of the Duchess (Chapel Hill, NC, 1968).

WINDEATT, B. A. (ed. and trans.), Chaucer's Dream Poetry: Sources and Analogues, Chaucer Studies 8 (Cambridge, 1982).

WINGATE, S. D., *The Mediaeval Latin Versions of the Aristotelian Scientific Corpus, with Special Reference to the Biological Works* (London, 1931).

WINNY, J., *Chaucer's Dream-Poems* (New York, 1973).

WOLFF, W., *The Dream—Mirror of Conscience: A History of Dream Interpretation from 2000 B.C. and a New Theory of Dream Synthesis* (New York, 1952).

WRIGHT, S., 'Deguileville's *Pèlerinage de Vie Humaine* as "Contrepartie Edifiante" of the *Roman de la Rose*', *PQ* 68 (1989), 399–422.

WRIGHT, T., *The Passions of the Minde in Generall* (London, 1621).

Wynnere and Wastoure, ed. S. Trigg, EETS os 297 (Oxford, 1990).

YOUNG, D. P., *Something of Great Constancy: The Art of 'A Midsummer Night's Dream'* (New Haven, 1966).

ZINK, M., 'The Allegorical Poem as Interior Memoir', in *Images of Power: Medieval History/Discourse/Literature*, ed. K. Brownlee and S. G. Nichols, Yale French Studies 70 (New Haven, 1986), 100–26.

Index